ISTANB

A Traveller

Sue Rollin
and **Jane Streetly**

CW00816032

Garnet
PUBLISHING

ISTANBUL: A Traveller's Guide

Published by
Garnet Publishing Limited
8 Southern Court, South Street
Reading RG1 4QS, UK
Tel: +44 (0) 118 959 7847
Fax: +44 (0) 118 959 7356
E-mail: enquiries@garnetpublishing.co.uk
Website: www.garnetpublishing.co.uk

Copyright
© Sue Rollin and Jane Streetly 2005

First edition

ISBN 1 85964 151 2

British Library Cataloguing-in-Publication
Data. A catalogue record for this book is
available from the British Library.

Credits
Editorial
Anna Hines, Emma Hawker
Maps: Karen Rose

Design
David Rose

Production
Typesetting: Samantha Barden
Illustrations: Janette Hill
Maps: Geoprojects UK Ltd., Julia Lunn
Reprographics: Nick Holroyd

Photography
Sue Rollin and Jane Streetly: pages 18, 31,
38, 39, 43, 61, 68, 71, 85, 94, 100, 103, 109,
111, 118, 119, 126, 128, 138, 144, 145, 146,
148, 152, 165, 169, 172, 185, 186, 189, 193,
205, 206, 208, 212, 214, 222
Corel Corporation: pages iii, 112, 131, 160,
179, 198, 201, 226
PhotoDisc: page viii
Andes Press Agency: Mike Cadman: pages
28, 29, 58
Andes Press Agency: C & D Hill: pages 47,
75, 114, 140, 163, 177, 199
Andes Press Agency: Carlos Reyes-Manzo:
pages 102, 217

Printed and bound
in Lebanon by International Press

Contents

PREFACE

Istanbul, Constantinople, Byzantium: three names for the same city, redolent of its past history as capital of two mighty empires for 1,600 years, and still today one of the great cities of the world. Istanbul is extraordinary – East meets West here, the only city in the world located astride two continents. Around it, the waters of the Marmara Sea mingle with those of the Golden Horn and of the Bosphorus. The famous skyline reflects its past; the six minarets of the Blue Mosque and the impressive size of the Süleymaniye Mosque strain to rival the great dome of St Sophia – in turn church, mosque and museum. But there is far more to discover on a visit to Istanbul.

Written as a series of walks, this book covers much of the historic city on foot, allowing visitors to soak up its unique atmosphere along the way. And the best way to explore Istanbul is on foot – in the back streets there are still many of the characteristic old wooden houses which once made the city so prone to disastrous fires. Relax in a café or tea-house, enjoy the bustle of street life, or stroll through the colourful markets in search of a bargain. Here and there you will find an old stone fountain, a bath-house or a Byzantine church, distinguished by its ornamental brick-work, but long since converted to a mosque. Istanbul has always been a cultural melting-pot, its different peoples each adding a layer to the richness of city life.

There is much else to enjoy in Istanbul: the cuisine is richly varied and there are hundreds of different restaurants to choose from. Shopping too is an experience: carpet hunters should be prepared to bargain over a glass of tea, some may prefer to wander around the labyrinthine Covered Bazaar, but there are also the shops of Istiklal Caddesi, once la Grande Rue de Pera, the height of fashion among nineteenth-century European residents of Constantinople, and still lined with the imposing façades of their former embassies. For the footsore, there are taxis, buses, the efficient modern tram and, of course, innumerable ferries crisscrossing their way up the Bosphorus. A trip up these narrow straits past castles and ornate Ottoman mansions and palaces, stopping for lunch at a waterside fish restaurant, is a must. Whatever you choose to do during your stay in Istanbul, we hope that you will enjoy yourselves exploring this wonderful city as much as we have.

Turkish people are renowned for their generosity and hospitality, and we have certainly found this to be the case during the research and writing of this book. While staying in Istanbul many people went out of their way to help us. We would particularly like to thank Şeniz Terem and Gülbikem Ronay of Unitur for not only organizing our travel and accommodation so efficiently, but also for their friendship and many kindnesses. Esat Yalçin of Carat Tours was likewise generous and helpful. For a tremendous welcome and constant subsequent hospitality, with delightful insights into Istanbul's nightlife and culinary delights, we thank Renan and Osman Gedikoğlu. Sally Kemble enthusiastically shared her own discoveries and knowledge of the city with us on foot, while Müge Özbay passed on much helpful information and showed us some of her favourite places. In the UK we would like to thank our friends Emma Bodossian and Lesley Scouller who helped us via their contacts in the travel business, Maggie Oliphant who recommended some Istanbul restaurants and Ayla Yurdacan Wyse who corrected our Turkish spelling and helped with the section on Turkish food and drink. We are also grateful to Jane Angelini for help in updating and to Mike and Heather Streetly for testing some of the walks and making useful suggestions. Our editors Emma Hawker and Anna Hines were always helpful, interested and pleasant to work with. Last, but not least, researching this book would not have been the same without the inimitable contributions of Uwe Kosa and the companionship of Stuart Young who explored the bazaars far beyond the call of duty, and provided some revealing insights into the architecture of the Süleymaniye Mosque.

HISTORY

The Byzantine period

Byzantium, Constantinople, Istanbul: each of these names has its own resonance. The capital of two mighty empires which spanned almost 1,600 years, the city was first named Byzantium after Byzas the Greek who, according to Herodotus, founded it in the seventh century BC. Walls were raised around the acropolis on the point where the Topkapı Palace now stands. Byzantium paid tribute to Rome from the second century BC and was later incorporated into the Roman Empire, but retained its status as a free city. It was sacked by Septimius Severus in 196 AD for siding with his rival and then rebuilt along Roman

BYZANTINE EMPERORS

324–337	Constantine the Great	685–695	Justinian II
337–361	Constantius	695–698	Leontius
361–363	Julian the Apostate	698–705	Tiberius III
363–364	Jovian	705–711	Justinian II (again)
364–378	Valens	711–713	Phillipicus Bardanes
379–395	Theodosius the Great	713–715	Anastasius II
395–408	Arcadius	715–717	Theodosius III
408–450	Theodosius II	717–741	Leo III
450–457	Marcian	741–775	Constantine V
457–474	Leo I	775–780	Leo IV
474	Leo II	780–797	Constantine VI
474–491	Zeno	797–802	Eirene
491–518	Anastasius	802–811	Nicephorus I
518–527	Justin I	811–813	Michael I
527–565	Justinian the Great	813–820	Leo V
565–578	Justin II	820–829	Michael II
578–582	Tiberius II	829–842	Theophilus
582–602	Maurice	842–867	Michael III
602–610	Phocas	867–886	Basil I
610–641	Heraclius	886–912	Leo VI
641	Constantine II	912–913	Alexander
641	Heracleonas	913–959	Constantine VII
641–668	Constantine III		Porphyrogenitus
668–685	Constantine IV	919–944	Romanus I Lecapenus

lines with temples, baths, a hippo-drome and new walls, covering an area twice the size of the early settlement. The Romans had soon grasped the strategic importance of the site, but it was not until the fourth century that Constantine the Great named this his New Rome, the Christian capital of the Roman Empire. Rome had had its day. New walls, marked out

Constantine the Great

959–963	Romanus II
963–969	Nicephorus II Phocas
969–976	John I Tzimisces
976–1025	Basil II
1025–1028	Constantine VIII
1028–1034	Romanus III Argyrus
1034–1041	Michael IV
1041–1042	Michael V
1042	Theodora and Zoe
1042–1055	Constantine IX
1055–1056	Theodora (again)
1056–1057	Michael VI
1057–1059	Isaac I Comnenus
1059–1067	Constantine X Ducas
1067–1071	Romanus IV Diogenes
1071–1078	Michael VII Ducas
1078–1081	Nicephorus III Botaniates
1081–1118	Alexius I Comnenus
1118–1143	John II Comnenus
1143–1180	Manuel I Comnenus
1180–1183	Alexius II Comnenus
1183–1185	Andronicus I Comnenus
1185–1195	Isaac II Angelus
1195–1203	Alexius III Angelus
1203–1204	Isaac II Angelus and Alexius IV
1204	Alexius V Ducas Murtzupholos
1204–1222	Theodore I Lascaris
1222–1254	John III Ducas Vatatzes
1254–1258	Theodore II Lascaris
1258–1259	John IV Lascaris
1259–1282	Michael VIII Paleologus
1282–1328	Andronicus II Paleologus
1328–1341	Andronicus III Paleologus
1341–1391	John V Paleologus
1347–1355	John VI Cantacuzenos
1376–1379	Andronicus IV Paleologus
1390	John VII Paleologus
1391–1425	Manuel II Paleologus
1425–1448	John VIII Paleologus
1448–1453	Constantine XI Paleologus

by the emperor himself, hugely increased the size of the city. On 11 May 330, it was dedicated in a splendid ceremony and from then on was known as Constantinople, although the people and the empire were still known as 'Byzantine'. And Constantinople it remained, long after it had fallen to Mehmet the Conqueror, first of the Ottoman sultans to reign from here. Whatever the name,

Mehmet the Conqueror

this has always been a marvellous city, not only for the site, surrounded by water and mighty walls in one of the prettiest settings anywhere, but also for its long and great history. It is replete with remnants of past ages in the form of Byzantine cisterns, Roman aqueducts and fora, Ottoman mosques and, as prominent as ever on the skyline, Justinian's great church of St Sophia, that later became a mosque and finally a museum, thus illustrating the changing fortunes of the city.

Constantinople was above all a Christian city, and many of the monuments which survive from this time are churches. But there were also secular buildings: the fourth-century Aqueduct of Valens, the forum of Constantine, the Great Palace and, of course, the Hippodrome, focus of city life. In the fifth century Theodosius II raised the tremendous city walls, which for so many centuries had withstood the attacks of Slavs, Bulgars, Huns, Arabs and many other besieging forces, and which are still one of the most impressive sights of Istanbul. Many other buildings have not survived, such as Constantine's great church of the Holy Apostles, which stood on the hill near the Fatıh Mosque. On a smaller scale, the palace workshops produced beautiful works of art, finely carved ivory panels, icons and illuminated manuscripts. Constantine had founded the city as New Rome, and yet, despite its Roman background, in the capital's streets Greek was the spoken language, as elsewhere in the Hellenistic East since the conquests of Alexander. Latin had its uses: 'the ruins of the Latin speech were darkly preserved in the terms of jurisprudence and acclamations of the palace' writes Gibbon. In other words, Latin was the language of the law, codified under Justinian. Greek, however, was the language spoken and, in later days, the Byzantines were known as the Greeks in the West. This difference was further accentuated when Theodosius I divided his empire between his two sons on his death in 395; Arcadius became emperor of the east and his ten-year-old brother Honorius ruled in Italy.

As Constantinople grew so did the Christian Church, which came to play an increasingly important part in daily life until religion and politics were inseparable. Up to the fifth century the emperors were crowned by the army, but now the Patriarch assumed this responsibility. As it strove to assert itself, the church had to contend, not only with paganism (even in the sixth century Justinian's great servant Tribonian, responsible for codification of the law, was a pagan), but with many Christian heresies, particularly in the eastern provinces. As early as 325 Constantine summoned the Council of Nicaea, over which he presided, to deal with one such heresy. The problem recurred time and again, however, as the Nestorian and Monophysite heresies and later the Iconoclastic crisis tore the church apart. In all this the emperor played a key role, since he was deemed to be God's representative on earth, equal of the apostles. There were further religious difficulties between Rome and Constantinople, with the Patriarch of the latter often a bitter rival of the Pope.

The sixth century was a Golden Age for Constantinople. Justinian's long reign (527–565) and liking for great monuments reshaped the city. The devastation

Justinian

wreaked by the Nika riots of January 532 (see p. 26) was seized as an opportunity to make his mark, and a new St Sophia began to rise on the site of the old. When complete, it would dominate the city. At the same time, Justinian's brilliant general Belisarius was busy reclaiming territory for the empire in North Africa and Italy, for which he was awarded a triumph in the Hippodrome. By now a triumph was a rare event, but splendid games and festivals took place in the Hippodrome, always a focus of city life. Like Rome, chariot racing was a favourite sport and the circus factions were powerful bodies, serving sometimes as a city militia: a fifth-century inscription in the Theodosian walls records the involvement of the Reds in repair work after an earthquake. Justinian's wife Theodora was the daughter of a bear-keeper for the Greens, but later changed her allegiance to the Blues. Closely-regulated guilds ran the trades, which had their own quarters, a custom inherited by the Ottomans and which persists today. Next to the Hippodrome and connected to it was the Great Palace, chief imperial residence. Mosaics from the colonnaded path linking the two are on show at the Mosaic Museum. There were also a number of other royal palaces both within and without the city walls.

A low point in Byzantine history was reached with the reign of the usurper Phocas in the early seventh century. The Persians overran many of the empire's eastern possessions and twice reached Chalcedon (modern Kadiköy) across the water. Heraclius, who had replaced Phocas and spent most of his reign fighting in the east, finally won a resounding victory against the Persians in 627. He made a triumphant return to the city in 628, entering through the Golden Gate in a splendid procession which included four elephants. The True Cross, won back from the Persians, was taken to St Sophia where a service of thanksgiving was held. These celebrations were somewhat premature, for a new power was rising in the East. For too long the Arabian frontier had been neglected and the forces of Islam now erupted out of Arabia and proceeded northwards, destroying the Persian Empire and taking over Egypt, Syria and Palestine. Within a century the Arabs had also moved into North Africa and Spain, but by this time the empire's attention was focused on a devastating crisis at home, which threatened to tear apart what was left of the empire (see p. 35).

Sadly, the struggles of the Iconoclastic period (717–845) have meant that no art of this period has survived, and much more besides was lost. Meanwhile, power struggles between Rome and Constantinople culminated in the coronation of Charlemagne, who was crowned Holy Roman Emperor on Christmas Day 800 by Pope Leo III in an affront to the Byzantine Empire. Charlemagne subsequently sent an embassy to the empress Eirene with a proposal of marriage. Had she accepted, and not been deposed

BYZANTINE *ADJ.*

adj. Relating to *Byzantium:* rigidly hierarchic, intricate, tortuous

The court at Constantinople was famed for its pomp and circumstance: one emperor, Constantine Porphyrogenitus (913–959), wrote a *Book of Ceremonies*, which gives details of the extraordinary ritual surrounding the person of the emperor, God's representative on earth. For example, on the feast of the emperor's name-day, the elaborate ceremony described involved a dance of high-ranking officials after the dinner:

> the Domestic of the Schools presents on his right hand the book of permission. The prefect of the table steps down and takes it, and gives it to the chamberlain in charge of the water ... The prefect of the table then turns and stretches out his right hand, opens his fingers in the form of rays and closes them again to form a bunch; and the Domestic of the Schools begins to dance with the Domestic of the Numeri, the Demarch, the tribunes, the vicars and the Demotes turning three times round the table ...

and so it continues in a ritual of extraordinary elaboration. In *The Decline and Fall of the Roman Empire*, Gibbon mutters darkly that the emperors were unduly influenced by eastern tradition, whereby forms of flattery such as hyperbolic titles ('your sublime Magnitude') were commonplace. The emperor was perceived to be on a different plane to his subjects. The hierarchy was certainly mystifying, particularly as it changed so much in the thousand years or more of the empire. Titles like 'clarissimi', 'spectabiles', 'illustres' and 'gloriosi', or 'drungarius of the fleet', 'eparch of the city' and 'logothete of the drome' have a wonderful resonance. Many other fantastic titles and personages fill the history of Byzantium and continued to influence the Ottomans on their arrival in Constantinople. Eunuchs were a prominent feature of both empires; since they could have no offspring they tended to be most loyal subjects, and rose to high rank in both church and state. Often, the sons of a deposed emperor or younger brother were subjected to castration to prevent any future claim to the throne. While a cruel punishment, it was better than the alternatives of blinding, slitting of the tongue or loss of one's nose (rhinokopia), all common practice in Byzantium. In later days, particularly after the Latin occupation of the thirteenth century, the capital declined, the city lost much of its population and the court much of its splendour.

shortly after, the history and shape of Europe might have been quite different. Eirene temporarily restored the icons, but she bankrupted the empire. This was the time of two other great foreign rulers: Haroun ar-Rashid, the Abbasid caliph ruled in Baghdad, and the Bulgars had been united under their khan, the great Krum. Both threatened the empire, indeed Krum managed to wipe out an entire Byzantine army, killing the emperor in the process and forever after using the skull of the unfortunate Nicephorus as a drinking cup. Despite fighting the Arabs for most of his reign, the last iconoclastic emperor, Theophilus, was fascinated with Islamic culture and by tales of the splendours of the Abbasid court. Having built the Magnaura Palace, he had a wonderful golden tree constructed over his throne full of mechanical birds 'guarded by gilded lions who beat the ground with their tails and emitted dreadful roars', according to one tenth-century ambassador to the court. On Easter Sunday 867 the huge apse mosaic of the Virgin and Child in St Sophia was unveiled, marking a formal end to iconoclasm.

In the same year a man of lowly origins, Basil the Macedonian, murdered Michael III (also known as 'the Sot') and came to power, founding a new dynasty. Despite this inauspicious beginning, he reigned for almost twenty years and both his political and artistic achievements were great. With boundless energy he repaired St Sophia, the church of the Holy Apostles and many other churches and palaces, and built the Nea, or new church, within the palace grounds. With gilded domes and splendid mosaics it was a fine sight, but sadly none of Basil's work remains. His son Leo VI (Leo the Wise), rather more of an intellectual, succeeded him and was responsible for codifying the law. This was an enormous task which was last undertaken by Justinian in the sixth century when Latin was still used for legal matters. Both Leo and his brother Alexander, a famous drunkard, feature in the mosaics of St Sophia.

The splendidly named Basil the Bulgar-Slayer (976–1025) won back the whole of the Balkans from the Bulgars and, in a long and successful reign, proved himself both a brilliant general and careful administrator. The marriage of his sister to Prince Vladimir of Kiev marked the conversion of the Russians to Christianity. Basil never married and his death marked the beginning of a long, slow decline for the empire. In 1054 the final split between the Church of Rome and the Eastern (Orthodox) Church occurred when three papal legates in Constantinople excommunicated the Patriarch after a long and bitter wrangle between Pope Leo IX and the Patriarch. The empress Theodora's death in 1056 marked the end of the Macedonian dynasty and a new dynasty, the Comneni, began with the coronation of Isaac Comnenus in 1057. Ominous changes were taking place in the East where a new power was rising. The arrival of the Seljuks was the beginning of the end. At the battle of Manzikert in 1071 the Byzantine army was routed by Alp Arslan, with the ensuing loss of much of Anatolia to the Turks.

This was an unmitigated disaster and the empire was fortunate indeed that an able emperor should have acceded to the throne shortly afterwards. Alexius Comnenus provided a firm hand for almost forty years and did much to restore the empire's fortunes. The first Crusade began with an appeal by Alexius to the West for help against the Turks. Ultimately this was a disaster for Constantinople, for it was an unholy alliance of the Fourth Crusade cleverly manipulated by the crafty Venetian doge, Dandolo, which was diverted to Constantinople and sacked it in 1204. The Venetians and Genoese had long traded in the Byzantine Empire and, while Alexius had wooed the Venetians, his grandson

Manuel evicted them from their district in Constantinople. This was to prove a very costly mistake.

After the Restoration the city was ruined and under-populated, and it never recovered from the depredations of the Franks and Venetians. The Paleologue dynasty presided over a final flourish, but these were the twilight years of the Byzantine Empire, now reduced to a rump state around the city. The magnificent mosaics in St Sophia and St Saviour in Chora are a tribute to the artistic revival of the times. It was now the turn of the Genoese to prosper and for a while they had the upper hand over Venice; these two great trading powers were often at war during this time. The Genoese received a grant of land in Galata from the emperor. Allowed considerable autonomy, the Genoese grew very powerful; proof of this strength can be seen by the way they lost no time in fortifying their quarter, against orders. The Galata tower was added in the fourteenth century; Genoese occupation of the Byzantine castle at the top of the Bosphorus dates from this period.

A new enemy had appeared in the fourteenth century and was beginning to encroach on the remains of the Byzantine Empire. By the time of his death in 1324 the founder of the Ottoman Empire, Osman Gazi, had conquered

THE FOURTH CRUSADE

The Fourth Crusade began with the best of intentions; called by Pope Innocent III, it was intended to attack Egypt. The Venetians agreed to provide ships, but the Crusade was unable to pay the money it owed them and, by way of compensation, agreed to attack the port of Zara, recently lost by the Venetians to the Hungarians. An attack by Crusaders on a Christian city was a controversial move, but in a dramatic flourish the doge himself offered to go, and sewed on the cross at the altar of St Mark's Cathedral. The Pope in reply excommunicated the entire Crusade, but Zara fell in 1202 to this combined force. At this time the deposed Byzantine emperor Isaac Angelus appeared in Venice, begging for help to reclaim his throne from Alexius III. (The latter had favoured the Genoese and Pisans, so Venice's trading interests were directly involved.) A sum of 200,000 marks was promised in return for help, very rashly as it transpired, and also for material help with the Crusades and union of the churches. The Crusaders (some of whom had disagreed with this diversion and left) arrived at Chalcedon on 24 June 1203. They then crossed over to take Galata on 6 July before turning to the city, where the doge Dandolo, over

eighty years old and almost totally blind, led his fleet up the Golden Horn to attack the great walls at the weak point where land and sea walls meet near the Blachernae Palace. The attackers were successful and Constantinople was stormed. Alexius III fled on 17 July and Isaac and his father were crowned co-emperors, but were unable to keep their promises of financial reward. In April 1204 the Crusaders, who had been camping outside the city walls and who cannot have failed to appreciate the great wealth and beauty of the city, decided to seize this great prize. After further fighting they took Constantinople on 13 April 1204 and one of their number, Baldwin, was crowned emperor the following month.

Thus began the Latin occupation of Constantinople. The spoils of three days of rampage and looting were shared out: officially, of 900,000 marks-worth of booty, 500,000 went to Venice and three-eighths of the empire, including St Sophia and various strategic harbours. Venice's rivals Genoa and Pisa were excluded from trade with the empire. The emperor got a quarter of the city and of the empire, while the rest went to the Franks, who were responsible for melting down the great silver iconostasis of St Sophia. Unlike the Franks, who were more interested in gold, the Venetians had a discerning eye for works of art – and Constantinople was full of these. The sixth-century bronze quadriga from the Hippodrome went to grace the façade of St Mark's Cathedral, the famous icon of the Virgin Nicopoiea which the Byzantine emperors carried into battle was taken, and a wonderful collection of Byzantine art now housed in the Treasury of St Mark's also came from the looted city. Dandolo did not live long to enjoy his triumph, for he died the following year. A part of his sarcophagus can be seen in the South Gallery of St Sophia. The Latin occupation lasted for nearly sixty years and left Constantinople a shadow of its once mighty self. The city reverted quite suddenly to Greek rule in 1261, when it fell to an opportunistic attack; now the boot was on the other foot and the Genoese traders gained the ascendant over Venice.

most of the neighbouring province of Bithynia. His successor Orhan Gazi, the first to call himself sultan, made Bursa his capital in 1326. Weakened by internal dissent, disease and disaster (the Black Death hit Constantinople in 1347, killing almost one-third of the population; the year before part of the dome of St Sophia had collapsed), their appeals for help ignored by the West, the Byzantine Empire was now lurching towards its end. Constantinople was now ignominiously reduced to paying tribute to the Ottomans, who had encircled it. The castle of Anadolu Hisarı was built on the Bosphorus by Beyazıt I who besieged Constantinople. It was saved by the Mongols who invaded Asia Minor and defeated the Turks, capturing the sultan. A contemporary account by a visitor to Constantinople in 1400 reveals the state of the city:

Though the circuit of the walls is thus very great and the area spacious, the city is not throughout very densely populated. There are within its compass many hills and valleys where cornfields and orchards are found ... Everywhere throughout the city there are many great palaces, churches and monasteries, but most of them are now in ruin.

Desperate for Rome's help, the emperor agreed to a union of the churches, but this was never accepted by the Greek clergy or the public at large.

In 1451 Mehmet (later styled 'the Conqueror') succeeded his father Murat II and immediately set about building a castle opposite

Anadolu Hisarı. Rumeli Hisarı was built with great speed in one year and the Turks, with a stranglehold on the Bosphorus, could now move in for the kill. Siege preparations began on both sides, but the great city was starved of fighting men and vulnerable. The Genoese provided a small contingent and their leader John Giustiniani played a key role during the siege, but calls for help to European powers went unanswered.

Theodosius II

OTTOMAN SULTANS

c.1281-1326	Osman Gazi	1623-1640	Murat IV
c.1326-1362	Orhan Gazi	1640-1648	Ibrahim I
1362-1389	Murat I		('the Mad')
1389-1402	Beyazıt I (Yıldırım or 'the Thunderbolt')	1648-1687	Mehmet IV
		1687-1691	Süleyman II
1402-1413	*Interregnum*	1691-1695	Ahmet II
1413-1421	Mehmet I	1695-1703	Mustafa II
1421-1451	Murat II	1703-1730	Ahmet III
1451-1481	Mehmet II (Fatıh or 'the Conqueror')	1730-1754	Mahmut I
		1754-1757	Osman III
1481-1512	Beyazıt II	1757-1774	Mustafa III
1512-1520	Selim I (Yavuz or 'the Grim')	1774-1789	Abdül Hamit I
		1789-1807	Selim III
1520-1566	Süleyman I ('the Magnificent')	1807-1808	Mustafa IV
		1808-1839	Mahmut II
1566-1574	Selim II ('the Sot')	1839-1861	Abdül Mecit I
1574-1595	Murat III	1861-1876	Abdül Aziz
1595-1603	Mehmet III	1876	Murat V
1603-1617	Ahmet I	1876-1909	Abdül Hamit II
1617-1618	Mustafa I	1909-1918	Mehmet V Reşat
1618-1622	Osman II	1918-1922	Mehmet VI
1622-1623	Mustafa I (second reign)	1922-1924	Abdül Mecit (II) (caliph only)

The Ottoman period

In March 1453 the Ottoman fleet sailed up the Dardanelles into the Sea of Marmara, with orders to ensure no supplies reached Constantinople by sea. At the same time Mehmet began to march his army through Thrace towards the city. On Easter Monday, 2 April, when the defenders sighted the first Turkish troops, Emperor Constantine ordered the destruction of the bridges across the moat and closed the city gates. The same day, a Genoese engineer fixed a great chain on wooden floats across the entrance to the Golden Horn. On 6 April the Ottoman troops were in their final positions before the Theodosian walls, the defenders had moved to their allotted stations and the siege began. For over seven long weeks the Turkish cannons mercilessly bombarded the great walls of Constantinople, and every night the Christians courageously did what they could to repair the damage. Though the Byzantines and Genoese were outnumbered ten to one they defended their city bravely.

During the third week of the siege Mehmet played his master card. Under cover of darkness teams of oxen dragged part of the Ottoman fleet along wooden rollers over the high ridge between the Bosphorus and the Golden Horn. On 22 April the city awoke to the terrifying sight of around fifty Turkish ships in the harbour, within the chain. Though prospects must have seemed bleak, the Byzantines had everything to fight for. They redeployed as many soldiers as could be spared to the defence of the Sea Walls along the Horn and the Christian fleet, still a force to be reckoned with, anchored at the chain to prevent the two parts of the Ottoman navy joining up and to welcome any relieving flotilla that might arrive. However, no relief was forthcoming and three hours before daybreak on 29 May Sultan Mehmet ordered the final all-out assault, a simultaneous attack on the Land and Sea Walls. It was a desperate battle, but finally Constantinople's great Land Walls, which had withstood so many attacks, were breached and the Turks poured into the city. Constantine died fighting alongside his men.

By noon the city was completely in Turkish hands and in the early afternoon Sultan Mehmet, riding a white horse, made his triumphant entry as Fatıh, 'the Conqueror'. In line with tradition he allowed his troops to loot and pillage for three days, and as he rode down the main street towards St Sophia the scene was of devastation, terror and carnage. One of Mehmet's first acts was to convert St Sophia, the great cathedral of Byzantium, into a mosque, and the following Friday he attended Muslim prayers there. The Conqueror had achieved his life's ambition, Constantinople was his, and immediately he instigated a rebuilding and repopulation programme so that the new capital of the Ottoman Empire would become the greatest of all Islamic cities. For the stability of the dynasty he introduced a fratricide law whereby it was deemed proper for a new sultan to eliminate all his brothers on accession to the throne.

Under Mehmet and his son Beyazıt II Constantinople was transformed. As Turks, Greeks, Armenians and Sephardic Jews were brought in, trade and commerce thrived and the city became lively and cosmopolitan. Along with St Sophia, other churches were converted into mosques and graced with minarets, the church of the Holy Apostles was demolished to make room for Mehmet's own splendid mosque complex on the fourth hill, and Beyazıt built his imperial mosque in the market district beside the new Covered Bazaar. Nearby was Mehmet's first palace, the Eski Saray or Old Palace where the sultan resided until his workmen had completed

the luxurious pavilions and gardens of the Topkapı Palace on the first hill. Mehmet's conquests did not stop at Constantinople. He led his army deeper into Europe and made Serbia and Bosnia Ottoman provinces.

Selim I, who forced his father Beyazıt to abdicate in 1512, earned the nickname Yavuz, 'Grim' or 'Resolute', because of his stern and unyielding character. He acquired such a reputation for executing his viziers that 'May you be a vizier of Selim' became a common curse formula. Selim was highly successful on the battlefield. After eliminating all his rivals including three of his own sons, he decisively defeated the shah of Iran in 1514, and added Eastern Anatolia to the empire. Next it was the turn of the Mameluk sultan of Egypt, who was overthrown in 1517 and hanged from one of the gates of Cairo. Egypt, Syria and Arabia, with the holy cities of Mecca and Medina, were brought within the Ottoman realm and after Selim received the keys of the Ka'ba, the sacred black stone, from the Sherif of Mecca he assumed the title 'Caliph of God on Earth'. He brought the Prophet's robe and other sacred relics back to Constantinople where they were enshrined in a special suite of rooms in Topkapı Palace called the 'Pavilion of the

Holy Mantle'. Thenceforth Constantinople could really claim to be the capital of Islam.

Selim's beautiful mosque on Istanbul's Fifth Hill was completed by his eldest son Süleyman the Magnificent (1520–1566), during whose reign both Ottoman art and architecture and the Ottoman Empire reached their peak. Under

Süleyman the Magnificent

corsair admirals like Barbarossa, the Turks asserted their naval power in the Mediterranean and the Red Sea, and even challenged the Portuguese in the Indian Ocean. Western Christendom watched with trepidation as the Ottoman army captured Belgrade in 1521, routed the Hungarians at Mohacs in 1526, then overran the whole of Hungary and in 1529 reached the gates of Vienna. Here, however, Ottoman expansion into

Europe was finally halted, for after 28 days Süleyman was forced to abandon the siege.

Much of the wealth of empire was used to adorn Constantinople with splendid buildings and works of art. Sinan, greatest and most prolific of all imperial architects (see p. 96), was commissioned to design or restore over 300 structures in Istanbul alone. His masterpiece, the Süleymaniye, which dominates the Third Hill and is surrounded by a vast complex of dependencies, epitomizes the Ottoman Golden Age. Süleyman is buried there alongside his wife, the beautiful and powerful Roxelana, whose influence over the sultan was so great it was rumoured she had bewitched him. Certainly she engineered the strangulation of Süleyman's eldest son Mustafa so her own son Selim would succeed to the throne.

With Selim, who was nicknamed 'the Sot', there began the era known as the 'Sultanate of Women' (1566–1652) during which the sultans spent most of their time in the palace rather than on the battlefield and the harem increased in size and importance. A series of strong-willed queen mothers and royal favourites exercised the real power behind the throne while affairs of state were managed by powerful Grand Viziers. By the reign of Ahmet I (1603–17) Mehmet's fratricide law had been abolished, but as the royal princes were still considered a threat they were no longer appointed as governors in the provinces with their own entourage and their own armies. Instead they were confined to a part of the palace known as 'the Cage', whence they only emerged (if at all) to ascend the throne, with no experience of the world outside. The Ottoman Empire had begun its slow but steady decline, but this was certainly not obvious to the outside observer. Though the state was bankrupt after long and unsuccessful wars with Austria and Persia, Ahmet commissioned the largest of all the great imperial mosques, known today as the Blue Mosque, unique in Turkey with its six minarets. Istanbul had more mosques than any other city in the Muslim world, their grey and white domes and minarets rising above the red-roofed houses to create the city's incomparable skyline.

In 1683 Mehmet IV failed disastrously in the second attempt to capture Vienna; Austria, Poland and Venice then formed a Holy League and declared war against the sultan. The Turks were forced to relinquish many of their Balkan conquests and in 1699 signed the humiliating Treaty of Karlowitz which marked the end of an era in the history of the Ottoman Empire. More defeats were to follow, more land was lost and it was clear there would be no return to the Golden Age of conquest. During the eighteenth century, exorbitant taxes levied to pay for the extravaganzas and luxury of the imperial court led to popular unrest. Ahmet III (1703–30), cruel but cultivated, presided over the 'Tulip Age' (see p. 208) organizing spectacular spring festivals to celebrate the blossoming of Turkey's favourite flower. This was the era of the baroque, when Istanbul was peppered with pretty curvular fountains and graced with flamboyant mosques like Laleli Camii and the Nuruosmaniye.

Selim III, who came to the throne in 1789 and was influenced by the progressive ideas of the French Revolution, was the first sultan to recognize the serious need for reform. However, his attempts to modernize the armed forces triggered a revolt of the Janissaries. This resulted in Selim's abdication and finally his murder, which was brutally carried out by the Chief Black Eunuch and his men in the Harem music room. It was left to Selim's cousin Mahmut II to deal with the Janissaries who rose in open rebellion soon after he acceded to the throne in 1808. After quelling the uprising Mahmut bided his time until he was in a strong enough position to approve a decree abolishing the

Janissary corps. Friday 16 June 1826 was thenceforth known as the day of the 'Auspicious Event' (see p. 106).

Mahmut's baroque mosque by the Bosphorus, the Nusretiye (Victory) Camii celebrates his triumph. It was designed by Kirkor Balian, the first in a dynasty of Armenian architects who were responsible for so many of the exuberant nineteenth-century mosques and palaces along the Bosphorus. Mahmut's son Abdül Mecit commissioned the ostentatious marble palace of Dolmabahçe which was formally opened by a great banquet held on 13 July 1856 to celebrate the end of the Crimean War. High society moved to the Bosphorus shores, where the sultan also built other palaces for himself and his daughters.

Though Abdül Mecit was committed to the reform process his extravagances virtually ruined the empire, for the government took out foreign loans at high interest rates which it was unable to repay. Meanwhile the reform movement gathered momentum and in 1877 Abdül Hamit II (1876–1909) was advised to accept a constitution and convene the first Ottoman parliament. The same year Russia declared war on Turkey and by the beginning of 1878 the Russian army was within ten miles of Istanbul. Under the

Treaty of Berlin the European powers managed to check Russian ambitions in the Balkans and rescue the Ottoman Empire from extinction, but the writing was on the wall. Abdül Hamit dissolved parliament but was himself deposed in 1909 by the liberal movement known as the 'Young Turks'. Their Committee of Union and Progress under Enver Pasha took control of government and the new sultan, Mehmet V Reşat became a mere puppet.

In 1914 Turkey entered the First World War on the side of Germany and four years later had to suffer the consequences of defeat. On 30 October 1918 an armistice was signed between Britain and Turkey, Istanbul was placed under Allied occupation, and plans were drafted for the dismemberment of the Ottoman Empire. Sultan Mehmet VI had no option but to accept the Treaty of Sèvres, which reduced Ottoman territory to Istanbul and part of Anatolia. At this point the Turkish people rallied to the call of the Turkish nationalists led by Mustafa Kemal (later known as Atatürk) who launched a war of resistance against the Allies and their peace terms. In 1920 Mustafa Kemal established a nationalist parliament, the Grand National Assembly, in Ankara, in opposition to the sultan's puppet government in

Istanbul. Finally, at the Lausanne peace conference, he obtained from the Allies new frontiers for Turkey, which thenceforth comprised the whole of Anatolia and a strip of Europe including Edirne. The Turkish National Assembly formally abolished the Ottoman sultanate and proclaimed a new Turkish Republic with Atatürk as its first president and Ankara as the capital. Sultan Mehmet VI left for exile aboard a British warship, and though his brother Abdül Mecit (II) retained the position of caliph, in 1924 the caliphate was abolished and he too was forced to leave the country. The Ottoman Empire was extinct and for the first time in 1600 years Istanbul had lost its status as a capital city.

Modern Istanbul is less cosmopolitan than it used to be, for the European embassies packed up long ago and moved to Ankara and most of the Greeks, Armenians and Jews have also departed. Instead, hundreds of thousands of Anatolians have poured into the city in search of work, causing a population expansion which seems out of control. Modern flats, office blocks and giant hotels have replaced most of the old wooden houses and spread over the green hillsides along the Bosphorus and Sea of Marmara. Despite the changes Istanbul remains one of the most vibrant and fascinating

cities in the world: Asian and European, a bridge between two continents. A stroll through the streets soon reveals lively and colourful bazaars and markets, palaces, mansions, mosques and churches, the magnificent heritage of two great empires, the Byzantine and the Ottoman.

Flag seller near Yeni Valide Camii

WALKING TOURS

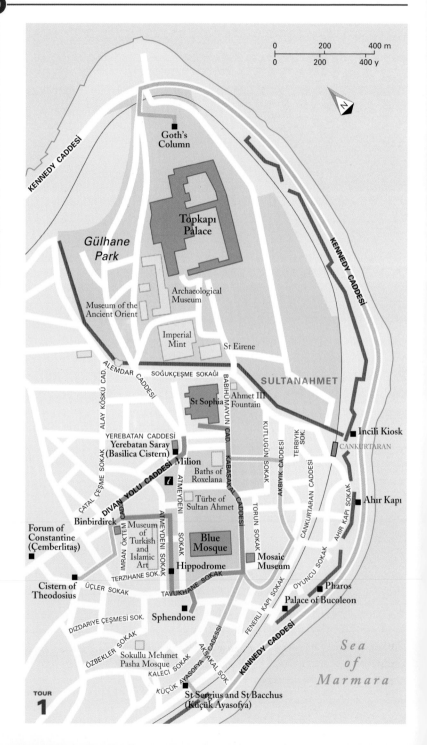

0   200   400 m
0   200   400 y

KENNEDY CADDESİ

Goth's Column

KENNEDY CADDESİ

Topkapı Palace

Gülhane Park

Archaeological Museum

Museum of the Ancient Orient

Imperial Mint

St Eirene

ALEMDAR CADDESİ

SOĞUKÇEŞME SOKAĞI

SULTANAHMET

ALAY KÖŞKÜ CAD.

BABIHÜMAYUN CAD.

St Sophia

Ahmet III Fountain

İncili Kiosk

YEREBATAN CADDESİ

Yerebatan Saray (Basilica Cistern)

CANKURTARAN

KUTLUGÜN SOKAK

TERBIYIK SOK.

Milion

ÇATAL ÇEŞME SOKAK

DIVAN YOLU CADDESİ

Baths of Roxelana

KABASAKAL CADDESİ

AKBIYIK CADDESİ

Ahır Kapı

AHIR KAPI SOKAK

ATMEYDANI

Türbe of Sultan Ahmet

TORUN SOKAK

CANKURTARAN CADDESİ

Forum of Constantine (Çemberlitaş)

Binbirdirek

Museum of Turkish and Islamic Art

IMRAN ÖKTEM CAD.

ATMEYDANI SOKAK

Blue Mosque

Mosaic Museum

OYUNCU SOKAK

Pharos

Palace of Bucoleon

Cistern of Theodosius

ÜÇLER SOKAK

TERZIHANE SOK.

Hippodrome

TAVUKHANE SOKAK

FENERLİ KAPI SOKAK

Sphendone

DIZDARIYE ÇEŞMESİ SOK.

Sea of Marmara

ÖZBEKLER SOKAK

Sokullu Mehmet Pasha Mosque

KALECİ SOKAK

KÜÇÜK AYASOFYA

AKSAKAL SOKAK

AKSAKAL CADDESİ

KENNEDY CADDESİ

St Sergius and St Bacchus (Küçük Ayasofya)

TOUR
1

The early Byzantine city

'Formed by nature for the centre and capital of a great monarchy' is Gibbon's description of Constantinople. This walk focuses on the original Roman city, laid out by Septimius Severus some years after his troops had sacked old Byzantium, and resplendently enlarged by Constantine and Justinian. The Topkapı Palace now stands over the acropolis of the small, pre-Roman city. Septimius Severus moved the walls westwards as it more than doubled in size and a Hippodrome, baths, temples and squares were laid out. But it was Constantine who made this New Rome, Christian capital of the empire, tracing out the line of the walls himself with a lance, somewhere beyond where the Fatıh Mosque now stands on the site of Constantine's church of the Holy Apostles. And it was Justinian who raised what is still a landmark of the famous Istanbul skyline, the tremendous architectural and religious statement which is the great church of St Sophia. By this time Constantinople was a worthy rival to Rome – indeed, within a century of its dedication in 330, the city's population was half a million. It had its own Senate and was embellished with theatres, colonnaded streets, churches and squares.

A focal point and the setting of many a dramatic moment in history was the Hippodrome, where emperors were crowned and, on occasion, beheaded, to the clamour of the mob. The Great Palace (actually a complex of palace buildings dating from different periods) grew up on the slopes overlooking the Sea of Marmara. As the city grew, so its boundaries moved outwards, culminating in the magnificent Theodosian walls which remained invulnerable for many centuries. Emperors left their mark in monuments ranging from grand fora, churches and columns to more prosaic cisterns, walls and aqueducts. The Aqueduct of Valens no longer brings water to Istanbul, but parts of the Byzantine water system were in use as late as the

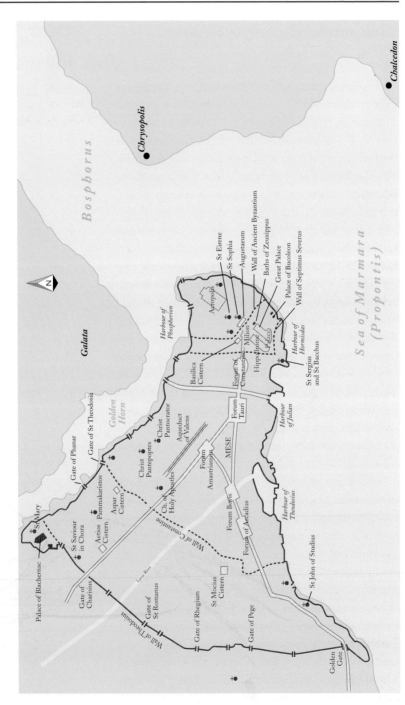

- Chalcedon
- Chrysopolis
- Bosphorus
- Galata
- Golden Horn
- St Mary
- Palace of Blachernae
- St Saviour in Chora
- Aetios Cistern
- Aspar Cistern
- Pammakaristos
- Gate of Phanar
- Gate of St Theodosia
- Christ Pantocrator
- Christ Pantepoptes
- Aqueduct of Valens
- Harbour of Phosphorion
- St Eirene
- St Sophia
- Augustaeum
- Wall of Ancient Byzantium
- Baths of Zeuxippus
- Great Palace
- Palace of Bucoleon
- Wall of Septimus Severus
- Acropolis
- Milion
- Hippodrome
- Palace
- Harbour of Hermisdas
- St Sergius and St Bacchus
- Basilica Cistern
- Forum of Constantine
- Forum Tauri
- MESE
- Forum Amastrianum
- Ch. of Holy Apostles
- Wall of Constantine
- Lycus River
- Forum Bovis
- Forum of Arcadius
- Harbour of Julian
- Harbour of Theodosius
- St John of Studius
- Sea of Marmara (Propontis)
- Gate of Charisius
- Gate of St Romanus
- Gate of Rhegium
- St Mocius Cistern
- Gate of Pege
- Wall of Theodosius
- Golden Gate

BYZANTINE CONSTANTINOPLE

nineteenth century. Much more of this period remains underground, although recent excavations of some beautiful frescoes and what may have been the archives of the Great Palace serve as a reminder of the wealth of history over which thousands of people tread daily.

Next to a brick *taksim* (water distribution centre) an apparently insignificant fragment of stone excavated in the early twentieth century marks the point from which all distances were measured. The **Milion** (from Miliarum Aureum or Golden Milestone) probably predates Constantine's reign and may mark the original Thracian Gate into the city. A monumental tetrapylon (gateway with four openings), it was apparently crowned with a part of the True Cross, discovered in Jerusalem by Constantine's mother, the Empress (Augusta) Helena, after whom the adjacent great square or Augustaeum was named. The Augustaeum covered the earlier Severan Square, in turn probably built over the agora of the original Greek city. From here the *mese*, a colonnaded street, led westwards along the present course of Divan Yolu and out to the city walls.

Along the way the *mese* ran through the magnificent oval **Forum of Constantine**, adorned with statues of pagan gods and Christian saints in a fascinating blend of religions. To cap it all, Constantine placed a column in the centre with a bronze statue of himself as Apollo holding sceptre and globe. A crown of rays blazed from his head. Certainly this was a man with a large ego; his tomb in the specially-built church of the Holy Apostles was placed within a circle of twelve sarcophagi representing the Twelve Apostles, with whom he deemed himself equal. Nowadays; all that remains of his forum is a rather dingy and truncated column, bound with the rusty hoops to which its Turkish name, Çemberlitaş, refers. Beyond here the *mese* continued on to the Forum Tauri (Forum of Theodosius), a once-splendid affair judging by the huge columns decorated with an unusual 'peacock's eye' relief. These were part of a triumphal arch, and now lie piled by the road beyond the Beyazıt mosque complex. Here the road forked, one branch running out to the Golden Gate through the Forum Bovis and Forum of Arcadius and the other following the aqueduct to emerge at the Gate of Charisius, near the church of St Saviour in Chora.

Round the corner from the Milion is the entrance to **Yerebatan Saray**, also called the Basilica Cistern after a nearby square. Open 9 am–5.30 pm, it is one of a number of surviving Byzantine cisterns. As with any large city an adequate water supply was essential and an extensive water storage and distribution network ensured this. Yerebatan is now a justifiably popular tourist spot – a trip to the damp and atmospheric world below comes as a welcome relief on a baking summer's day. Concerts are given down here in summer, and there is a small café. Yerebatan has a capacity of 80,000m^3 and measures 138m by 64m, although one section is now walled-off. Follow the steps down to see the impressive brick-vaulting of the ceiling and the forest of columns (336 in all), taking the walkway between them which passes a reused 'peacock's eye' column of the type found at the Forum Tauri. At the far end descend a few more steps to see two colossal stone Medusa's heads serving as column bases – presumably they were pressed into service when the cistern was rebuilt in the sixth century under Justinian. You emerge by an exit some distance downhill from the entrance.

There are two other Byzantine cisterns nearby: **Binbirdirek** (the Cistern of Philoxenes) is the nearest. Located across the Hippodrome on Oktem Cad., it has been converted to house a café, bar and restaurant (entrance fee includes a non-alcoholic drink). Binbirdirek means 'one thousand and one columns' – definitely a case of poetic licence! Its double columns, on some of which the mason's marks scratched into the stone are still visible, are girdled by stone ties. Most of the floor has been raised but a section in the centre shows the original depth. Just a two-minute walk from here is the less-frequented **Cistern of Theodosius** in the large Eminönü Belediye Baskangli building. Technically it is not open to the public, but the watchman may let you in and switch the lights on. This is a far smaller cistern: a mere thirty-two columns support the roof. In the right-hand corner there is a channel which apparently leads to Binbirdirek, and, diagonally opposite, one going to the cistern at Laleli – all part of the water grid which once supplied the city.

In the direction of the Hippodrome lie the ruins of two fifth-century palaces, one of which was later converted to become the **Martyrium of St Euphemia** of Chalcedon. Murdered in 303 her relics are now in the Greek Patriarchate at Fener. Now lying within the grounds of the large building next door, not much can be seen of this structure, formerly the fifth-century palace of the eunuch Antiochus, *praepositus sacri cubiculi* (Grand Chamberlain) to the emperor. There are some remains visible of the adjacent **Palace of Lausos** with its vestibule and seven-apsed hall, though much of the area has been landscaped and bricked over.

Atmeydan (the 'Square of Horses'), the present name of the **Hippodrome**, preserves the memory of its past, but three monuments and part of its tremendous foundations are all that now remain. Constantine enlarged the original Severan hippodrome to hold up to 100,000 spectators and adorned it with statues and columns brought from the corners of the empire as war trophies and objects of worship. Three of these now remain, though many more once stood along the *spina* or centre of the track. Almost 500m in length, the Hippodrome's main entrance was at the north end, while the Royal Box or *Kathisma* was probably on the east, with access to the palace. The southern end (*sphendone*) was semicircular, and it is these impressive foundations which are still visible. Construction of the Blue Mosque in the seventeenth century led to the demolition of the Hippodrome, but some of its stones had doubtless already been robbed for other buildings.

BREAD AND CIRCUSES

Juvenal's famous nostrum for appeasement of the mob was as true of Constantinople as of Rome. While chariot-racing was a favourite spectator sport, it also involved serious politics. Charioteers raced in quadrigas (drawn by four horses) under different colours, red, white, blue and green, each of which was associated with a different faction. The Reds and Whites were later absorbed by the Blues and Greens and rivalry between the two factions was intense. The Blues tended to be conservative and more orthodox in religion, while the Greens drew a lot of members from trade and industry, many from the eastern provinces. Consequently the Greens also had associations with the Monophysite heresy (see p. 36) prevalent there. During times of crisis, the factions could be pressed into service, for example, to repair the walls of the city. In the Archaeological Museum are two statue bases commemorating the famous charioteer Porphyrius – a total of seven once stood along the *spina* of the Hippodrome, erected in his honour by the factions. A good charioteer could make a lot of money – 25 races was the standard number for a festival day. Apart from the races there would be dancing and music and possibly circus games. Like football hooliganism in the twentieth century, rivalry among the factions occasionally spilled out into the streets to disastrous effect.

During the Nika riots of 532, the factions were most dangerously united in their dissatisfaction with Justinian. The emperor was already unpopular for having increased taxation by running a more efficient tax collection service when, in January 532 he made the mistake of punishing both factions for rioting at the Hippodrome. At the races three days later the crowd began chanting 'Nika, Nika' (meaning 'Win', it was normally shouted at the charioteers) before pouring out onto the streets to wreak havoc. Days later the city was in ruins and the panicked emperor was packing his bags. Had it not been for the cool head of his wife Theodora who, in a stirring speech ('the throne is a glorious sepulchre'), urged him to stay and fight, and the courage of his great general Belisarius, Justinian might well have lost his throne. Belisarius gathered troops loyal to him and led them into the Hippodrome to confront the rioters, who had already appointed themselves a new emperor. The eunuch Narses, in charge of the Imperial Bodyguard, blocked the exits as the slaughter began.

In all, it is thought that 30,000 rioters died in the massacre, and the power of the factions was broken. The city was devastated. St Sophia lay smouldering in ruins and, doubtless grateful to God for his narrow escape, Justinian decided to build a magnificent replacement. So it is that we have a disgruntled mob of the sixth century to thank for one of the most beautiful buildings in Christendom.

The Hippodrome

One cannot underestimate the importance of the Hippodrome in the early Byzantine period. It dominated daily life in the city. Not only were there chariot-races, but also triumphs, circuses, festivals and, all too often for many an emperor, uncontrollable riots. Some idea of what went on in here can be gained from a closer look at the scenes carved on the stone base of the **obelisk**. By far the oldest of the three remaining monuments, it dates to the reign of Pharaoh Thutmose III. Shipped here on Constantine's orders, it broke during transport and only this top third remains. Finally, in 390, it was erected on the orders of Theodosius I – the north face of the base shows scenes of soldiers labouring to raise it with winches and ropes under the emperor's supervision. A fourth-century description of the raising of an obelisk in Rome speaks of the obelisk being 'gradually hauled up through the empty air, where it hung suspended for a long time, till at last the efforts of many thousand men turning what looked like millstones placed it in position'. The west face shows the emperor receiving the homage of captive Persians (identifiable by their hats) and long-haired Goths. Goths are also shown among the emperor's guard – at this time they were moving into the empire. To the south a chariot race is being watched; below the royal box spectators raise their hands as though cheering on their team. Finally, on the east side, Theodosius holds out the laurel wreath; with him are his sons Honorius and Arcadius, between whom the empire was divided on his death. Below them graceful, if weathered, dancers and musicians enliven the spectacle. The Latin and Greek inscriptions refer to the raising of the obelisk, but differ slightly over the time this took.

Next to the obelisk stands the battered bronze **Serpentine Column** mentioned by Herodotus. Made by the grateful Greeks from the booty and armour of the defeated Persian side at the battle of Plataea in 479 BC, Constantine brought it here from its home in the Temple of Apollo at Delphi. The three intertwined serpents lost their heads, so the story goes, to a drunken Polish diplomat in the eighteenth century, but one head is on show in the Archaeological Museum. The last monument is the **Column of Constantine Porphyrogenitus**, or the Brazen Column. The Greek inscription at the base says that it was under this tenth-century emperor that the column was restored and clad in bronze and compares it, rather hopefully, to the Colossus of Rhodes. Time and the activities of the Janissaries, who tested their climbing skills on this column, have taken their toll of it.

For a look at the impressive walls and foundations of the Hippodrome's *sphendone* (semi-circular

The obelisk

end), walk down to Nakilbent Park and follow the curving wall round. Houses have been cleared from its base and the brick arches are clearly visible, as are the brick and stone courses above them – a school now stands at the top, a good 15m above.

A five-minute walk from here is the **Mosaic Museum** (open 9 am–4.30 pm, closed Monday) which houses on two levels a collection of mosaics from the Great Palace. Excavated in the 1930s, they have since been restored by a team of Austrian archaeologists. The main panel, a 170m x 180m section, was part of a colonnaded walk between the palace and the Hippodrome's *Kathisma*. It is thought to date from Justinian's reign, when the peristyle was restored; the whole floor being probably seven or eight times as large as this stretch. The work is fine, the detail is vivid, and there is a distinct comic touch to some vignettes. By the entrance a man tumbles off his donkey which kicks its heels in glee; next to this is a well-known image of two chubby little boys astride a humpless camel. The main panel shows a multitude of animals; note the monkey catching birds with a stick covered in lime. There are numerous references to Greek myths and many battles between animals and men.

At last we turn to Justinian's crowning glory, the great **Church of St Sophia**, the Holy Wisdom (open 9 am–4.30 pm; closed on Monday). Impossible to ignore, the bulk of its massive dome still dominates the city and is rivalled only by the nearby Blue Mosque and the Süleymaniye which, in striving to compete with it, have created Istanbul's glorious skyline. Built in the sixth century, St Sophia has survived earthquake, fire and the depredations of the Fourth Crusade to outlast the two great empires under which it was first a church and later a mosque, finally becoming a museum in 1935. The massive buttresses were added later to cope with the tremendous stresses imposed by its shallow dome, as were the four minarets, which were added at various times after the Conquest:

St Sophia

Mehmet erected the first in the south-east corner, Beyazıt another in the south-west. Until the sixteenth century, the Baths of Zeuxippus stood on the site of the Haseki Hürrem Baths, between the church and the baths was the great square of the Augustaeum. From here the cluster of buildings forming the Great Palace spread down the slopes to the Sea of Marmara. These included the palaces of the Magnaura, the Daphne, Bucoleon and the Mangana. The main entrance to the palace, the Chalke, was adorned with a golden icon of Christ over its great bronze doors. It was the removal of this icon which triggered the eighth-century Iconoclastic crisis.

The present church is the third on this site – it was built in 532–37 after the destruction of the second St Sophia, during the Nika riots of 532. A monumental statue of Justinian astride a horse stood outside until the sixteenth century; on completion of the church he is said to have exclaimed 'Solomon, I have rivalled you!' and certainly his reign was a time of exciting innovation in architecture, particularly in church buildings.

Work began almost immediately after the riots. The task of designing the church was entrusted to two men: Anthemius of Tralles, who was a physicist and mechanical engineer, and the mathematician Isidorus of Miletus. Anthemius died within the year and the work was finished by Isidorus. Despite some difficulties (the first dome was too low and soon collapsed) their brilliant combination of the more traditional rectangular basilica with the dome creates a tremendous sense of space from inside. It was not a completely new idea, but the size and the opulence of the building were unparalleled.

The courtyard entrance formed an atrium to the church. Before entering the building, look at the frieze of sheep and the column bases in the excavation trench on the left. This is part of the second, fifth-century 'Theodosian' church (the first church of St Sophia was completed in 360). Pass through the **outer narthex**, which is divided into nine bays, to the **narthex** proper. This is decorated with beautiful marble panels, which have been skilfully split into thin leaves to create symmetrical patterns – a theme continued in the church. Initially the church was decorated with plain gold mosaic ground and floral motifs, some of which survive on the vaulted ceiling here; the figurative mosaics all date from the post-Iconoclastic period. Of the doors leading through into the nave the central **Imperial Gate** was reserved for the emperor, patriarch and procession. Over this gate a mosaic shows Christ enthroned before a kneeling figure, probably the emperor Leo VI (886–912) from whose reign the mosaic dates. Leo's repentant attitude is warranted – desperate for an heir he made a scandalous fourth marriage to his mistress, the beautiful Zoë Carbonopsina ('the Black-Eyed') to ecclesiastical outrage. The inscription is from St John 10:7 ('I am the door of the sheep').

St Sophia, interior

Not even the ugly scaffolding inside can detract from the magnificence of St Sophia's interior; when the surfaces overhead were complete with 30 million golden tesserae, all carefully angled to catch the light from the dome and sparkling from the candlelight below, it must have been truly breathtaking. Look up at the soaring dome 56m overhead and at the four massive piers supporting it, and man seems a very small creature in the scale of things. This is precisely the effect intended by the Byzantines, who loved symbolism: the dome can be seen as representing the heavens above and the light streaming down as the light of God. Although Mark Twain, who visited in the nineteenth century while it was a mosque, disparagingly describes St Sophia as 'the rustiest old barn in heathendom' (adding for good measure that 'its dirt is much more wonderful than its dome'), there has since been much restoration and cleaning. Three types of tessera were used in the dome; stone, coloured glass and 'sandwich' type, where silver or gold leaf was inserted between two pieces of glass. Two huge semi-domes open at the east and west ends, lengthening the nave and the transition above, from the square walls to the round ribbed dome is assured by the pendentives. Those at the east end bear mosaic seraphim, while the pair opposite are painted in imitation of the originals.

At the back of the north aisle is the **Column of St Gregory**, which reputedly has healing powers; the lower part is sheathed in brass, but a hole has been worn through this by the fingers of countless eager pilgrims and curious tourists who mill around waiting their turn to touch it. Two huge Byzantine urns at the back of the nave were actually Ottoman additions, a gift of Murat III. The capitals of St Sophia are deservedly famed for their beauty; the wonderful carved tracery of acanthus and palm foliage bears the imperial monograms of Justinian and Theodora and extends to the arcades above the capitals. Standing between the dome and the eastern semi-dome, and looking at the soffit of the dome's eastern arch, it is possible to make out the faint outline of what was once a mosaic of the Virgin. A square of red and green granite and porphyry set into the floor in the south-east part of the nave marks the spot where the emperor's throne stood. The mosaic of the Virgin and Child in the apse is dated to 867 and heralds the end of the iconoclastic phase, when images were banned and destroyed. This is the first post-iconoclastic mosaic in St Sophia and the tone of the inscription is defiant: 'These icons the deceivers once put down, the pious emperors have restored.' On the lower right wall of the arch around the apse is a large mosaic of the archangel Gabriel, but only a few feathers remain of St Michael, his counterpart on the left.

In May 1453, on entering the vanquished city, the young Mehmet the Conqueror rode straight to St Sophia. Struck by its magnificence, he gave orders for it not to be looted, but rather converted to a mosque. Figurative mosaics were plastered over, but not much else was altered – not even the name. A *mihrab* and *minber* were added, as were the sultan's *loge* (the present *loge* is nineteenth-century) and a minaret at the south-eastern corner – the other three were added in the 1570s. Huge calligraphic shields that hang over the nave date from the nineteenth-century restoration by the Swiss Fossati brothers; these bear the names of Allah, Muhammad and the first four caliphs. A Qur'anic inscription in the nave appropriately describes God as the light of heaven and earth.

ICONOCLASM

Religious controversies were nothing new in the Byzantine Empire, although the Iconoclastic crisis of the eighth and ninth centuries was one of the worst and had far-reaching consequences. Given the power of the church, religion was, inevitably, closely linked to politics. Ever since Christianity became the official religion it had struggled against a series of heresies, mostly to do with the nature of Christ, whether he could be both man and God at the same time and what his precise relationship with God was. Arians, Nestorians, Monophysites and Monotheletes fought tooth and nail to have their particular brand of theology prevail, especially during the fourth and fifth centuries. One bemused fourth century pagan wrote 'no wild beasts are such dangerous enemies to man as Christians are to one another'. In all this the emperor was sometimes mediator, sometimes allied with a particular group. These abstruse arguments were particularly heated in the eastern provinces, where many of them had taken firm root, to the exasperation of the Western Church. It is hard now to understand how such fine points of theology could have been so important to the man in the street, but it was undoubtedly so: 'If you ask a man for change he will give you a piece of philosophy concerning the Begotten and the Unbegotten; if you enquire the price of a loaf he replies: "The Father is great and the Son inferior"' writes Gregory of Nyssa in the late fourth century.

Iconoclasm (the destruction of religious images), was in part a legacy of Monophysitism; if Christ is divine, how can he be portrayed as a human? Doubtless it was also influenced by the deep-rooted distrust of the 'graven image', so typical of the neighbouring Semitic religions. It is interesting that it should have been an eastern emperor, Leo III, who triggered the crisis in 726 by giving orders for the icon of Christ over the Palace Gate to be taken down. This instantly created a riot, but was followed a few years later by an imperial edict banning icons. Not long before, the Umayyad caliph had also banned images. Leo also seems to have interpreted a recent earthquake as a sign of God's displeasure with icon worshippers. Veneration of icons had become increasingly important since the time of Justinian and, once again, this controversy led to a clash between the Eastern and Western Churches. The timing was unfortunate, because with the growing security threat to Rome of the Lombards, and a lack of attention from the preoccupied iconoclastic emperors, the West now turned to the Franks for support. Ultimately, this alliance would lead to the crowning of Charlemagne as Holy Roman Emperor on Christmas Day 800 and the subsequent great divide between the Orthodox or Eastern Church and the Western Church based in Rome.

Meanwhile, in the East the battle raged; monks in particular were persecuted by the iconoclasts and opposition was centred in the monasteries and convents. The great champion of their cause was John of Damascus, who, in a series of great addresses, argued persuasively that the icon was not an idol but a symbol, intended to mediate between the beholder and God, and a channel for prayers: 'Christ is venerated not in the image but with the image.' Leo's son Constantine V ordered the destruction of all religious icons after a church council in 754. It was a woman, the empress Eirene, ruling as regent for her young son, who took the first steps towards the restoration of the images in the 780s. (Indeed, women probably played an important part in the preservation of icons, which, being portable and easily hidden, continued to be venerated in many a household even through the times of persecution.) Iconoclasm was itself declared a heresy under Eirene and, although there was a subsequent backlash and brief return to iconoclasm, (again under an eastern emperor, Leo V), the movement had been much weakened. The sensible Michael II put a stop to persecution of iconodules, as the opponents of iconoclasm were known, and forbade discussion of the subject. The last iconoclast emperor, Theophilus, died in 742, but in alienating Rome and the West, iconoclasm caused irremediable damage to relations between Constantinople and Rome.

**St Sophia,
Deesis mosaic**

The **galleries** are reached from the narthex, and their mosaics well repay the climb. Views of the nave are particularly good from the green marble circle and verd antique columns in the centre of the west gallery where the empress' throne supposedly stood. Lurking in a dark corner of the north gallery, on the east face of the pier furthest from the apse, is a mosaic of the emperor Alexander (912–13), gorgeous in jewels and finery but in real life a drunken sot. Alternative versions of his death have him dying after a drunken polo match or after making pagan sacrifices in the Hippodrome; at any rate, his reign was mercifully brief. Walk round to the south gallery and eastwards through the 'Gates of Heaven and Hell' – a stone screen stretching across the passage. Inside on the right is the stunning late thirteenth-century **'Deesis' mosaic**. In a final flowering of Byzantine art it shows a very human Christ with John the Baptist and the Virgin Mary, their soulful faces expressing great love and sadness. Turn now towards the apse; at the end of the next bay, set into the floor on the right is part of a sarcophagus. 'Henricus Dandolo' it reads, in reference to the doge of Venice who was responsible for the

disastrous diversion of the Fourth Crusade to Constantinople (see p. 10).

From here look across the nave at the tympanum
of the north arch (which sags noticeably from the
great weight of the dome), where there are three more
ninth-century mosaics. From the apse westwards are
St Ignatius Theophorus (a second-century bishop of
Antioch who was fed to the beasts in Rome), St John
Chrysostom and St Ignatius the Younger. St John
Chrysostom (the 'golden-mouthed') was Patriarch of
Constantinople. A stirring but blunt preacher, his exile
prompted the riots which led to the destruction of
the first church in 404; he had criticized the court and
called the empress Eudocia a Jezebel.

Continue on to the end of the gallery for the last
two mosaics, which are on the east wall. On the right
is the Virgin Mary with the infant Christ, flanked by
the emperor John II Comnenus and his pious wife
Eirene. This mosaic dates from 1118, although it is
thought that the image of the emperor's son Alexius
on the right was added a few years later when he
became co-emperor.

Nearest to the apse is a mosaic somewhat cruder
in style, but with an interesting story. Again Christ is
shown flanked by an emperor and empress bearing

**St Sophia,
mosaic showing
John II
Comnenus and
Eirene**

gold and a scroll respectively. They are identified as the empress Zoë, who ruled for a while in her own right with her sister Theodora, and her third husband Constantine IX Monomachus. This version of the mosaic probably dates to 1042, when she married him, but the heads of the figures have been changed as well as the inscriptions referring to Constantine. It is likely that the faces of all three husbands were shown in succession! Certainly Zoë had a colourful life – married for the first time at fifty, to ensure the succession, she is reputed to have killed that husband with the aid of a lover who then acceded to the throne. On his death, at the ripe old age of sixty, she married Constantine, having obviously acquired a taste for nuptials.

Leave the church through the **Vestibule of the Warriors,** where the emperor's bodyguard would wait for him during services. Over the door outside is a tenth-century mosaic of the Virgin and Child with the two greatest Byzantine emperors flanking her. Constantine offers her a representation of the city and Justinian a model of the church. The courtyard contains a number of Ottoman tombs (*türbes*) (see p. 155) – note the old Baptistery immediately to the left, which was converted to the tomb of Mustafa I and later Ibrahim. Other imperial tombs include those of Selim II (built by Sinan in 1577 and decorated with Iznik tiles), of Murat III and Mehmet III. These tombs are shared with other family relations, including large numbers of younger sons slaughtered by incoming sultans (their elder brothers) who, on accession, regularly removed any possible rivals to the throne. Fratricide was a well-established tradition in the Ottoman Empire for many centuries; the large numbers of children fathered by some sultans made this quite a task. Murat III was the record-holder with fifty-six children.

Those who are not yet footsore can now head for the **Church of St Sergius and St Bacchus** (may be closed for restoration), contemporary with St Sophia, finishing off with a stroll along the Land Walls past the scant remains of the Palace of Bucoleon. Some of the vaulting of the Magnaura Palace can be seen from Akbiyik Cad. or via the patio behind the carpet shop on Kutlugün Sok. The obliging proprietor will switch on lights so that you can descend into the cool of the vaults where excavations are being carried out. Some of the back streets between here and the railway are very colourful, with old wooden houses in desperate need of repair. The church itself, now a mosque known as Küçük ('little') Aya Sofya, lies horribly close to the railway and cracks from the vibrations are spreading across its dome. Built on a cramped site between the earlier basilica church of St Peter and St Paul and the palace of Hormisdas, where Justinian lived before he became emperor, it was begun early in his reign and completed by 536. Legend has it that following his implication in a plot to kill his uncle, the emperor, these saints appeared to the emperor in a dream, claiming Justinian was innocent. Grateful that his life had been spared, Justinian erected this church in honour of the soldier saints. Like St Sophia, this charming building broke with the traditional basilica plan for churches; in plan it is an octagon set slightly crookedly within a rectangle. A 'pumpkin' dome rises over the central space with galleries below – the effect of this dome is striking from the outside. The beautiful lettering of the inscription over the capitals (it honours Justinian, Theodora and St Sergius) and their monogram on the laceworked capitals are now obscured under a heavy coat of whitewash. Crosses on most capitals were erased following its sixteenth-century conversion to a mosque.

A path from here leads under the railway and through a gate to the busy main road along the Sea of Marmara. The **Sea Walls** joined with the Theodosian Land Walls at the marble tower, rendering Constantinople one of the most impregnable of cities. Although they were largely destroyed by the building of the railway and have been badly repaired in places, there are still some fine stretches of wall along the busy highway, including this stretch. Houses have been built right up to and even into the walls.

A five-minute walk east is the **Cracked Gate** (Çatladı Kapı), marked by a carved stone cornice to the left, where Justinian and Theodora's monogram can be seen on the right of the marble entrance to the gate which led to the **Palace of Bucoleon**. In the later Byzantine period the emperors moved down here, but nothing remains of its former grandeur beyond the large windows which give onto the sea, three of which still have their marble frames. Re-used capitals from a pre-Christian building, probably a temple, were incorporated into the lower wall.

Just beyond the palace is the **Pharos**, the tower which once served as the lighthouse. A five-minute walk will bring you to the **Stable Gate** (Ahır Kapı), through which we re-enter the city. At nearby Cankurtaran Meydan you can enjoy a cool drink or, if the time is right, a well-deserved meal. Alternatively, continue on for fifteen minutes to the **Incili Kiosk**, a solitary Ottoman pavilion of the Topkapı Palace projecting from the walls. Just next to this the decorative brickwork, niches and arched entrance in the walls are all that remains of the twelfth-century **Church of St Saviour Philanthropus**. Nearby was once the eleventh-century palace of the Mangana, all but obliterated by the railway.

A ten-minute walk brings you to **Gülhane Park**. Inside among trees up on the left stands a lone column known as the **Goth's Column**. It commemorates a victory over the Goths – the inscription is still partly legible – and is probably one of the oldest surviving monuments in the city. Nearby, with pleasant views across to the Asian shore, is a welcome line of tea-houses. If you stop to rest your aching feet here on the promontory, think of the founders of this enduring city likewise gazing across to the settlements at Chalcedon and Chrysopolis so many centuries ago.

The Great Walls of Constantinople

TOUR

2

'The ride by the walls of the city, on the land side, is beautiful', wrote Lord Byron in 1810. 'I have seen the ruins of Athens, of Ephesus and Delphi. I have traversed great part of Turkey, and many other parts of Europe, and some of Asia; but I never beheld a work of nature or art which yielded an impression like the prospect on each side from the Seven Towers to the end of the Golden Horn.'

Despite some ugly renovation the great land walls of Constantinople, built in striking striped masonry with narrow bands of tiles between broader sections of neatly cut limestone blocks, are still one of the city's most majestic monuments. A stroll or clamber along all or part of these dignified fortifications, which tell such an epic story, is well worthwhile.

It all started with Constantine, one of whose first priorities was to ensure the defences of his new capital. In line with Roman tradition he probably took his spear and traced the line of the city walls himself, walking across the promontory and along the shores of the Sea of Marmara and the Golden Horn. The new

Theodosian walls

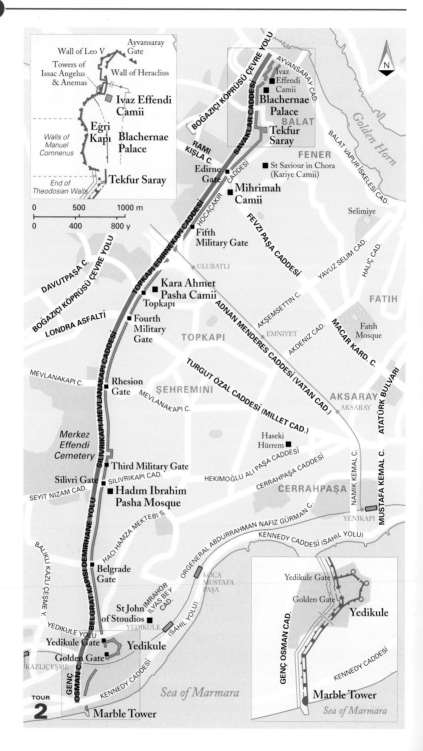

TOUR 2

walls enclosed an area over four times that of the old Graeco-Roman town of Byzantium. Incentives to attract residents to Constantinople included free bread distribution and tax exemptions for building contractors. For the upper classes there were elegant mansions with income from country estates attached. So successful was Constantinople that soon its population had spilled way beyond the walls, and when barbarian attack threatened at the beginning of the fifth century, something had to be done quickly. Theodosius II promptly decided to build a new line of fortifications to include the outer surburbs. His great defences, 6km long, doubled the size of Constantinople and effectively protected its population for the next 1,000 years.

Constantine's original land and sea fortifications probably consisted of a single high wall punctuated by strong towers. Theodosius adopted the same pattern for his first ramparts, which were completed in 413 but seriously damaged by earthquake in 447, just as Attila and his Huns were advancing on Constantinople. There was a rapid response to the emergency – the Hippodrome circus factions provided labour and within two months the city had a formidable new triple fortification system, comprising a double wall and a ditch. Most awesome was the 12m high solid inner wall (*teichos*), with a crenellated parapet walk and ninety-six massive rectangular and octagonal towers. A 15m wide road (*periblos*) in front was used for rapid deployment of soldiers and protected by an 8m high outer rampart (*proteichisma*) with casemates for archers and ninety-six smaller towers. Beyond was an outer terrace (*parateichon*) and the battlemented scarp of a deep ditch (*taphros*), which could be flooded in times of danger. To repel attackers, the defenders of the city catapulted arrows and bolts from the parapet of the inner wall and used massive machines to hurl stone balls and other missiles from open-air platforms at the top of the inner towers, including the lethal concoction known as 'Greek fire', a highly combustible chemical fluid which ignited on impact.

Constantinople's land defences were one of the most successful fortification systems ever devised, standing firm against the Goths, Huns, Avars, Slavs, Serbs and Bulgars. When the Crusaders seized and pillaged the city in 1204 they broke in through the weaker sea defences along the Golden Horn, leaving the Land Walls intact. It was not until 1453, when they were pounded by the great cannons of Sultan Mehmet which shot huge balls with gunpowder (a new weapon marking the effective beginning of modern warfare) that the Theodosian walls were finally breached. Even then they withstood a merciless battering for fifty-five days before they succumbed. Today, though ruined and cracked by the ravages of war and time, the great walls still stand to an impressive height, an evocative reminder of the glorious history of Byzantium.

By the Sea of Marmara, where the Land and Sea Walls joined, is the **Marble Tower**. Now separated from the rest of the walls by the busy highway along the shore, this tower, which is partly revetted in marble, is different from the others in the defence system. It may have served over time as an imperial sea pavilion and a prison. North of the main road is the first of the great octagonal towers of the inner defences and a small arched gate with the monogram of Christ above. This is one of four gates in the Theodosian walls which were reserved for the military and led only to the outer ramparts. In addition, there were six main gates leading to smaller gates in the outer wall which were closed by portcullises and approached by bridges over the ditch. Beyond the gate a fairly well-preserved stretch of wall passes through a dirty, litter-strewn area and is then cut by a road and a railway. Inside the wall, the road crosses the railway and continues to **Yedikule**, the **Fortress of the Seven Towers**.

Yedikule (open 9 am–4 pm, except Wednesday, may be closed for restoration) is a five-sided fortified enclosure with four Byzantine and three Ottoman towers connected by strong, high walls; it comprises a

Yedikule Fortress

section of the Theodosian fortifications and an extension added on the city side by Mehmet the Conqueror in the fifteenth century. During Ottoman times Yedikule was a notorious prison where foreign envoys were incarcerated and deposed sultans and other enemies of the ruling sultan were executed. Their heads and corpses were flung outside to be eaten by dogs, or down a well to be flushed into the sea. Inside is an open courtyard with the remains of a small mosque for the garrison. Several stairways lead up to the ramparts and the round Ottoman towers. On a clear day, walk round the ramparts for wonderful views of Istanbul and the Byzantine Land Walls; take a torch to explore inside the dark, rather sinister towers.

Within the Byzantine wall at the far end of the courtyard two huge square towers of Proconnesian marble flank the famous **Golden Gate**, which once had gilded metal doors. This was the most splendid of all the entrances to Constantinople, through which triumphant Byzantine emperors rode on return from campaign, or on their way to be crowned in St Sophia. The Golden Gate was originally built by Theodosius I around 390 as a grand triumphal arch on the Via Egnatia, 2km outside the Constantinian walls. A few decades later it was incorporated into the new fortifications of

Theodosius II, who also built a smaller marble gate just in front, joined to the city walls as part of the defence system. The triple arch of the Golden Gate can best be seen from outside Yedikule (if the door to the exterior is open), and there is also a good view from the top of its southern tower (entered from ground level). Two of the three arches are now bricked-up, but the door jambs and lintels are still in place – the façade was once decorated with sculpture, some pieces of which are in the Istanbul Archaeological Museum.

The last Byzantine emperor to ride in triumph through the Golden Gate was Michael VIII Palaeologus, after Constantinople had been recaptured from the Latins in 1261. He then proceeded to the **Stoudion**, the church and monastery of St John of Stoudios, following the chariot which bore the sacred icon of the Virgin Hodegetria (see p. 65), the protectress of the city, traditionally painted by St Luke. A thanksgiving service was held in the church, with the icon on the altar. Founded in the mid-fifth century by a wealthy senator named Stoudios, the Stoudion was one of the foremost intellectual and artistic centres of Byzantium, and during the eighth century it was the main centre of resistance to iconoclasm. Its library was famous and copying manuscripts was considered a great honour, though smudges or mistakes were severely punished. Monastic life was strict; no female animals were allowed in, monks attended seven services a day and often kept all-night vigil, they had no personal property and were only allowed meat for health reasons. Even melancholy was a sin – the penance was 150 genuflexions and 500 'kyrie eleisons' a day until the monk cheered up! At the end of the fifteenth century, the church was converted into a mosque (known locally as Imrahor Camii). It was abandoned after serious earthquake damage in 1894.

The Stoudion is about 500m from Yedikule, just off the main road (Imrahor Ilyas Bey Cad.) to the right. Though roofless and overgrown, it has a certain dilapidated grandeur. Through a gate in the wall (usually locked) is a courtyard with two abandoned houses and a Muslim cemetery, formerly the atrium of the church. From here you can look into the narthex and the nave, which are kept closed. The middle bay of the narthex has four columns with acanthus capitals and a carved entablature and both narthex and nave had a magnificent *opus sectile* floor and walls revetted with marble. Fine verd antique columns divided the nave and aisles (the north row is still standing) and above the aisles and narthex there was a gallery. Light flooded into the apse through five large windows.

Just north of the Fortress of the Seven Towers is **Yedikule Gate**, a small city gate built during the last years of Byzantium after the Golden Gate had been walled up for defence. Above it on the inside there is an imperial eagle in white marble. Yedikule Gate is still in use, and sometimes has its own local self-appointed traffic warden. Beyond, there is an impressive and unrestored stretch of the Theodosian fortifications – well-tended market gardens occupy the area of the ditch and behind the casemated outer rampart rises the inner wall, its huge towers scarred with evocative jagged cracks. In striking contrast is the **Belgrade Gate**, rebuilt in pristine white stone and red brick. Here you can climb up to the parapet and the top of the towers for views of the city and ramparts.

Next comes the **Silivri Gate**, a good place to see some of the many inscriptions which record imperial repairs to the fortifications. In Byzantine times it was called the Spring Gate because there was a Christian church outside which enclosed a sacred spring. On the outer wall of the north gate-tower is an inscription of Basil II (976–1025) and Constantine VIII (1025–8) and opposite on the south gate-tower is an inscription dated 1438. Between the gates and on the inner wall of the south tower are two further inscriptions. It was through the Silivri Gate that the first contingent of Byzantine troops forced their way into the city in

July 1261, paving the way for the recapture of Constantinople from the hated Latin usurpers.

Close to the gate is the **Mosque of Hadım Ibrahim Pasha**, one of Süleyman the Magnificent's Grand Viziers, built by Sinan in 1551. It is a charming, modest mosque of brick and stone – the five-domed portico has handsome inscriptive Iznik tiles above the windows and the dome over the lofty prayer hall is supported on elegant shell squinches. The marble *mihrab* and *minber* are of fine workmanship. In the garden is the open *türbe* of Ibrahim Pasha with a marble cenotaph.

Not far from the Silivri Gate two huge collapsed towers mark the **Third Military Gate**, and beyond is the **Sigma**, a curious curve in the walls so-called because it is shaped like the Greek letter sigma. Several hundred metres further on is the best-preserved Theodosian gate in the walls, the **Rhesion Gate** or **Yeni Mevlevihane Kapı**. It bears some interesting inscriptions recording repairs over the centuries. The upper inscription on the outer lintel dates to Basil II (976–1025) and Constantine VIII (1025–8) and the four-line inscription below refers to Justin II (565–78), his wife Sophia and the eunuch general Narses. On the north corbel we read of the Reds, one of the Hippodrome factions, and the Praetorian prefect Constantine who rebuilt the wall in only two months after the 447 earthquake; a feat, we are told, that not even Pallas Athene, goddess of war, could have managed.

A long stretch of wall, in good condition, takes us past the closed up **Fourth Military Gate** and across Millet Cad., a busy main road that breaches the fortifications, to **Topkapı** (cannon gate) formerly called the **Gate of Romanos**. Near this gate is a charming mosque, the **Kara Ahmet Pasha Camii**, built by Sinan in 1554 for another of Süleyman's Grand Viziers who briefly took office from his brother-in-law Rüstem Pasha until the latter had him executed for treason. Kara Ahmet's pious foundation included a special unit (*zaviye*) with sixteen cells for pious recluses to pray for the Pasha's soul! A pretty triangular garden leads to a spacious arcaded courtyard, with verd antique, granite and marble columns and a low polygonal *şadırvan* covered with an iron grille. In the lunettes over the niches in the porch are some lovely Iznik tiles in green, yellow, blue, turquoise, black and white. In Kara Ahmet Pasha Camii, Sinan used the plan of a hexagon inscribed within a rectangle for the first time. Six antique columns support the central dome and there is some fine early paintwork in deep red, dark blue and gold on the ceilings of the western bays.

Topkapı was named after the huge cannons built by Urban, the Hungarian engineer who worked for Mehmet the Conqueror (see p. 53). It was destroyed in 1453 by Urban's cannons, as was the next gate, the Edirne Kapı, and many sections of the fortifications between. This was the most vulnerable stretch of Constantinople's land defences, which here descend to the valley of the river Lycus, its course marked today by Vatan Cad., a busy boulevard which breaches the walls. Beyond Vatan Cad. is the **Fifth Military Gate**, with a worn inscription on the lintel recording a fifth century repair. In Turkish this gate is called **Hücum Kapı**, Gate of the Assault, for this is where the Turkish Janissaries first breached the walls of Constantinople during the final battle on 29 May 1453. Constantine XI was seen near here in the last stages of the conflict, fighting bravely alongside his soldiers. As you walk up the hill towards the Edirne Gate, look back to the valley, scene of that momentous battle and imagine the thundering of the cannon, the clouds of black smoke and the destruction wrought by the immense cannonballs.

It was through the **Edirne Gate**, known in Byzantium as the **Charsios Gate**, that Mehmet the Conqueror rode in triumph on 29 May 1453, as recorded in an inscription on the wall alongside. Inside the gate is **Mihrimah Camii**, one of the loveliest imperial mosques in Istanbul, built by Sinan for

Princess Mihrimah, Süleyman the Magnificent's favourite daughter and wife of his powerful Grand Vizier, Rüstem Pasha. It crowns the Sixth Hill, the highest point in the old city, and is raised on a platform so its slender minaret and great dome can be seen from afar. Access is from the main street via a stairway which leads under the gatehouse. To the right is the courtyard which has elegant low porticoes surrounding a well-kept garden with a graceful *şadırvan*. The mosque is preceded by an impressive porch supported on eight red and grey granite and marble columns, but it is inside the building that the genius of the architect becomes most apparent. The overall impression is of space and light, which pours into the mosque through some 200 windows, in the walls, in the tympana of the dome arches and in the base of the dome. Many of them are clear glass. The great central dome towers above the smaller cupolas of the lateral galleries, which rest on elegant arcades where skilful use is made of polychrome marble. Next to the *mihrab* is a fine white marble *minber*. Mihrimah Camii is one of Sinan's most imaginative and successful buildings, and in its day was considered revolutionary.

Just after the Edirne Gate a modern road breaches the Theodosian walls, which continue for a few hundred metres to the **Tekfur Saray** or palace of the Sovereign, better known as the palace of the Porphyrogenitus. This may have been an annexe of the nearby Blachernae Palace, the favourite imperial residence from the twelfth century until the fall of Constantinople. Although it is now a mere shell and has suffered some hideous reconstruction, the Tekfur Saray is an excellent example of Late Byzantine architecture. It probably dates from the early fourteenth century, the period of the Palaeologue Renaissance. Look at the building from outside and inside: it has three storeys and is wedged between the inner and outer fortifications. On the ground floor, which was vaulted, four arches on the north side open on to an outer courtyard. The two upper floors have rows of windows. From the first floor there was access to the parapet walk along the ramparts, while the top floor projects above the city walls. Particularly interesting are the rounded windows and geometric decoration in red brick and white marble, reminiscent of earlier Western architecture. After the Ottoman conquest the palace was used variously as an imperial menagerie for exotic animals, a brothel, a tile factory and a Jewish pauper hospital.

URBAN'S CANNON

The Fall of Constantinople in 1453 was at least partly due to the development of new weapons technology. Gunpowder had been invented in China in the ninth century, the Chinese had guns by 900 and cannons by 1259. A hundred years later the cannon had arrived in western Europe, and its value as a siege weapon was quickly realized. Though the early cannons were ineffective against solid masonry, there were developments and improvements until in summer 1452 a Hungarian called Urban travelled to Constantinople to offer his services to the emperor as an artillery engineer. Constantine's refusal to pay Urban the salary he required was perhaps his greatest mistake, for the Hungarian went straight to the enemy camp and told Sultan Mehmet he could build a cannon powerful enough to destroy the walls of Babylon.

Mehmet employed him immediately, and within three months he had constructed a huge cannon which was installed at Rumeli Hisarı and successfully sank a Venetian ship trying to run the blockade. Urban was then instructed to cast a cannon twice the size, and the result was a monster with a barrel 20cm thick and over 8m long which fired 270-pound cannon balls. Urban's cannon was transported from Adrianople to Constantinople on a cart drawn by 60 oxen with 200 men marching beside it, and wheeled into position opposite the weakest point of the walls in the Lycus valley. Other great cannons cast in the Ottoman foundries under Urban's direction were lined up alongside. On 12 April the bombardment began, and continued relentlessly for over six weeks. Though the cannons were unwieldy and often slid off their firing platforms into the mud, and though Urban's monster took so long to load it could only fire seven times a day, the results were devastating.

On 29 May the great Land Walls of Constantinople which had stood firm for over 1000 years were finally breached, the Turks swarmed into the city and fanned out on all sides to open the gates. Soon Turkish flags were flying where the imperial eagle had flown, and a few hours later Sultan Mehmet made his triumphant entry. Emperor Constantine may have died near here during the last stages of the battle, but his body was never found.

Shortly after the Tekfur Saray, the Theodosian walls come to an end and a later fortification system runs to the Golden Horn. The first section, built in the twelfth century by **Manuel Comnenus**, is a single massive wall with nine solid towers and one gate, the **Eğri Kapı** or Crooked Gate. In the cemetery outside the Eğri Kapı is the tomb of Haceti Hafir, companion of the Prophet Muhammad, who died here during the Arab campaigns of the seventh century.

At the third tower after the gate, the walls of Manuel Comnenus run into a later wall of inferior workmanship which is not bonded to the tower. From here, there is a lovely view down the last stretch of fortifications to the Golden Horn. A small walled-up gate in the ramparts a short distance down the road was probably an entrance to the **Blachernae Palace**, whose two huge towers and buttressed retaining wall form part of the defences. Between the Blachernae terrace and the Golden Horn there is once again a double wall. The inner defences were built by **Heraclius** in 627 when Constantinople was under attack by the Avars and Persians; the three strong polygonal towers are particularly well constructed. Later, in 813, when the Bulgars were threatening the city, **Leo V** strengthened the fortifications by building an outer wall with small square towers. Outside and between the walls is a religious complex comprising a mosque and cemetery with the tombs of three more companions of the Prophet Muhammad. By the Golden Horn the walls of Leo and Heraclius come together to join the sea ramparts and we have ended our walk along the Land Walls of Constantinople, one of the most impressive and effective defence systems ever devised.

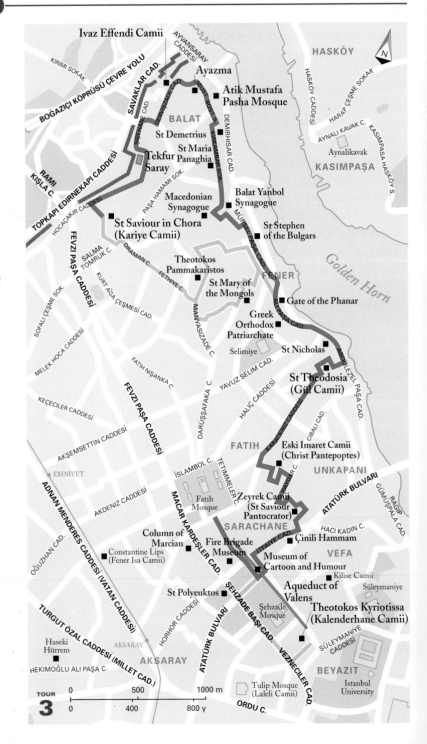

HASKÖY

Ivaz Effendi Camii

AYVANSARAY CADDESİ

Ayazma

Atik Mustafa
Pasha Mosque

KIRIMI SOKAK

BOĞAZİÇİ KÖPRÜSÜ ÇEVRE YOLU

SAVAKLAR CAD.

DEMİRCİZADE CAD.

MİLLET BOSTANI

KIRKAMBER SOK.

DEMİRHİSAR CAD.

HASKÖY CADDESİ

HARAP ÇEŞME SOKAK

AYNALI KAVAK C.

KASIMPAŞA HASKÖY S.

BALAT

St Demetrius

St Maria
Panaghia

Tekfur
Saray

Aynalikavak

KASIMPAŞA

RAMİ
KIŞLA C.

TOPKAPI EDİRNEKAPI CADDESİ

HOCAÇAKIR CADDESİ

PAŞA HAMAMI SOK.

Macedonian
Synagogue

Balat Yanbol
Synagogue

MÜRSEL PAŞA CAD.

St Saviour in Chora
(Kariye Camii)

St Stephen
of the Bulgars

FEVZİ PAŞA CADDESİ

SALMA
TOMRUK C.

DRAMAN C.

FETHİYE C.

KURT AĞA ÇEŞMESİ CAD.

Theotokos
Pammakaristos

St Mary of
the Mongols

FENER

Golden Horn

Gate of the Phanar

SOFALI ÇEŞME SOK.

MANYASİZADE C.

Greek
Orthodox
Patriarchate

ALİ PAŞA CAD.

MELEK HOCA CADDESİ

FATİH NİŞANKA C.

Selimiye

St Nicholas

ABDÜLEZEL PAŞA CAD.

KEÇECİLER CADDESİ

DARÜŞŞAFAKA C.

YAVUZ SELİM CAD.

HALİÇ CADDESİ

St Theodosia
(Gül Camii)

FEVZİ PAŞA CADDESİ

AKŞEMSETTİN CADDESİ

KARADENİZ CADDESİ

CİBALİ CAD.

FATİH

Eski Imaret Camii
(Christ Pantepoptes)

UNKAPANI

EMNİYET

AKDENİZ CADDESİ

İSLAMBOL C.

TETİMMELER C.

HAYDAR C.

ATATÜRK BULVARI

RAGIP GÜMÜŞPALA CAD.

ADNAN MENDERES CADDESİ (VATAN CADDESİ)

OĞUZHAN CAD.

MACAR KARDEŞLER CAD.

Fatih
Mosque

Zeyrek Camii
(St Saviour
Pantocrator)

SARACHANE

İTFAİYE CAD.

Çinili Hammam

HACI KADIN C.

VEFA

Column of
Marcian

Fire Brigade
Museum

Museum of
Cartoon and Humour

Kilise Camii

Süleymaniye

Constantine Lips
(Fener Isa Camii)

St Polyeuktos

ŞEHZADE BAŞI CAD.

Aqueduct of
Valens

Theotokos Kyriotissa
(Kalenderhane Camii)

HORHOR CADDESİ

TURGUT ÖZAL CADDESİ (MİLLET CAD.)

Haseki
Hürrem

AKSARAY

AKSARAY

Şehzade
Mosque

VEZNECİLER CAD.

SÜLEYMANİYE CADDESİ

BEYAZIT

ATATÜRK BULVARI

HEKİMOĞLU ALİ PAŞA C.

Istanbul
University

TOUR
3

0   500   1000 m

0   400   800 y

Tulip Mosque
(Laleli Camii)

ORDU C.

The later Byzantine city

When Don Ruy Gonzales de Clavijo, Spanish envoy to Tamerlane in Samarkand, visited Constantinople in 1403 he was told that within the city there were '3,000 churches, great and small'. Though this may be an exaggeration, there are references to around 350 monasteries and 500 churches in Constantinople, so it is not surprising that religious buildings made a strong impression on visitors. Churches, the most visible expression of Byzantine culture, gave Constantinople its special atmosphere and character. This walk focuses on the later Byzantine churches, built from the eleventh century onwards on the slopes of the Fourth, Fifth and Sixth Hills, and along the Golden Horn in the picturesque districts of Fener and Balat. Constantinople by that time already had a splendid heritage of grand churches, the great basilicas of the Stoudion and St Eirene, the cruciform church of the Holy Apostles, where the emperors were buried, and the vast domed cathedral of St Sophia. Changing fashions meant there was no further call for buildings on such a grand scale and later Byzantine churches tend to be smaller, though usually quite high in relation to their ground area and dominated by one or more domes.

Some, like the Greek Orthodox Patriarchate, the Vatican of Greek Orthodox Christianity, are still functioning churches, though with ever-dwindling congregations. For these, Sunday morning is often the best time to visit, when you may be lucky enough to coincide with a service. Other churches were converted into mosques after the conquest, including the imposing church of the monastery of Christ Pantocrator overlooking the Golden Horn. Not to be missed is the Kariye Camii (church of St Saviour in Chora), now a museum, which boasts exquisite Late Byzantine mosaics and frescoes.

This area of Constantinople was particularly popular with the later Byzantine emperors. Alexius

Comnenus (1081–1118) abandoned the Great Palace by the Hippodrome for the Blachernae Palace close to the city walls. Though in 1204 the Blachernae suffered the ravages of the Crusaders, who stole most of its magnificent contents, it was subsequently repaired and remained the imperial residence until the fall of Constantinople in 1453. Today, little is left of the palace but enough churches survive in this part of town to give us some impression of the later Byzantine city.

We begin our walk at one of Istanbul's most dramatic landmarks, the **Aqueduct of Valens**, which spans the valley between the Third and Fourth Hills. Built in around 370 as part of a new water supply system for the expanding city, it is a masterpiece of Roman engineering. From the western end, up Kıztaşı Cad., there are nice views across to the Şehzade and Süleymaniye mosques. As you walk down the hill alongside the aqueduct, note that it is supported first on single and then on double arches until it reaches an impressive height of 18.5m where it crosses the busy Atatürk Bulvarı. In front of the aqueduct on Itfaiye Cad. is the **Fire Brigade Museum** (Itfaiye Müzesi: open 9 am–4 pm, except Sunday, admission free) well worth a short visit to see the early fire wagons and

Aqueduct of Valens

carts, firemens' uniforms and collection of nineteenth- and early twentieth-century pumps. Founded in 1872, the fire service was indispensible to Istanbul, where fires spread with horrifying speed through the closely-packed wooden houses, and could literally burn for weeks. For example, a fire which began on 3 May 1756 was not finally extinguished until 6 July and consumed several thousand buildings.

Not far from the museum are two early Byzantine monuments. At the lower end of Kıztaşı Cad., the **Column of Marcian** (Kıztaşı) has definitely seen better days, though you can still make out a damaged inscription and two worn winged victories on the pedestal. There are eagles around the plinth at the top, which once supported a statue of the fifth-century emperor. Marcian's Column lay on the processional route from the Forum of Theodosius to the church of the Holy Apostles.

On the same route was an impressive basilica dedicated to **St Polyeuktos**, a Roman soldier martyred in 251 for his Christian faith – its overgrown ruins are in front of the aqueduct, in a small park across Şehzadebaşi Cad. This church was commissioned by Princess Anicia Juliana, wealthy heiress of the Theodosian family, and completed in 527. Around the nave, narthex and courtyard was carved a long poem extolling the foundress, her royal lineage and her splendid church, which for ten years, until surpassed by Justinian's St Sophia, must have been the most sumptuous in Constantinople. Several pieces of dec-oration, including a peacock niche with part of the poem, are in the Archaeological Museum and gardens, but the Crusaders stole many of St Polyeuktos' rich contents. They include the famous porphyry group of four figures (part of a foot was discovered during excavations of the church) and several capitals and carved piers now in St Mark's, Venice.

Nearby, towards the eastern end of the aqueduct, is the beautifully restored twelfth-century church of

Theotokos Kyriotissa; this was converted into a mosque shortly after the Conquest and is known as **Kalenderhane Camii**. Now well below street level, it is a charming red brick church, cruciform in plan, and preceded by a narthex and exonarthex, which still show traces of original Byzantine painting although the faces have been disfigured. Some of the fine marble wall panelling and carved decoration has been preserved in the nave. During archaeological investigation and restoration of the church important finds were made, including a rare pre-iconoclastic mosaic and thirteenth century frescoes of St Francis, which represent the only works of art found *in situ* from the period of the Latin occupation. These are now in the Istanbul Archaeological Museum.

Pass along Atatürk Bulvarı beneath the aqueduct and on the left is the **Museum of Cartoon and Humour**, housed in the charming *medrese* of Gazanfer Ağa (1599), chief of the white eunuchs under Mehmet III (open 10 am–6 pm, admission free). If the exhibits (mainly modern cartoons) are not to everyone's taste, from the courtyard there is a good view of the aqueduct, towering impressively above the domes of the Ottoman building. Here along Kovacilar Sok. are several once grand but now dilapidated, wooden houses; turn right at the top along **Itfaiye Cad.**, where there is a lively **meat market**. Rows of carcasses hang in the windows and the butchers sport bright red aprons. Other shops sell traditional white cheeses with herbs, and if you need a rest or a drink look for a nice shady tea house. Further down the road, as the market finishes, the sixteenth-century **Çinili Hammam** (Tiled Bath) was designed by the great Ottoman architect Sinan for Admiral Hayrettin Pasha, known to the West as Barbarossa. It is a fine high-domed double bath, still in use.

Turn left into Zeyrek Cad., then first right, for the church of the monastery of **St Saviour Pantocrator** (**Molla Zeyrek Camii**), formerly one of the most splendid Byzantine sanctuaries in the city (not always open outside prayer times). High above the Golden Horn, this is a poor but picturesque neighbourhood, with dilapidated wooden houses. Behind the church an area has been cleared for the upmarket Zeyrekhane Restaurant (open 9 am–midnight, except Monday, no alcohol); from the terrace there are superb views across the valley to the Beyazıt Tower, the Süleymaniye and Şehzade Mosques, and over the Golden Horn to Pera and Galata.

Below the monastery complex was one of Constantinople's huge cisterns which came to be called the 'Elephant Stables'. Parts of this massive structure can clearly be seen on the left of Atatürk Bulvarı as it descends from the Aqueduct of Valens to the Golden Horn. Medieval Constantinople boasted several grand monasteries, imperial foundations with schools, hospitals, hospices and orphanages attached. St Saviour

Church of the Pantocrator

Pantocrator was the dynastic monastery of the Comneni family, founded in the early twelfth century by Empress Eirene, whose portrait is in St Sophia. It was lavishly endowed, housing several hundred monks, and included a hospice for the aged as well as a hospital with wards for different diseases.

Only the church survives today; it is an excellent example of medieval Byzantine architecture which is in desperate need of restoration, though it has been partly re-roofed in lead and the ugly concrete overlay is being removed. Walk around the outside of the building to note the multiple apses, the tall, slender niches and windows, and the dog-tooth mouldings below the eaves. Mortar originally covered the brickwork. St Saviour Pantocrator is a triple church; the south church was exclusively for the monks, while the public attended the north church, which was dedicated to the Virgin of Mercy and the focus of a weekly procession of icons. Between was the double-domed mortuary chapel of the imperial family, dedicated to St Michael, where the monastery's foundress, Empress Eirene, and various emperors of the Comneni and Palaeologue dynasties were buried. North and south churches are both triple-apsed and crowned by a dome which rested on four columns within a square, a popular later Byzantine design. During the Ottoman period when the church was converted into a mosque, the columns were replaced by stone piers and part of the outer narthex demolished.

Investigations by the Byzantine Institute have revealed traces of the Pantocrator's former splendour. Hundreds of fragments of brightly coloured stained glass were discovered, some of which are displayed in the Istanbul Archaeological Museum. The south church and mortuary chapel have elegant *opus sectile* pavements with geometric, floral and animal designs, currently covered with carpet and boarding, as this part of the church is used for Muslim prayer. Traces of mosaic survive in the soffit of a window in the north church, which has a nicely moulded cornice, but is otherwise in a desolate state.

Not far from the Pantocrator is the smaller church of **Christ Pantepoptes**, the 'All-Seeing', founded in about 1100 by the formidable Anna Dalassena, a pious and compassionate woman who wielded considerable power during the reign of her son Alexius I Comnenus. Known as **Eski Imaret Camii** or 'Old Kitchen Mosque' it was used for a while as a kitchen and dining hall for students attached to the mosque of the Conqueror. Inside, most of the Byzantine decoration is painted over, though there are still crosses on a couple of capitals in the gallery and on the central door to the outer narthex. Outside, the building retains much of its Byzantine charm. It has a lovely tiled roof and twelve-sided dome, dog-tooth mouldings below the cornice and above the dome windows, and Greek key and rosette patterns in the brickwork.

On Vakif Mektebi Sok. at the bottom of the hill, the former church of **St Theodosia**, now the **Gül Camii** or 'Rose Mosque', has a special place in the final pages of Byzantine history. On the eve of the Ottoman conquest, local women adorned the church with roses and a large congregation gathered for a vigil of prayer. When the Turkish soldiers broke in after dawn they found the believers praying in vain for the salvation of their beleaguered city. The name of the mosque preserves a memory of the rose garlands. Despite some Ottoman modifications the church of St Theodosia retains many of its original Byzantine features – note in particular the blind niches on the exterior of the apses, and the galleries inside the church.

Nearby, **St Nicholas**, patron saint of sailors, has a church within the old Byzantine Sea Walls along the waterfront. It is usually closed, but if you ring the doorbell the caretaker may let you in. Marble paving and columns grace the portico, over the door a ship bears the name of the church, and St Nicholas is shown rescuing sailors from the perils of the sea.

Numerous icons inside the church depict St Nicholas and St George.

Just beyond St Nicholas is a stretch of the Sea Walls with the small arched **Gate of St Theodosia** (Aya Kapı). A short walk along Sadrazem Ali Pasha Cad. leads you to the **Greek Orthodox Patriarchate**, on this site since 1601. This is the stronghold of Greek Orthodox Christianity, a beleaguered remnant of the Byzantine Empire, for the Patriarch of Istanbul (who nowadays must be a Turkish citizen) is still the spiritual head of the Orthodox Church. The current incumbent, Bartholomew, was enthroned in 1991; he has a small flock, but services are held regularly, with all the ritual and paraphernalia of Orthodoxy, and at times the congregation is swelled by visitors and diplomats. The main gate to the enclosure is welded firmly shut, in memory of Patriarch Gregory V, who was hanged here for treason when the Greek War of Independence broke out in 1821. Today's entrance is to the left; across the courtyard is the church of St George, built in 1720 to replace an earlier sanctuary. Gifts from the Orthodox community ensure that this small basilica is well cared for; glittering chandeliers illumine the gilded iconostasis and the inlaid patriarchal throne, which may date from the Byzantine period. On the south wall are the relics of St Omonia, St Theophano and St Euphemia of Chalcedon, and a piece of the Column of Flagellation. Among the icons which decorate the walls and screen is a precious copy of the Virgin Hodegetria, in mosaic on board, commissioned around 1060 by John Comnenus (brother of Emperor Isaac Comnenus) and his wife Anna Dalassena for the monastery of Theotokos Pammakaristos (see p. 65).

Near the Patriarchate was once the **Gate of the Phanar** (lighthouse) in the Byzantine walls. This district is still called **Fener**, after the long-vanished gate. During Ottoman times Fener was a wealthy quarter, populated by Greek merchants and traders, the Feneriotes, who enjoyed the special protection of

THE VIRGIN HODEGETRIA

In the fifth century the empress Eudocia, wife of Theodosius II, brought a portrait of the Mother of God, which St Luke reputedly painted during her lifetime, from Palestine to Constantinople. The standing Virgin was holding her child in her left arm and pointing to him with her right, a pose known as *hodegetria* or 'the guide who shows the way'. This painting became the most prized and most copied of all icons, and was believed to miraculously protect the city. It was covered in silver plate encrusted with precious stones. During Lent the Hodegetria was carried from its shrine near the Great Palace to the church of the Mother of God of Blachernae; it also went regularly to the burial chapel at the monastery of Christ Pantocrator for com-memorations of deceased emperors. When an emperor celebrated a military victory, he saluted the Hodegetria, which then preceded him on a gilded silver chariot drawn by four white horses along the parade route from the Golden Gate to St Sophia. Otherwise, every Tuesday the icon made an excursion around Constantinople, mounted on a wooden pallet.

It must have been a colourful and emotive occasion, for according to Stephen of Novgorod: 'All the people from the city congregate … they sing a very beautiful chant in front of it, while all the people cry out with tears, "kyrie eleison". They place the icon on the shoulders of one man … and he stretches out his arms as if being crucified, and then they bind up his eyes … Two deacons carry the flabella in front of the icon, and others the canopy.'

In April 1453, at the beginning of the final siege of Constantinople, the icon of the Hodegetria was taken to the church of St Saviour in Chora, near the Land Walls, so its presence might inspire the defenders. This time, however, its miraculous powers failed. On 29 May 1453 the Turkish forces breached the defences and poured into the city. Some of the soldiers forced their way into the Chora, stripped it of its treasures and hacked the icon into pieces. Finally the protectress had deserted her city.

the sultan. There is still a small Greek community in Fener. Today it is a poor and run-down but charming part of the city, which time seems to have passed by. Dilapidated old houses line the steep and narrow streets, where scruffy children play and washing hangs overhead. By the waterfront tattered stretches of the old walls are incorporated into later buildings.

An interesting detour can be made to two churches on the hill above the Patriarchate. On the way to the **Theotokos Panayiotissa** (All-Holy Mother of God), popularly known as **St Mary of the Mongols**, note the monstrous late nineteenth-century red brick building of the former **Greek High School**, which dominates the Fener skyline. The church, which is painted deep pink and has an unusual little red and white belfry, is in a walled courtyard. Ring the bell to enter. St Mary of the Mongols was founded by Princess Maria Palaeologina, daughter of Michael VIII, who in 1265 sent her to marry the Mongol Khan Hülägü, grandson of Ghengis Khan and founder of the Ilkhanid Empire in Persia, with whom Michael had concluded a treaty. Hülägü died that year so she married his son Abaqa, but when he was poisoned in 1282 Maria returned to Constantinople. There she became a nun to circumvent her father's attempts to marry her off to yet another Mongol khan, founded a convent and built the small church which bears her name.

After the Conquest, Sultan Mehmet granted the church to his Greek architect, Christodoulos. A copy of the Conqueror's *firman* (imperial decree) is on the wall to the left of the entrance. Among the icons in the sanctuary is a portable mosaic of the Virgin and Child, probably eleventh century in date. As you look around, notice that the south side of the church is a later and rather incongruous early twentieth-century extension.

Not far from St Mary of the Mongols is the twelfth-century Byzantine church of the **Theotokos Pammakaristos** (Joyous Mother of God), seat of the Greek Orthodox Patriarchate from 1455–1568 and converted into a mosque five years later by Murat III, who called it **Fethiye Camii** ('Mosque of the Conquest') to celebrate his victories over Georgia and Azerbaijan. Viewed from outside, this is a typical tall stone and brick church of the Palaeologue Renaissance, with several domes. On the south façade a carved epigram commemorates General Michael Doukas Glabas Tarchaniotes, a scion of one the great imperial families of the Late Byzantine period. He reconstructed the church towards the end of the thirteenth century and was buried in the parecclesion which his widow, Maria Blachena, added against the south wall. This funerary chapel, beautifully restored, is now a museum and houses some fine mosaics. Unfortunately it is usually closed; the keys are with the directorate at St Sophia, who are not at all helpful. In the dome Christ Pantocrator is surrounded by twelve prophets and in the apse Christ is flanked by the Virgin and St John the Baptist, with the four archangels in the vault. To the left of the apse St James, St Clement and St Metrophanes represent the Patriarchates of Jerusalem, Rome and Constantinople, while to the right appear three bishops, St Gregory the Theologian, St Cyril and St Athanasius. Other mosaics depict saints and bishops, and the one surviving narrative scene shows the Baptism of Christ.

The rest of the church is still a functioning mosque; the apse area has been altered to orient the *mihrab* towards Mecca, and given a new dome, while the domed nave and vaulted double narthex retain much of the original Byzantine fabric.

From Fethiye Camii you can go directly to St Saviour in Chora (Kariye Camii) or explore more churches along the Golden Horn. **St Stephen of the Bulgars**, sandwiched between two busy roads, is one of the most familiar landmarks on the waterfront. Close inspection reveals that St Stephen's is no ordinary church, for it is constructed entirely of cast-iron plates! These were prefabricated in Vienna, then shipped down the Danube and across the Black Sea to Istanbul in 1871, after the Bulgarian church had declared its independence from the Greek Orthodox Patriarchate of Constantinople. The Greeks immediately pronounced an anathema upon it which was not revoked until 1945! Today there are only a few hundred Bulgarian Orthodox in Istanbul, but services are occasionally held in the church and there should be a caretaker in the well-kept garden to let you in. By the door and elsewhere on the building is the name of its creator, R.P.H. Waagner, who was also responsible for a twin church in Vienna, destroyed during the Second World War. As your eyes adjust to the dim light inside St Stephen's, note the elaborate iron mouldings and impressive coffered ceiling, all rusting badly, and climb to the vaulted upper gallery for a good view down on the nave.

About 250m north of the Bulgarian church is a dirty and dilapidated **Feneriote Ottoman Greek mansion**, once an impressive stone and brick building. Most of the lower part is now below street level; the upper storeys project on stone consoles and the attic has an elaborate double cornice with rows of brick

St Stephen of the Bulgars

chevrons. From the late seventeenth century this was the Constantinople residence for the representative of St Catherine's Monastery in Sinai. Next to the mansion, the gateway to the church of **St John the Baptist** is permanently closed; it is marked by a roundel containing a cross and crook alongside a hand in low relief. Just beyond on the left was the **Balat Gate** in the Byzantine walls, its name a corruption of 'palation' (palace) for it was formerly one of the gates that led to the Blachernae Palace. A relief of Nike (Victory) from the Balat Gate is in the Archaeological Museum. As with Fener, this area takes its name from the gate; Balat used to be a Jewish quarter, though now there are few Jews left speaking the Ladino tongue of their Spanish Sephardic ancestors. There are still two operating synagogues in Balat, the **Balat Yanbol Synagogue** at the end of Lapçinci Sok. (only open for special festivals) and the **Macedonian Synagogue** at the end of Vodina Cad., opposite Duriye Sok.

Along Kırkambar Sok. there are a couple of churches, both eighteenth century but on the site of earlier buildings. **St Maria Panaghia** is a well-kept little church with a number of interesting old icons, while **St Demetrius**, which bears the distinction of having served as the patriarchal church for four years (1597–1601), has a beautifully carved iconostasis. Sadly, many of its icons have been stripped or stolen in recent years. St Demetrius is directly behind the Byzantine walls, and alongside the church is a well-tended kitchen garden. Further along the road a minaret marks another small Byzantine church, now the **Atik Mustafa Pasha Mosque** and just beyond, on a corner, is the entrance to the famous **Ayazma of the Blachernae**. The sacred spring (*ayazma*) and church, once one of the most important shrines in Constantinople, which housed the robe and mantle of the Virgin, are at the end of a walled garden. Though the current buildings are nineteenth century, there has been a church here since 451, when Empress Pulcheria, wife of Marcian, enclosed the spring. Our Lady of Blachernae, or the Blacherniotissa, to whom the church was dedicated, appeared on the city walls to save Constantinople from the Avars in 627, an occasion which is celebrated to this day. Inside this unusual two-level church there are several distinctive icons of the Blacherniotissa with her hands raised, while on the lower level is the sacred spring and a marble cistern which dispenses the holy water. Services are held here every Friday morning.

From the Ayazma turn left and then right into Dervişzade Sok. As you climb the hill, notice the scattered ruins of Byzantine walls on both sides of the road, remains of the once magnificent **Blachernae Palace**, imperial residence during the Late Byzantine period. It is worth looking into the **Ivaz Effendi Camii**, a charming small sixteenth-century mosque attributed by some to Sinan which has superb Iznik tiles in the *mihrab*. Behind the mosque is a tower which also belonged to the Blachernae Palace, and steps lead down to an undercroft kept permanently closed. Traditionally this is the **Prison of Anemas**, where several unfortunate emperors were imprisoned, tortured and executed. On the terrace alongside there is a tea house and splendid views of the Land Walls and the Golden Horn.

From here wind your way uphill past Eğri Kapı (Crooked Gate) in the Land Walls to the **Tekfur Saray** (see p. 52). If you then follow the street inside the walls, bear left at the fork and turn first left you come to the **Kariye Mosque** (9 am–4 pm, except Wednesday), one of the jewels of the Palaeologue Renaissance. Be prepared for crowds, especially in the high tourist season. Maria Dukas, mother-in-law of Alexius I Comnenus, restored the original church and monastery of **St Saviour in Chora** in the early twelfth century, when the nearby Blachernae Palace became popular. Alexius' son, Isaac Comnenus, further remodelled the church, which again fell into disrepair during the Latin occupation. Around 1310–1320 the great 'Renaissance' scholar Theodore Metochites, treasurer and prime minister under Andronicus II Palaeologus, created the building we see today and was responsible for its magnificent decoration. Theodore was a self-made man who worked his way up the ladder of the Byzantine civil service; later in life he fell from favour and retired to the monastery of the Chora as a penniless monk. Metochites' portrait is inside his church, and he was buried in the mortuary chapel. After the Conquest the church became a mosque; the mosaics and frescoes were painted over and remained covered until 1948–58, when they were cleaned and restored by the Byzantine Institute of America.

In his church Theodore Metochites wanted 'to relate in mosaics and paintings how the Lord Himself … became a mortal man on our behalf'. His imagery

Kariye Mosque

PLAN OF KARIYE MOSQUE

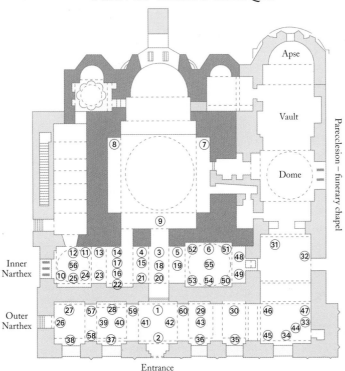

Apse

Vault

Pareeclesion – funerary chapel

Dome

Inner Narthex

Outer Narthex

Entrance

1	Christ Pantocrator
2	The Virgin Mary
3	The Founder Dedicating his Church
4	St Peter
5	St Paul
6	Christ and the Virgin Mary
7	The Virgin Mary
8	Jesus Christ
9	The Dormition of the Virgin Mary
10	Joachim's Offerings Rejected
11	Joachim Praying
12	The Annunciation of St Anne
13	The Meeting of St Anne and Joachim
14	The Birth of the Virgin
15	The First Seven Steps of the Virgin Mary
16	The Virgin Mary Blessed by the Priests
17	The Virgin Mary Embraced by Her Parents
18	The Presentation of the Virgin in the Temple
19	The Virgin Mary Being Fed by an Angel
20	The Virgin Receiving the Skein
21	Zacharias Praying before the Rods of the Suitors
22	The Virgin Mary is Entrusted to Joseph
23	Joseph, Taking the Virgin Mary to his House
24	The Annunciation to the Virgin Mary
25	Joseph Leaving Home
26	Joseph's Dream and Journey to Bethlehem
27	The Enrolment for Taxation
28	The Nativity
29	Three Wise Men before King Herod
30	The Enquiry of Herod

31	The Return of the Wise Men
32	The Flight into Egypt
33 – 34	The Massacre of the Innocents
35	The Mourning Mothers
36	The Flight of Elizabeth and St John
37	The Return of the Holy Family from Egypt
38	Christ is taken to Jerusalem for the Passover
39	St John the Baptist Bearing Witness of Christ
40	The Temptation
41	The Wedding at Cana
42	The Feeding of the Multitude
43	Christ Healing a Leper
44	Christ Healing the Paralytic at Capernaum
45	Christ and the Samaritan Woman at the Well
46	The Paralytic Carrying his Bed
47	The Cure of the Man Born Blind
48	Christ Heals the Man with the Withered Hand
49	Christ Cures the Leper
50	Christ Healing a Deaf and Dumb Man
51	Christ Healing the Woman with a Haemorrhage
52	Christ Raising Peter's Mother-in-Law from her Bed
53	Christ Healing Two Blind Men
54	Christ Healing a Group of the Lame and Sick
55	The Genealogy of Christ
56	Religious and Noble Ancestors of Christ
57	St Anne Holding the Virgin Mary
58	Joachim
59	Mary and the Christ-Child
60	St John the Baptist

broadly follows a scheme developed in the tenth century, whereby the church interior is conceived as a microcosm of the Christian world, with heaven above and earth below. In this arrangement Christ and the Virgin occupy the summit of the building, narrative scenes of their lives cover the upper parts of the walls, while below the saints represent intermediaries between heaven and earth.

As you enter the church, straight ahead above the door to the inner narthex is a fine portrait of (1) Christ Pantocrator, a concept which means 'All-Holder' and refers to His encompassing and sustaining nature. Holding the Gospel in his left hand and blessing with his right, he is described as 'Jesus Christ, Dwelling-Place [Chora] of the Living'. Opposite, above the entrance door, (2) the Virgin Mary raises her hands in prayer like our Lady of Blachernae. Her title is 'Mother of God, Dwelling-Place [Chora] of the Uncontainable'. Both titles play on the name of the church and are repeated in other panels. The prominent position of these mosaics suggest the church was dedicated to both Christ and the Virgin. Pass into the inner narthex and above the entrance to the nave is (3) Theodore Metochites, in elaborate silk robes and an extraordinary hat, presenting a model of his church to Christ. Left of the door (4) St Peter clutches the keys to heaven, and on the right (5) St Paul holds the Gospel. Before going into the nave look at (6) the magnificent devotional panel on the wall to the right of St Paul, which shows the Virgin interceding with Christ. Below are two smaller figures: a posthumous portrait of Isaac Comnenus, who restored the church in the twelfth century, and a black-robed figure of a nun called Melane, Lady of the Mongols. She is usually identified as Maria Palaeologina, who returned to Constantinople in 1282 after the death of her husband, the Mongol Khan Abaqa (see p. 66) and later became a nun.

The lower walls in the nave are revetted in splendid marble, but only three mosaic panels remain.

On either side of the apse are (7) a variant of the Virgin Hodegetria and (8) Christ holding the gospels open at St Matthew 11:28 'Come to me, all you who labour and are overburdened, and I will give you rest.' Above the door from the narthex is a beautiful rendering of (9) the Dormition of the Virgin. She lies on a bier, mourned by the apostles and church fathers, while beside her Christ holds an infant in swaddling clothes representing her soul. Above hovers a winged seraph. We must assume that originally there was a portrait of Christ Pantocrator in the dome, and a number of major narrative scenes including the Annunciation, Nativity, Baptism, Transfiguration, Crucifixion and Ascension in the pendentives and adjacent areas.

To compensate for the loss of the nave mosaics there are magnificent narrative cycles of the life of Christ and of the Virgin in the inner and outer narthex. These are drawn from the canonical Gospels and apocryphal writings, particularly (in the case of the Virgin) the Protoevangelium of James, which was popular in the later medieval period and the inspiration for so many picture cycles of this kind. Biblical quotations describe most of the scenes. The colours are rich and vivid, the figures slender and graceful, the gestures expressive. In contrast to the crowded compositions of earlier periods there are open landscapes and judiciously placed architectural features.

The narrative series of the life of the Virgin covers three bays of the inner narthex. The story begins in the north bay, north-west pendentive, with (10) the High Priest Zacharias' rejection of Joachim's offerings, because though rich he is childless. In the pendentive opposite (11), Joachim is praying in the wilderness. Meanwhile, in (12) the Annunciation of St Anne, an angel comes to their garden, where birds nest in the trees beside a water basin, to tell Joachim's wife she will bear a child. When the couple meet (13) they

Kariye Mosque, ceiling of inner narthex

embrace with joy at the news. After the birth (14), servants attend St Anne and prepare to wash the Virgin. Joachim stands at the door. Only six months old (15), Mary takes her first seven steps towards her mother. The nurse's shawl encircles her head in classical style while the trees blow in the breeze. Two scenes in the vault show (16) Joachim taking the child on her first birthday to be blessed by the priests, and (17) Mary embraced by her parents. The peacocks represent incorruptibility and everlasting life. In the vault of the third bay (18) Joachim and Anne present Mary, three years old, to the High Priest. Behind the priest she is in the Temple receiving food from an angel, a scene repeated (19) in the soffit of the arch between the third and fourth bays.

In the lunette above the door (20) Mary receives a skein of scarlet wool from the High Priest to weave part of the veil for the Temple. When it was decided the twelve-year-old Mary should be married, Zacharias, the High Priest, assembled the widowers, took a rod from each, (21) placed them on the altar and prayed for a sign. Joseph's rod sprouted shoots (22), so Mary was entrusted to him. Joseph looks behind (23) as Mary follows him home. The Annunciation of the Virgin (24) shows Mary, now sixteen years old, carrying a pitcher to draw water from a well when she is surprised by an angel who announces her destiny. A final scene (25) depicts Joseph the carpenter leaving with his son to work away from home.

Pass to the northern lunette of the outer narthex for the beginning of the Christ story, and proceed clockwise. Joseph dreams that the angel tells him Mary has conceived by the Holy Spirit (26), then the couple journey to Bethlehem for the census. Mary rides a donkey while Joseph walks behind. On arrival (27), the family come before the governor to register. Quirinius is on his throne while a clerk inscribes the names on an elegant scroll. Mary reclines gracefully at the centre of the Nativity scene (28) and the new-born Child lies in a cave beneath a beam of heavenly light. The extra-biblical detail of the cave is typical in Byzantine art. Angels adore the Child, and the ox and ass peer into the manger. On the left the Child is washed, while Joseph sits pensively in the centre foreground and on the right an angel announces the news to the shepherds.

In the lunette on the right of the door to the inner narthex (29) the three Wise Men journey to Jerusalem and are summoned before Herod. (30) A partly destroyed panel shows King Herod on his throne asking the priests and scribes where Christ is to be born. Only traces remain of the next scenes (31, 32), which must have shown the Return of the Wise Men and the Flight of the Holy Family into Egypt.

The story continues (33, 34) on the southern lunette of the outer narthex and the first lunette of the western wall, with a poignant rendering of the Massacre of the Innocents. Herod, enthroned, is ordering the slaughter of all male children up to two years old, while the soldiers viciously carry out his instructions and desperate mothers witness the horror of the scene. (35) A group of women then mourn the death of their children. (36) The next scene shows the escape of Elizabeth and her infant son, John the Baptist, from the massacre. As a Roman soldier holds out his sword to strike, a mountain opens up to give them refuge. In the first panel past the entrance (37) Joseph, returning from Egypt, is told by an angel to beware Herod's successor Archelaus. So, carrying Jesus on his shoulders and followed by Mary, Joseph turns from his path to settle in Nazareth, depicted on the lower right of the scene. (38) In the last scene of Christ's childhood the twelve-year-old boy with his parents and two half-brothers travel to the walled city of Jerusalem for the Passover.

Christ's story continues with scenes of his ministry. These run from north to south in the vaults of the outer narthex and then pass to the southern bay of the inner narthex. Many of the panels in the outer narthex are fragmentary or destroyed. Among the best-preserved and most interesting are (39) John the Baptist, dressed in skins and short robes, showing Christ to the crowd by the River Jordan and (40) four vignettes of the Temptation, with a running dialogue between Christ and the little dark brown and black devil. Satan holds out a stone to tempt Christ to turn it into bread, he offers him all the kingdoms in the world (represented by kings wearing crowns at the bottom of the scene), and Jesus is shown standing on the temple of Jerusalem while Satan dares him to jump down. In the next vault there are the scanty remains of (41) the Wedding at Cana, where Jesus stands with his mother while servants follow his instructions and fill the stone water jars, and (42) the Feeding of the Multitude where people are eating from baskets of bread. In the adjacent bay there are fragments of (43) Christ healing a leper (only his spotty legs are visible). The fifth vault is bare but in the dome alongside there were originally scenes of a number of miracles. (44) Christ healing the paralytic at Capernaum is reasonably complete and the mosaics in the pendentives are in better condition; they depict (45) Christ and the Samaritan woman at the well, (46) the paralytic carrying his bed and (47) the cure of the man born blind.

Pass from the bay before the parecclesion, where there are mere traces of four scenes in the dome, into the southern dome chamber of the inner narthex for some of the best mosaics of this cycle. On the soffit of the arch (48) Christ heals the man with the withered hand and (49) cures the leper, who is covered in unsightly spots. Four charming scenes grace the pendentives: (50) Christ healing the deaf and dumb man, who is holding his hand to his ear, (51) Christ healing the woman with a haemorrhage, who is prostrate before him touching his robe, (52) Christ raising Peter's mother-in-law from her bed and (53) Christ coming forward to heal two blind men seated beneath a tree. The western lunette shows (54) Christ with the apostles healing a crowd of the lame, crippled and sick.

In the crown of the dome is (55) a medallion of Christ Pantocrator, while his ancestors are ranged in the flutes below – Adam to Jacob in the top row, Jacob's twelve sons and some others in the lower zone. Now pass to the northern bay of the inner narthex where there is (56) a medallion of the Virgin and Child in the centre of the dome, with sixteen kings of the house of David, including David himself and Solomon, below her. Other ancestors outside the genealogy, among them Joshua and Moses, are in the lower row.

Return to the outer narthex and note the portrait busts and full-length figures of martyr-saints in the soffits of the arches. In addition there were saints in the wall panels between the bays. Most of those which survive were precursors of Christ – (57) St Anne holding the infant Mary, opposite (58) her husband Joachim, (59) Mary and the Christ-Child, and on the other side of the door (60) a fragment of St John the Baptist.

Now go into the parecclesion, the funerary chapel built by Metochites alongside his church and decorated with superb frescoes. There, below the cornice, is a long frieze of saints and martyrs, identified by inscriptions. Many are soldier-saints in military dress, and in the apse six early bishops wear a type of chasuble with dark crosses on a white background, introduced in the eleventh century. In the Orthodox tradition, the faithful would first venerate the images of the saints, who are at an accessible height and act as intercessors between God and man. Worshippers would bow, then touch and kiss the image, address their prayers to the holy figure and perhaps light a candle.

Above the Church Fathers, in the semi-dome of the apse, is a magnificent representation of the Anastasis (Resurrection) or Christ's Descent into Hell, surely one of the finest of all Byzantine works of art. A Byzantine favourite, this dramatic story is told in the apocryphal Gospel of Nicodemus. Christ in the centre has broken down the gates of Hell and Satan lies bound before him surrounded by fragments of the bars, locks, and chains of bondage. With his right hand Christ pulls Adam from his tomb and with his left hand he raises Eve. Behind Adam stand the bearded John the Baptist, David, Solomon and other righteous kings, while behind Eve is Abel with a crook and a group of the just.

Two miracles of Christ, both with a resurrection theme, are depicted in the arch: the daughter of Jairus restored to life, and the raising of the Widow's Son. A superb scene of the Last Judgement covers the central vault. Christ, encircled by a halo of light, is flanked by John the Baptist and the Virgin interceding on behalf of humanity. Alongside are the twelve apostles seated as judges with angels behind. Above Christ, an angel carries the Scroll of Heaven inscribed with the sun, moon and stars, and choirs of the elect fill the clouds. Below him Adam and Eve bow down before a throne left empty for the Second Coming. Underneath, angels weigh the souls in the balance and the condemned are led away to be consumed in the river of fire which flows from beneath Christ's feet. In the pendentive is the Rich Man in Hell, and this theme spills over onto the adjacent lunette where four rather unclear panels depict various torments of the damned. Below Christ and to his right the elect are invited into Paradise, and on the adjacent lunette St Peter leads them to the Gate where they are welcomed by the Good Thief who points to the Virgin enthroned. In the pendentive Abraham holds the beggar Lazarus on his lap.

The beautiful dome of the parecclesion has a central medallion of the Virgin and Child surrounded by angels. On the pendentives are four poets writing verses, and the walls and arches below have various Old Testament scenes. On the north wall is Jacob's Ladder, which nicely follows the curve of the lunette; alongside and in the soffit of the arch is the Story of Moses and the Burning Bush. On the south wall the Ark of the Covenant is moved to Solomon's Temple.

Most of the scenes in the parecclesion, as appropriate in a funerary chapel, concern death or resurrection. The four niches originally contained sarcophagi. General Michael Torkikes (a close friend of Metochites) was placed in the south wall of the domed chamber, and Metochites himself, the man to whom we owe the church and its magnificent decoration, was almost certainly buried in the tomb opposite. This has a nicely carved marble canopy.

THE MONASTERY CHURCH OF CONSTANTINE LIPS

Alongside the busy Vatan Cad., about half-way between the Byzantine Land Walls and Aksaray Square, is the handsome Byzantine church of Constantine Lips, which used to be attached to a large monastery. It was converted into a mosque in 1496 and is known locally as Fener Isa Camii or 'mosque of the lamp of Isa', after the head of a dervish lodge which took over the monastic buildings. Constantine Lips is an interesting Middle Byzantine sanctuary, comprising two churches, a funerary chapel, and a double narthex. Constantine Lips, who was admiral of the Byzantine fleet, dedicated the north church and monastery to the Mother of God in 907, ten years before he was killed in action. Emperor Leo VI attended the dedication. Perhaps the establishment suffered during the Latin occupation of Constantinople, for it was refounded by the empress Theodora, wife of Michael VIII Palaeologus in the late thirteenth century.

Theodora enlarged the foundation by attaching another church to the south and enclosing the complex on the south and west by a vaulted exonarthex. Though the building has suffered Ottoman modifications and the monastery has been destroyed, Constantine Lips is worth a visit. It has a charming brick exterior, with two high domes, tall windows and blind arches. Note the chevrons on the south church and the colonnettes which frame the windows, also the four unusual tiny chapels on the roof of the north church, which were reached via a stair tower south of the narthex. The north church was triple-apsed and flanked by two side chapels; the north chapel is destroyed, and the original columns which supported the dome have been replaced by arches. The southern side chapel became the northern aisle of Theodora's south church; now only traces remain of the triple arcades which once separated the nave from the aisles to the north, west and south. Theodora, her sons Prince Constantine and Emperor Andronicus II, and several other members of the Palaeologue dynasty were interred in the funerary chapel to the south of the church, which is currently closed. Some of the original decoration of the church survives on the cornice and window frames, and there are various pieces from Constantine Lips in the Istanbul Archaeological Museum, including an exceptionally fine icon of St Eudocia in coloured stone and glass inlaid in marble.

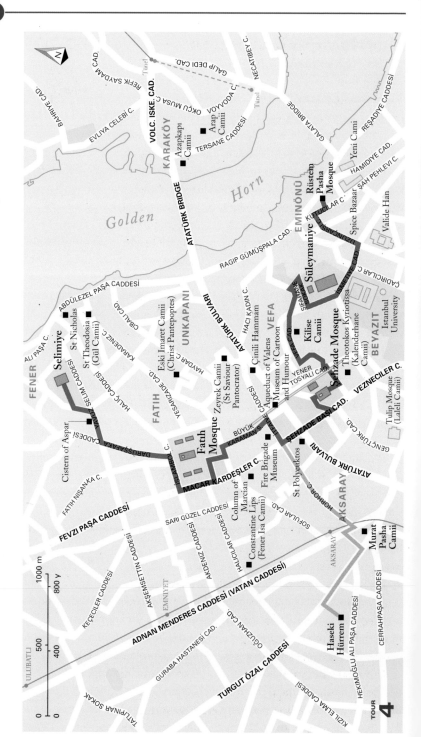

The mosques of Istanbul

TOUR 4

One of the first tasks facing Mehmet the Conqueror in the aftermath of his victory was the need to turn the capital of a Christian empire into an Islamic city. St Sophia's conversion to a mosque was an important symbol, but much more was needed: pre-conquest Constantinople had dwindled as its fortunes waned, and many of its buildings and public places were dilapidated. Immigrants were attracted with grants of land as Mehmet launched an ambitious programme of building and reconstruction. On the site of the church of the Holy Apostles he built his own imperial mosque, but he also commissioned two palaces, the fortress of Yedikule, the Grand Bazaar (built over the Byzantine shopping street, the Makros Embolos) and numerous other lesser works. Later sultans, their mothers, viziers and other notables were to follow suit and the Istanbul skyline gradually assumed its familiar minaretted outline.

As the mosques went up, so the remnants of the Byzantine Empire came down – the already dilapidated Forum of Theodosius (Forum Tauri) became the site of Beyazıt's mosque complex, the Hippodrome fell into disrepair, its stones were taken for other buildings and finally the Blue Mosque rose over it. Church bells were silenced. The church of the Holy Apostles and other churches, such as the Pantocrator and St Saviour in Chora, were converted to mosques. The large mosques include a number of other dependencies such as kitchens, schools, hospitals and libraries, and the *türbe* (mausoleum) of the founder; the whole complex is called a *külliye*. Baths and markets sprang up around these busy centres – the Çarşamba ('Wednesday') market outside the Fatıh (Conqueror) Mosque, is one such example. In fact, the Islamic city revolved around the major mosque complexes; the administrative units into which the city was divided were usually named after the largest mosque in the area.

To gain some idea of the variety and splendour of Istanbul's mosques one should visit a range of them, preferably not on a Friday or when prayers are being said. This walk includes one of the earliest (the fifteenth-century Murat Pasha Camii) and some of the great imperial mosques, charting the development of the greatest of all Ottoman architects, Sinan. We begin at one of the most beautiful but less-frequented mosques in Istanbul. A ten-minute walk downhill from the Fatıh mosque complex, passing the impressive cistern of Aspar (which now contains a sports centre) is the **Selimiye**, the Selimiye I. Yavuz Selim (Selim the Grim) earned his sobriquet from his reputation for mercilessness both at home and abroad; while sultan he executed approximately one vizier a year. Having forced his father Beyazıt to abdicate in 1512 (Beyazıt died very shortly afterwards in suspicious circumstances), he took the throne and spent most of the rest of his reign on campaign. His mosque was completed in 1522 by his son, Süleyman the Magnificent.

Enter the mosque precinct, passing on the right a little red and white *mektep* (primary school). The fine marble-flagged mosque courtyard has pretty Iznik tiles (see p. 101) in the lunettes over the windows. The colours used here and inside, green, turquoise, yellow and dark blue, are characteristic of the early period of Iznik production. Red and white voussoirs (wedge-shaped stones in an arch) rise over the stalactite capitals of the portico columns. Cross to the north side where there is a peaceful terrace with lovely views down over the Golden Horn and its shipyards. Inside the mosque the simple, austere style is striking; the large, shallow dome is supported on four arches pierced by windows. The single chamber is uncluttered with aisles and columns and the decoration is equally restrained, but effective. If it is not prayer-time, have a look at the beautiful painted wooden ceiling of the loge in the far left corner – a red, blue and gold border encloses a pattern of floral motifs. There are more beautiful Iznik

tiles in the lunettes and altogether the Selimiye is a lovely but unshowy imperial mosque.

Selimiye – courtyard lunette

Access to the *türbe*s (open 9.30 am–4.30 pm, closed Mondays) is through a gate in the south-east corner of the precinct. On the way, note the dervish wing (*tabhane*) on the south side of the mosque. Many mosques provided accommodation for wandering dervishes on pilgrimage to holy sites. The first *türbe* is that of Selim himself; a suitably imposing catafalque behind railings, inset with mother-of-pearl. Two lovely tile panels in blues, yellow and green flank the entrance; the *cuerda seca* technique gives very clear definition to the shapes. Other *türbe*s include those of Abdül Mecit I and of some of the children of Süleyman the Magnificent.

Now walk up the hill to the grand complex of the Conqueror himself, the **Fatıh Mosque**. It is worth timing this walk to coincide with the Wednesday market which operates in the streets around the complex, stopping for lunch or a snack at one of the many little restaurants in the food market on the west side or simply enjoying the bustle and colour of the vegetable stalls laden with everything from huge golden quinces and chanterelle mushrooms in November to apricots and melons in summer; mind out for the barrow boys wheeling their stacks of pastry through

FATIH MOSQUE COMPLEX

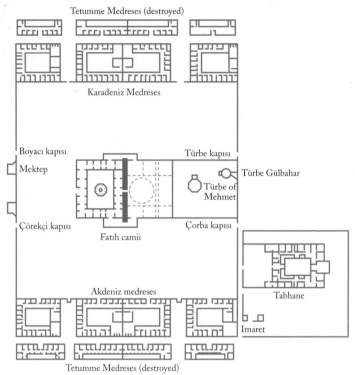

Tetumme Medreses (destroyed)

Karadeniz Medreses

Boyacı kapısı

Mektep

Çörekçi kapısı

Türbe kapısı

Türbe Gülbahar

Türbe of Mehmet

Fatıh camii

Çorba kapısı

Akdeniz medreses

Tabhane

Imaret

Tetumme Medreses (destroyed)

the crowded streets. Enter the mosque complex from here through the Boyacı Kapısı (Painter's Gate) or Çörekçi Kapısı (Muffin-Maker's Gate).

Mehmet had doubtless soon identified the Fourth Hill as a prime site for a monument intended to dominate the city. Constantine too had chosen it for the church of the Holy Apostles, looted in the Fourth Crusade, in ruins by the fifteenth century, and then replaced by a leather market. Work began on the mosque in 1463, and took seven years. This makes the Fatıh Mosque the first of Istanbul's imperial mosques, but the original building, which is known to have had a very large dome, was destroyed in the earthquake of 1766 and rebuilt by Mustafa III to a different plan. The courtyard, however, survived the earthquake and the other *külliye* buildings were restored rather than rebuilt.

MOSQUES

Mosque design was influenced by a number of factors, ranging from liturgical and religious requirements to what was doubtless a competitive urge – the challenge of building a mosque to rival St Sophia. While the clusters of many smaller domes around the central dome, so characteristic of Istanbul's Ottoman mosques, may distinguish them from that great landmark, the similarities are also apparent – the mosque of Kılıç Ali Pasha Camii in Galata, built by Sinan himself, is unashamedly modelled on St Sophia.

Mosques generally have a courtyard with a central *şadırvan* (fountain) or taps against the wall for the ritual ablutions required before prayer-time. Latecomers may also say their prayers on the raised portico along the entrance wall of the mosque. Minarets, from where the muezzin would give the call to prayer, vary in number from one to six; imperial mosques were entitled to two, but the Blue Mosque alone has six. Even St Sophia and the Süleymaniye have only four. Minaret style has altered over the years; the original square minaret later became round, while the caps were once shorter and have gradually tapered. In the late eighteenth century their bases began to swell bulbously. One charming mosque feature, especially popular in the baroque period, is the stone dovecote or bird-house which may occasionally be spotted high up on the exterior courtyard walls. The Ayazma Mosque in Üsküdar has a number of elaborate birdhouses, both on the courtyard walls and the walls of the mosque itself, as does Laleli Mosque.

Inside a mosque look for the *mihrab*, a niche in the *qibla* wall which faces towards Mecca. Nearby there will be a *minber* (pulpit) for the Friday sermon (the imam never sits right at the top – this place is reserved for Muhammad). Sometimes there is also a rather prosaic grandfather clock against this wall. Overhead, calligraphic roundels on the pendentives or on large boards bear the names of Allah, Muhammad, the first four caliphs and often Hussein and Hassan, the Prophet's grandsons. The sultan's loge or box with its own entrance is usually to the left, and the platform from which the müezzins may chant is on the right. There may also be a library (*kütüphane*) in or attached to the mosque and the founder's *türbe* (mausoleum) lies in an adjacent cemetery garden.

A *külliye* (mosque complex) has other buildings attached, such as a hospital (*daruşşifa*), a college (*medrese*: mosques played an important part in the education system), *caravansaray*, *tabhane* (accommodation for wandering dervishes), *mektep* (primary school), *kütüphane* (library), *timarhane* (asylum) and *imaret* (kitchen). The kitchen at Eyüp still functions and on a Friday the kitchen workers can be seen ladling food out of enormous tureens to the poor and needy. A system of religious endowments has meant that some of these complexes, such as the Süleymaniye, are extremely wealthy.

Of the fifteenth-century *külliye* buildings, the hospital, *caravansaray* and *mekteb* of the *külliye* have now disappeared and the *tabhane*, reputedly the most beautiful of the surviving structures, is now an Islamic school and off-limits for women. The two groups of four *medrese*s, named Karadeniz and Akdeniz after the Black Sea and the Mediterranean, were built to the same plan with nineteen cells and a *dershane* (lecture room) around a courtyard. Behind these *medrese*s were the smaller Tetümme *medrese*s. With more than one student to a cell, these colleges accommodated huge numbers; the kitchens must have been hard put to serve students, teachers and staff, and (as required by law) the poor and needy. Raised on vaults, the precinct of this imperial mosque was huge, allowing plenty of space for pilgrims to pitch their tents. The fine exterior of the courtyard includes an unusual detail: marble set into verd antique for the inscriptions over the windows. Inside, cypress trees and a pretty 'witch's cap' *şadırvan* complement the graceful verd antique columns around three sides of the portico. Massive red granite columns support the raised mosque porch, which has faience lunettes at both ends that are similar to but less attractive than those of the Selimiye. The minarets up to the first *şerefe* (balcony) are also original, as is a part of the cemetery wall and the Çorba Kapı or 'Soup Gate' – so-called because the kitchens were close by.

The eighteenth-century mosque was raised on the foundations of the original following an earthquake in 1766, but is thought to have been influenced by Sinan's Şehzade Mosque. Four massive piers support the dome, with galleries around three sides. The general impression is one of size and spaciousness. The *mihrab* with its marble *muqarnas* (honeycomb) decoration is original, for somehow it survived the earthquake. In the north east corner stands the sultan's loge. Plain and stained glass windows light the interior of the mosque which has beautiful inlaid wooden doors.

Mehmet's *türbe* (open 9.30 am–4.30 pm), a rather heavy baroque affair with a projecting wooden roof, stands in the garden beyond the eighteenth century **library**. Inside, the Conqueror's sarcophagus is swathed in green with heavy, ornate stencilling. Here, beware of touts who may attach themselves to you and then demand a gratuity; donations are expected at *türbe*s, but should be paid into a collection box by the entrance. The nearby *türbe* of Mehmet's consort Gülbahar is very plain.

Leave by the old Çorba Kapısı and, if the gate is open, sneak a quick glance into the *tabhane* on the right, famed for the beauty of its courtyard columns. Opposite is the early nineteenth-century *türbe* complex of Nakşidil, mother of the reforming sultan Mahmut II. Now follow the aqueduct down to Itfaiye Sok., turning right past the Fire Museum and left along Şehzadebaşı Cad. to the Şehzade Mosque. You may also like to visit the sweet little *medrese* of the **Gazanfer Ağa** (Chief White Eunuch), now housing the **Museum of Cartoon and Humour**. The execution of its founder in 1603 marked the ascendency of the black eunuchs in the closed world of the Topkapı Palace (see p. 115).

Often described as the apprentice work of Sinan, the **Şehzade Mosque** lies not far from the Süleymaniye, as though inviting comparison. Following the death from smallpox of the Şehzade (Crown Prince) Mehmet, work began on the mosque in 1543 and was completed in 1548. The two minarets denote an imperial mosque since, although it commemorates a prince, it was commissioned by his grief-stricken father, Süleyman the Magnificent. These minarets are beautifully and uniquely decorated with a pattern in relief and the odd red highlight – the external stonework of the Şehzade is altogether quite exceptional and much more striking than the interior. Also of note on the outside are the small ribbed domes; to anchor the mosque more securely, Sinan continued the thrust of its four great piers upwards through the roof, transforming them into these pretty towers. Unfortunately, the *türbe*s of the Şehzade and the Grand Viziers Ibrahim and Rüstem Pasha, which lie in the grounds here and are decorated with the most sumptuous Iznik tiles, are not currently open to the public.

The courtyard has a large *şadırvan* and marble and granite columns to support the portico. Inside the mosque, which has been recently restored, the lack of galleries provides greater space, partly filled by the four massive piers supporting the dome. The new paintwork is uninspiring, there is a marble *minber* and *mihrab*, and the plain stonework of the walls presents a sober contrast to the extravagant carving outside. Unfortunately, the noise of traffic on the busy road outside intrudes, but a restaurant has now opened in the former *medrese*, where one can relax and contemplate the minarets of the mosque. No alcohol is served, but the food is good. The cells have been turned into private dining rooms.

Murat Pasha camii and the Haseki Hürrem *külliye*

Anyone with a particular interest in mosque architecture may now wish to make a detour to look at one of the earliest surviving mosques in Istanbul, that of **Murat Pasha**, standing at what is today a very busy intersection. A simple rectangle with two domes and a single minaret, it provides an interesting link between the two empires. Its founder was a Christian convert from the family of the last Byzantine emperor, who went on to serve as a vizier to Fatih, dying in battle for his sultan. The mosque was built in the late 1460s and is one of only two of the so-called 'Bursa' type in the city. Brick and stone courses alternate up the walls, and the domed portico is supported on columns of granite and verd antique. Two rooms on either side provided accommodation for dervishes.

A ten-minute walk from here is the **Haseki Hürrem** *külliye* – Sinan's first important commission, although he may only have completed the partially built complex. This was a birthday present from Süleyman to Roxelana in 1538. The cramped site has meant that the dependencies are separated from the mosque by a road. Look for the kitchen chimneys rising above the wall as you approach the mosque. From this side you may like to peek inside the hospital (No. 26), still in use, to see the unusual octagonal courtyard. The entrance to the other buildings is through a wooden gate on the other side, beyond the wide, overhanging eaves of the *mektep*. On entering, turn right and pass this *mektep* with its open verandah to enter the pretty *medrese* courtyard. The *dershane* (lecture hall) is distinguished by its larger dome and the two bosses which protrude from the space between the arches. Slender columns, some decorated with rosettes on the capitals, support the portico. Opposite the gate lies the large rectangular courtyard of the *imaret* and to its right is the *darüşşifa*.

A derelict *tabhane* can be seen in the mosque grounds beyond here; the *mektep* (under restoration) and *imaret* (run down and locked) are off Dede Efendı Sok. next to a pleasant eighteenth-century *medrese*, now home to the Uighur Cultural Association.

Leave the mosque precinct by the back gate and walk through the aqueduct and up, passing on the left the nineteenth-century wood-panelled **Vefa Bozahanesi**, famous for its *boza*. This was the drink of the Janissaries, a bland semolina made of fermented millet. Wind along Vefa Türbesi Cad. to the eighteenth-century **Atik Effendı library** (open 8.30 am–5.00 pm, closed Sunday, Monday). A passageway leads to a courtyard, off which are rooms for accommodation and the library itself. Inside, bays splayed like the fingers of a hand ingeniously provide more light for the reader in this small space.

Continue on, looking right down Tirendaz Sok. for a view of the converted late Byzantine church of St Theodore, now known as **Kilise Camii,** and walk up the slope to emerge at the **Süleymaniye** complex with the tomb of Sinan to your left. In the street below the wall of the Suleymaniye beyond Sinan's tomb are the Salı and Rabı *medreses* (closed), and the derelict baths. Little ironmongers' shops in the vaults beneath the terrace are a reminder that previously this area would have been far livelier. This street can be seen equally well from the garden of the mosque precinct.

In 1550 Süleyman the Magnificent (the Lawgiver, to Turks) commissioned St Sophia's greatest rival on the Istanbul skyline. Any visit to Istanbul, however brief, would not be complete without a look at the Süleymaniye. For this is the work of Sinan's maturity, an enormous complex demonstrating both the architect's great technical skill and artistic flair. Most of the buildings of the *külliye* have been preserved, and Sinan's own tomb on the edge of the complex can also be visited. The endowments of a mosque are capable of making a great deal of money: shops, markets and

SÜLEYMANIYE MOSQUE COMPLEX

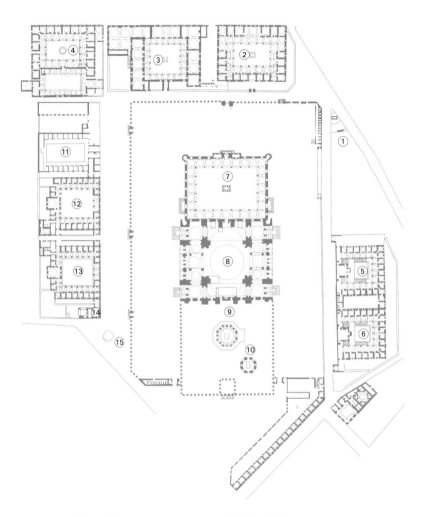

1 Türbe of Sinan
2 Caravansaray
3 Imaret
4 Mental Hospital
5 Salı Medrese
6 Rabı Medrese
7 Courtyard
8 Mosque
9 Türbe of Süleyman
10 Türbe of Roxelana
11 Tip Medrese
12 Sani Medrese
13 Evvel Medrese
14 Mektep
15 Taksim

Süleymaniye

other properties all contribute to its wealth, and the Süleymaniye is one of the country's wealthiest religious foundations. Now under government management it includes two hundred villages, a few mills and a couple of islands.

Turn right down the street to see three further buildings of the complex. The first on the right is the *caravansaray*, which is closed. Next to it is the *imaret*, currently the Darüzziyafe Restaurant, where you can get a good meal seated around the courtyard, although no alcohol is served. The former mental hospital next door is also closed.

From the road, climb to enter the mosque grounds by the steps in the centre of the western wall. A visit should begin at the impressive west entrance to the courtyard. The mosque stands on a vaulted terrace on the edge of the hill with its dependencies grouped around and below it. Apart from the decoration at the top and a few inscriptions the façade of the projecting gateway is sober. Unlike a cathedral, the entrance to an imperial mosque is masked by the courtyard, so it is usually the courtyard entrance which strives to impress the visitor. Note the fine tracery and turquoise studded band below the cap of the minarets at each corner of the courtyard. Before entering the courtyard, enjoy the wonderful views from the northern edge of the terrace of the Golden Horn, Galata and the Bosphorus. Note the domes of the Salı and Rabı *medreses* below. Inside the courtyard the sober style continues – there is a small, closed *şadırvan* and ten tiled, calligraphic panels over the windows along the mosque wall. A raised triple arch marks the entrance to the mosque, which is further adorned with fine stalactite stonework and a calligraphic panel over the door.

On entering the mosque the immediate impression is of space and a soaring dome. This is beautifully offset by the fine but restrained use of decorative elements. The side aisles contribute to the sense of airiness, being open with just a couple of columns between the arches while a gallery runs around the plain stone walls. Semi-domes support the dome itself at the *qibla* end and the west end. Part of the mosque is divided off for those at prayer. A certain Ibrahim the Drunkard was responsible for the fine stained glass; in the view of the authorities his dubious reputation was apparently balanced by his superb craftsmanship. Many Christian workmen were employed in the building of the mosque. The voussoirs of the arches are in grey and white or red and white, and a plain marble *mihrab* is matched by the *minber*. Contemporary Iznik tiles embellish the *mihrab* wall.

To visit the *türbe*s of Süleyman and Roxelana, leave the mosque through the courtyard (the tourist entrance) and walk around to the opposite end along the south side. Notice the double gallery with ablution fountains below as you walk – this is Sinan's ingenious solution to the problem of the great buttresses required to support the dome. The galleries both inside and outside

SINAN

The man who was to become the most famous
Ottoman architect, responsible for masterpieces such
as the Süleymaniye Mosque in Istanbul and the
Selimiye in Edirne, was probably born a Christian in
Anatolia in 1491 or 1492. He was recruited into the
devşirme, the levy of young boys, mainly from the
Balkan provinces and other Christian areas, who were
then given a rigourous training to fit them for a wealth
of jobs within the empire. Initially the system worked
well; without any family allegiance, these men served
their sultan faithfully. Corruption set in, however, once
concessions were made allowing Janissaries to marry
and their status to be passed on to their own sons. By
1520 Sinan was a Janissary, one of the sultan's élite
soldiers, and he served in battle at the siege of Mohacs
in 1526. His initial training was that of a military
engineer, but subsequently he was appointed Imperial
Architect to Süleyman the Magnificent, with whom his
name is inextricably linked. Sinan's great achievement
was to free Ottoman architecture from the hidebound
traditions and conservatism which were restricting its
development. He continued to experiment with

new solutions to old
problems throughout
his career, which was
an extremely long one
as he lived on well
into his nineties.
Having been given
permission, he built
himself a modest
tomb at this corner
of the Süleymaniye
precinct, under an
open stone shelter
with an inscription
over the grill.

successfully mask these ugly projections. Beyond the mosque turn left through a gate, walk down a path lined with gravestones and turn right (see p. 99).

The *türbe* of Süleyman (open 9.30 am–4.30 pm) is on the right and that of Roxelana lies ahead. There are superb tile panels flanking the entrance and within the *türbe*. Roxelana was probably born in Ruthenia, then a part of Poland. Although she was not deemed to be conventionally beautiful, Süleyman was greatly in love with her and indeed married her, in a break with Ottoman tradition. She was also responsible for another great change; she moved permanently into Topkapı Palace, which until then had been more of a male domain. The harem had been kept at the Eski (Old) Palace, although women did spend some time at the Topkapı. Roxelana's move led eventually to the whole of the sultan's harem joining him there, while the Old Palace was reserved for the harems of previous sultans. By the 1530s Roxelana wielded great power, so much so that she was able to engineer the downfall of Süleyman's great friend and trusted Grand Vizier, Ibrahim Pasha, who was strangled on the sultan's orders in 1536. She is also believed to have been responsible for turning Süleyman against his son Mustafa, to favour his sons by her instead. Mustafa was also killed on his father's orders in 1553. Roxelana may thus have done the empire a great disservice, for while Mustafa was widely admired and liked, her son Selim, who succeeded his father, was known to posterity as Selim the Sot. Roxelana herself died in 1558 and was buried here in the grounds of Süleyman's great mosque.

Tile panels flank the entrance to Süleyman's mausoleum, as they do his wife's. The interior comes as a surprise after the sobriety of the mosque: tiles cover the walls up to the windows and the pendentives. The shallow dome sparkles; it is studded with tiny pieces of ceramic, each apparently inset with rock crystal. A tiled calligraphic band runs above the windows, and eight marble columns add a further sense of opulence to this magnificent *türbe*. Other sarcophagi include those of Süleyman II, Ahmed II and Mihrimah.

By now a cup of tea or cold drink in one of the little tea houses along the southern edge may be an attractive idea before continuing on to look at the other parts of the complex, not all of which are open to the public. When the *külliye* was first established this was a little street of coffee and hashish houses and leather shops. Behind are two of the *medreses* of the complex and the library and the hospital, which is still a working hospital.

Now continue eastwards down the street, passing on the right the former *mektep* (now a children's library) and the *taksim* (water distribution point). Continue on past a couple of streets before turning left into Uzunçarşı Cad., which now descends towards the Golden Horn. This is the edge of the bazaar quarter, and the street is full of backgammon and musical instrument makers, among other little shops. Emerge at the bottom, opposite the narrow steps, up to the **Rüstem Pasha Mosque**.

There is one glorious exception in Sinan's career to his otherwise restrained use of the flamboyance of Iznik tiles. The building of a mosque for the Grand Vizier Rüstem Pasha coincided with the peak of Iznik tile production, and the appearance and mastery of the distinctive tomato-red or Armenian bole (a fine compact earthy clay). Rüstem Pasha, despite his dubious reputation, had consolidated his position by persuading the Sultan to give him the hand of his daughter, Princess Mihrimah, thus justifying his nickname 'the louse of fortune'. His mosque, despite its cramped location near the spice market, is stunning for the wealth of exquisite tiles with which it is covered. The **Rüstem Pasha** *medrese*, a pretty octagonal design of cells around a courtyard and fountain, is located some distance away uphill, towards the Nuruosmaniye Mosque on Hoca Hanı Sok.

GRAVESTONES

Conventions in the iconography of gravestones include the use of a flower to signify a woman, while mens' gravestones were marked with a turban, different styles indicating the wearer's rank. Those of children are smaller. It is also possible to date gravestones by the depiction of headgear: following the 'Auspicious Event' (the euphemism for the elimination of the Janissaries) in 1826 and the reforms of 1829, when turbans were banned and the fez introduced, all traces of the former élite force were removed. The very word 'Janissary' was banned, and the characteristic turbans which identified their gravestones were knocked off. Fezzes were in turn outlawed by Atatürk in 1925 so any gravestone with a fez can be dated to 1829–1925.

From Hasırcılar Sok., enter the Rüstem Pasha mosque precinct by steps leading up to one end of a courtyard with a tiled porch. There are four panels of tiles and two external *mihrab* niches. Note the particularly fine panel of a blossoming tree on a dark blue ground. The manganese purple used for the trunk and branches was later deemed too pale in tone and was discarded. One tile shows a stylized plan of Mecca, while the right-hand section is a complete jumble of leftovers. Even this foretaste does not prepare one for the overwhelming experience of the interior where, apart from the stone *minber* and columns, every inch of wall is covered with tiles up to the cornice. Five identical panels adorn the *mihrab*; trees spring from urns into blue cartouches surrounded by a wealth of floral decoration. Blue predominates, but red and turquoise are also much in evidence. The dome is supported on piers; the four arches and four semi-domes making an octagon. The side galleries are also tiled, whereas the back gallery is wooden with painted decoration. From the mosque precinct the enticing smells of the Spice

Rüstem Pasha, detail of tile from exterior wall

Bazaar beckon the visitor; a stroll through the streets and into the cool of its vaulted passageways, perhaps stopping for a bite at Pandeli's, provides a fitting end to this walk.

IZNIK TILES

Iznik (ancient Nicaea of the fourth-century Church Council which produced the Nicene Creed) is a lakeside town some fifty miles from Istanbul, which was once famed for its beautiful tiles. First appearing in the late fifteenth century, they reached their peak in the late sixteenth century. Initially influenced by the Chinese porcelain so prized by the sultans, Iznik gradually developed its own style, fusing decorative elements from Persia, China and central Asia. The palette of yellow, blue, turquoise and green which marks the earlier Iznik tiles, such as those in the Selimiye, later gave way to blues, turquoise and above all the famous tomato-red or Armenian bole, which was produced from clay rich in iron oxide. Persian craftsmen from Tabriz are thought to have been imported by the Ottomans to contribute their skills and artistry. Iznik tile panels are found in mosques, *türbe*s and the Topkapı Palace itself, as well as in museum collections around the world. In these tile panels, delightful floral fantasies complement realistic depictions of blossoming trees, carnations, rosebuds, hyacinths and, above all, tulips. Indeed, it is thought that the tulip accompanied the nomadic Turks on their journey west, and certainly it was a special and much-loved flower for them: there is even an era called the 'Tulip Period', and a baroque mosque in Istanbul known as the Tulip (Laleli) Mosque.

Production of Iznik tiles reached an artistic peak in the time of Süleyman the Magnificent. The tiles of Rüstem Pasha Mosque were produced at precisely this time, the crowning glory being the wonderful rich red of the Armenian bole highlighted against the blues and white ground of the mosque's thousands of tiles. Thereafter, technical and artistic mastery of these colours and glazes declined, and not even the sheer scale of the internal decoration of the Blue Mosque could equal the perfection of this earlier stage of tile production.

TOUR
5

Topkapı Palace

Topkapısaray, the imperial palace of the Ottoman sultans for over 400 years, is one of Istanbul's most fascinating and evocative monuments. Its location is perfect: high up on the promontory looking down to where the waters of the Bosphorus and the Golden Horn meet the Sea of Marmara, this was once the acropolis of the original Greek colony of Byzantium. From the beginning Mehmet the Conqueror recognized the potential of this prime site. Although he built a first palace near the Covered Bazaar, work began on another palace here on the acropolis only six years after the Conquest. This New Palace (Yenisaray) later became known as Topkapısaray after the Topkapı (Cannon Gate) in the ancient sea walls at the tip of the promontory.

After the Conquest Mehmet continued campaigning to consolidate and expand his empire, but by the 1460s he had time to devote himself to his new capital. Inspired by its splendid past, he determined to revive Constantinople, which had fallen into decline in

**Topkapı Palace
from the
Bosphorus**

the late Byzantine period. To do this, he had to both rebuild and repopulate the city. Traditionally the Ottoman capital had been where the sultan pitched his tent, but Mehmet, modelling himself on the grand Byzantine emperors, adopted Constantinople as his permanent capital and built within it his grand imperial palace.

Topkapı Palace was probably completed by 1465, although it was further embellished and developed by later sultans. It is a typical Oriental residence, with pavilions and courtyards set in beautiful gardens which ran down to the sea. A great wall surrounded the palace complex to guard its privacy. Unlike many western palaces it looks inwards on itself, above all in the harem, which was closed to all but a select few and consequently an endless source of fascination to outsiders.

Now a museum, Topkapısaray houses a glittering collection of treasures from the Ottoman past. Priceless jewels, exquisite ceramics, extravagant costumes – countless works of art are displayed in its pavilions, many of them produced in the palace workshops.

Outside the palace gate stands the **Fountain of Ahmet III**, which dates to 1728. Covered in a wealth of decoration, the roof has a central dome and corner turrets rise above the four *sebils*, with *çeşmes* in between; a projecting roof provides shade under its great eaves. Every inch of the fountain is covered in floral motifs, decorative calligraphy (including a poem about water), tiles and fine stonework in great contrast to the sobriety of classical Ottoman architecture. Ahmet III was known as the 'Tulip King' and the Tulip period bridged the gap between the classical period and Turkish baroque. An attendant behind the bars of the *sebil* would have handed out cups of water or

Tile from Topkapı Palace

TOPKAPI PALACE

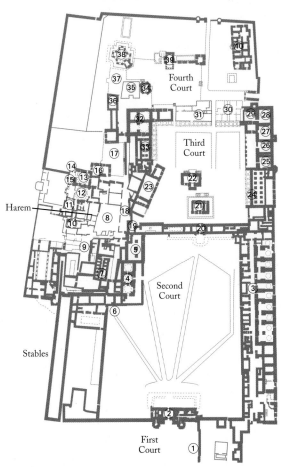

1	Executioner's Fountain	21	Throne Room
2	Gate of Salutation	22	Ahmet III Library
3	Kitchens	23	Palace School Mosque (New Library)
4	Divan	24	'Dormitory of the Expeditionary Force' (Costume Collection)
5	Inner Treasury	25	Treasury Room 1
6	Carriage Gate	26	Treasury Room 2
7	Quarters of the Black Eunuchs	27	Treasury Room 3
8	Courtyard of the Valide Sultan	28	Terrace
9	Courtyard of the Jariyes (female slaves)	29	Treasury Room 4
10	Apartments of the Valide Sultan	30	Chamber of the Pantry
11	Bedchamber of Abdül Hamit I	31	Chamber of the Treasury (Special exhibitions)
12	Imperial Hall	32	Pavilion of the Holy Mantle
13	Murat III Bedchamber	33	Privy Chamber (Portraits of the Sultans)
14	Ahmet I Library	34	Revan Kiosk
15	Ahmet I Dining Room	35	Pool and Fountain
16	Cage (Kafes)	36	Circumcision Chamber
17	Courtyard of the Favourites	37	Itfariye
18	Golden Road	38	Baghdad Kiosk
19	Birdcage Gate	39	Sofa Pavilion
20	Gate of Felicity	40	Mecidiye

sherbet for passers-by – nowadays, some of the *sebils* of Istanbul house little kiosks where one has to pay to slake one's thirst.

Turn now to the **Bab-ı Hümayün**, or Imperial Gate, built by Mehmet in 1478. Four of the inscriptions and his *tuğra* (monogram) date to this time. In the nineteenth century the upper storey was removed, marble panelling and further inscriptions added. Inside are guardrooms. By way of a deterrent, heads of the recently executed were displayed in niches flanking the gate.

THE FIRST COURT

Pass through the narrow arch into the first court of the palace, also known as the **Court of the Janissaries** since this was their place of assembly. This is not the palace proper, but a service area accessible to all. Relatively few buildings have survived in here: one is the sixth-century **Church of St Eirene**. Like St Sophia it was rebuilt after the Nika riots, but was converted to an arsenal in Ottoman times. Other than for the occasional concert, it is not open to the public. Nearby is a nineteenth-century mint and beyond is the path to the stables, the archaeological museum and Çinili Kiosk. Tickets for the palace can be bought at the ticket office on the right of this courtyard. Some distance beyond on this side was the **Executioner's Fountain**, where heads were displayed on two pillars. Curiously, the palace gardeners or *bostancis* also served as executioners and as the sultan's oarsmen. Executioners had their own guild and took part in the parades of the guilds. A more discreet form of execution was sometimes permitted for those within the inner circle of courtiers who had fallen from grace, and even the occasional sultan; they might be strangled with a bowstring or cord in private. Disgraced harem women were disposed of more perfunctorily, being placed in large sacks weighted with stones and thrown into the sea.

THE JANISSARIES AND THE 'AUSPICIOUS EVENT'

Janissary

The word 'Janissary' comes from the Turkish *yeni ceri*, meaning the 'new troops'. The origins of the Ottoman sultans' splendidly exotic guard are obscure, and they are first mentioned by Europeans shortly before the fall of Constantinople. Conscripted as young boys under a system known as the *devşirme* (gathering), this levy gradually grew more regular and began to occur on a seven-yearly basis. It took place mainly in Albania and the Balkan provinces; Christian boys were rounded up (Muslims could not be enslaved according to

the Qur'an), the best were selected and taken to Edirne, from where some went on to Istanbul. They were circumcised and converted. The very best went to the palace school, but there were other schools, both in Istanbul and the provinces.

Not all were destined to be soldiers, for some became administrators and rose to the very top, but all had a training in warfare (especially archery). They were taught trades like carpentry and engineering, and sometimes seem to have assisted in the building of mosques. The great Ottoman architect Sinan was trained as an army engineer in this way. A corps of guards comprised of slaves was not a new idea; there had been the Mameluks in Egypt, for example. The advantage of this system was that without any family ties the slaves were absolutely obedient. At first Janissaries were not allowed to marry, but later this prohibition was lifted and was doubtless one of the factors in the decline of the Janissaries as a military élite.

In Istanbul they were quartered at Et Meydan near Fatih Mosque. The barracks was called the *ocak* (hearth) because here the Janissaries received their food rations. Their huge copper kettles were most significant; when overturned, this rejection of their rations from the sultan signalled that they were no longer loyal to him. The Janissaries had close links with the Bektashi dervishes, whose lodges were clustered near the barracks. This sect was a curious dervish order, liberal in nature. Certain similarities with the Christian religion may have appealed to the Janissaries, many of whom were born into Christian families. Also the drinking of wine was permitted. There were also close financial links between the Janissaries and the Jews of Constantinople.

From early days the Janissaries were powerful and fractious; even Mehmet the Conqueror had to buy them off on a couple of occasions. From 12,000 men in the time of Süleyman the Magnificent, their numbers had swollen to 50,000 by the time of Murat III for by then they were allowed to marry and their sons could also become Janissaries. The levy disappeared in the early eighteenth century. The payroll was bloated due to the corrupt practices which were all too common; for example, many dead Janissaries continued to collect pay and a Janissary ration book was a valuable commodity. However, when it came to fighting, it was often difficult to persuade them to leave their trades and families.

The Janissaries were divided into *ortas*, a unit comparable to a brigade. Each *orta* had an emblem which the men would tattoo on

their arms. Embassies employed Janissary guards, and their flamboyant headgear struck many a traveller. They were also the city's firefighters. The need for reform was increasingly apparent as the force became corrupt, undisciplined and rebellious. Yet reform was extremely difficult; the Janissaries' way of fighting, while it contrasted badly with the disciplined manoeuvres of the modernized European armies, was something they refused to give up. The courage of the individual was what mattered, whereas drills and training smacked of the heretical to them. In this conviction they were supported by the conservative religious establishment and were strong enough to unseat sultans, if they were not appeased in time.

Consequently, early attempts at reforms in the eighteenth century failed, and when Selim III established a new army this was perceived as a great threat. The sultan was deposed in an insurrection in 1807 and was strangled in a power struggle the following year. Mahmut II (1808–39), who had nearly lost his life at the same time, wisely bided his time, building up the auxiliary units and new troops at a safe distance on the Asian shores and ensuring that he was in a strong position with powerful allies. He cleverly drove a wedge between the Janissaries and the religious leadership before finally making a move against the Janissaries – and when the move came, it was fast. In 1826 the new troops were formally established, and were cleverly modelled on the successful modern Egyptian troops. They were Muslims, not infidel Europeans. Their new guns were even blessed, in a sign of the clergy's approval of the new forces. Days later, however, the Janissaries overturned their kettles – insurrection had been predictable, but no one could have predicted how soon their end would come. Janissaries massed in the city, but so did opposing forces; engineers, bombardiers and other reformist units gathered in Topkapı Palace.

This time the clergy were on the sultan's side, all Muslims were urged at prayers to join in supporting him. With the people and the clergy on his side the sultan now opened the palace gates and his troops filed out; orderly and drilled, they advanced as the Janissaries fell back to their quarter, Et Meydan. With the barracks surrounded, the onslaught began; cannon were trained on the gate, and when this had been destroyed the troops poured in and set fire to the wooden buildings within. In scenes reminiscent of the slaughter of the circus factions in the Hippodrome after the Nika riots in the sixth century, the Janissaries were massacred. Those who managed to escape were rounded up and taken to the Hippodrome, where rebels were disposed of. There are no precise figures, but probably around 7,000 were killed in the city; many more were slaughtered in the provinces once the news spread.

The sultan declared that the very name 'Janissary' was henceforth banned, and their gravestones with the distinctive turbans were destroyed. Mahmut himself, as well as his troops, now took to wearing modern dress in a sign of the changing times. Subsequently known as the 'Auspicious Event', the destruction of the Janissaries was commemorated by the building of a mosque (the Nusretiye) near to Tophane, the modern arms factory built in the old arsenal.

THE SECOND COURT

The real palace entrance is the middle gate (Orta kapı) or **Gate of Salutation** (Bab-üs Selam). Fortified with twin towers, a parapet and two pairs of doors, the *tuğra* of Süleyman the Magnificent can be seen over the door. Inside the gatehouse, now the entrance to the palace, foreign dignitaries who had been fortunate enough to be granted an audience had to wait in the dark chambers on the right. Rooms on the other side included a cell for those awaiting execution.

None but the sultan might ride through here into the rarified atmosphere of the Second Courtyard, where silence in the sultan's presence was the rule (sign language replaced the spoken word) and cypress and plane trees, peacocks and even gazelles adorned the grounds. Paths lead away from the entrance to the Divan and harem on the left, straight ahead for the entrance to the inner palace and to the kitchens on the right.

The **kitchens** were probably deliberately placed on this side, where the prevailing wind would carry smells away, and they are one of the landmarks of the palace with their tremendous chimneys and domes rising over their ten great halls. After a fire in 1574 they were rebuilt and expanded by Sinan. By the late sixteenth century over 600 cooks were employed, cooking thousands of meals a day (in total, palace staff numbered some 5000 at this time). Now they house the priceless palace collection of ceramics, glass and silverware. The Ottomans built up one of the largest and finest porcelain collections outside China; there are 12,000 pieces, of which less than half can be shown at any time.

Across the courtyard is the **Divan**, easily spotted with its conical-roofed tower. This was where the council met regularly to decide on legal and administrative matters. It consists of three connected rooms, the Council Chamber being the corner room. The Divan gets its name from the low bench, which runs around three sides of the chamber. Iznik tiles decorate

Topkapı kitchens

the lower part of the walls. At first the sultan presided over the debates, but early on he withdrew, in a sign of his growing remoteness. Thenceforth, no one knew when he might be listening to debates from behind a curtained window in the tower, which came to be known as the **Sultan's Eye**.

Under this window sat the Grand Vizier, surrounded by other officials in strict order of precedence. Perhaps the tremendous hierarchical organization of the Byzantine Empire influenced the Ottomans, for prior to the fall of Constantinople the Ottoman court was not particularly marked by pomp and ceremony. In the palace, however, all was carefully regulated by complex ceremonies and carefully defined ranks. Officials were recognizable by both dress and colour: for example, the *ulema* (clergy) wore purple, viziers green and chamberlains scarlet. These distinctions also applied to the population at large, until the nineteenth-century members of other religions wore different coloured slippers and hats. When the Divan was in session (it met four times weekly), thousands of guards, Janissaries and functionaries filled this courtyard in a splendid but silent display. Next to the Council Chamber was the Divan archive and from here a door led into the office of the Grand Vizier.

Adjacent to the Divan was the domed **inner treasury**, a late fifteenth-century building renovated in the sixteenth century. Formerly all the revenue of the empire was received here and kept in underground vaults. The Janissaries' pay-day was another splendid occasion, when thousands of Janissaries stood here in silence to receive their dues. The chamber now houses a collection of Islamic arms. This includes Mameluk swords, Turkish helmets, matchlock rifles, swords, axes and lances and an impressive collection of huge 'tower rifles' for the defence of fortresses. In the left-hand corner is the sword of Mehmet the Conqueror, and there is also an executioner's sword on the back wall. Note the Persian and Tartar composite bows made of sinew on the outside, wood and horn on the inside for superb performance.

The Tressed Halberdiers had their barracks near here, adjacent to the harem. They served as Palace Guard and were also responsible for delivering firewood and heavy loads to the harem, hence the horsehair tresses of their headgear, which effectively blinded them.

The **Gate of Felicity** was rebuilt in the sixteenth century and given an eighteenth century overhaul. Initially this gate was known as the Sublime Porte, and ambassadors were accredited here. The Porte was later moved to the Grand Vizier's residence outside, but ambassadors continued to speak of the Sublime Porte in reference to the Ottoman government. It was in front of this gate that, in another splendid ceremony, the sultan was seated on his throne on accession. Three *tuğras* frame the door. Beyond was the sultan's private domain where few ever penetrated.

THE HAREM

You can only visit the Harem as part of a guided tour (open 9.30 am–3.30 pm, queue for tickets which are sold every half hour for the following forty-minute tour). Groups are large, tours are usually rushed because of the large number of visitors and only some sections are open to the public. Nonetheless, this part of the palace, a hidden centre of intrigue and power, should not be missed. Entrance is through the **Carriage Gate** where carriages waited to take women on their rare outings from the palace. The harem was heavily guarded by the black eunuchs; a small domed vestibule with cupboards for the guards' bedding leads into a guardroom revetted with beautiful seventeenth-century Kütahya tiles. From here the sultan could gain access to the Divan tower to eavesdrop on council debates in the room below.

Ahead are the quarters of the black eunuchs; left of the paved courtyard is a colonnaded porch

Tile from Topkapı Palace

Harem

through which you can look into their dormitory. At the peak of the harem's power, up to 700 eunuchs were employed here. In charge was the *Kislar Ağa* (Chief Black Eunuch) who had his own apartments. One of the richest, most powerful and feared imperial officials, he was ranked third in the state hierarchy after the Grand Vizier and the Sheikh ül-Islam. As supervisor of the princes' education, official inspector of the *vaqfs* (endowments) of the imperial mosques and the holy cities, commander of the halberdiers and member of the Privy Council, the *Kislar Ağa* had unrestricted access to the sultan at all times and was the harem's connection with the world outside its walls (see p. 115).

Pass through the main Harem door to another guardroom with a shelf on the left for food coming from the kitchens. Opposite is an entrance to the **courtyard of the Valide Sultan**, one of the largest of the harem. Continue down the long corridor which leads to the rectangular, arcaded courtyard of the women slaves, around which were baths and bedrooms for the girls, the harem kitchen, and the laundry. The harem required large numbers of female staff, and its hierarchy was fascinating. Harem girls were given to the sultan or bought for palace service, entering as *jariye*s (female slaves). They all received a training, but few ever shared the sultan's bed. Some senior women became *usta*s, the chief harem administrators. Rooms on the garden side of this courtyard were probably for such women as the Chief Laundress, the Treasurer, the Wet Nurse (considered to be related to the sultan) and the Mistress of the Harem, who trained the sultan's personal servants. Accomplished and beautiful girls might be apprenticed to the *usta*s and would hope to catch the sultan's eye, becoming *ikbal*s or favourites. Among their ranks a favoured few (up to six) rose to become *kadın*s, official concubines with their own apartments. The *haseki sultan* (favourite concubine) was ranked above the royal princesses and came second only to the sultan's mother or Valide Sultan.

Supreme among the women of the harem was the Valide Sultan, whose apartments are adjacent to the courtyard of the *jariye*s. From the **salon**, with its raised dining area, look through into the beautifully tiled bedroom and annexe. To its right is the prayer room. The salon has panels inlaid with mother-of-pearl and tortoiseshell, a domed and gilded ceiling and a beautiful fireplace. This was the heart of the harem in more ways than one. Not only was the Valide Sultan head of the harem household, but as guardian of the royal family and the only person to whom the sultan would bow, she received the highest stipend in the empire. Of all the women from the closed and claustrophobic world of the harem, she was the only real public figure, occasionally seen during ceremonial processions between palaces, mosques and gardens. The influence wielded by a powerful Valide Sultan extended far beyond the harem doors.

A corridor leads from these rooms past the Valide's baths to those of the sultan which are opposite the painted wooden doorway to the **bedchamber of Abdül Hamit I**. This marks the dividing line between the *haremlık* (women's area) and the *selamlık* (men's area). Note the elaborate taps on the marble basins of the baths, which are attributed to Sinan, as is the domed **Imperial Hall** alongside. This is the largest room in the harem, where dancers and blindfolded musicians entertained the sultan as he sat on his sumptuous throne, while the ladies of the harem gathered on the raised area below the musicians' gallery. The pendentives and soffits have been repainted in the original red, blue and gold, but the blue and white Delft wall tiles were added in the eighteenth century.

Behind the hall is a particularly fine suite of rooms, entered through a prettily tiled antechamber. **Murat III's domed bedchamber** which has been beautifully restored, is one of the best examples of sixteenth-century interior design. Built by Sinan in the 1570s, it boasts the most splendid Iznik tiles covering

The Harem, Imperial Hall, Topkapı Palace

the walls, set in the niches and framing the shelves, doors and windows. A calligraphic band runs right around the room. A dainty two-tiered fountain faces the exquisite bronze fireplace, surrounded by magnificent tile panels of blossom.

Ahmet I's library (1608) is a delightful light-filled room. From its windows there are wide vistas of the sparkling waters of the Bosphorus and the Golden Horn. Tortoiseshell and mother-of-pearl inlay embellish the wooden book cabinets while above are more magnificent blue and green tiles. Look through into **Ahmet III's dining room**. Built a century later than the library, the Turkish rococo decor of this tiny room reflects growing European influence. Every inch of the lacquered wooden panels is brightly painted with bowls of fruit and flowers in typical 'Tulip Period' style.

Off a corridor quaintly named the 'Consultation Place of the Jinns' is the double kiosk with a sinister history traditionally known as the *Kafes* or **Cage**, and reputedly the rooms where unfortunate Ottoman princes were held prisoner. Before 1607 princes were trained in the art of government and sent out to rule the provinces. However, on the death of a sultan his successor routinely murdered all of his own brothers to eliminate rivals to the throne. In the seventeenth century there was a radical change; henceforth the sultan tended to withdraw from public view, and his male relatives were forcibly confined to the harem. Here they received an education and were provided with sterile concubines as consolation. This meant that new sultans had very little experience of the outside world, and it was a factor in the decline of the Ottoman Empire. As some sultans produced vast numbers of offspring it is hard to imagine that the *kafes* could contain all the princes. While the idea of the 'Cage' captures the imagination, obviously this building would not suffice – Murat III had 103 children!

The chambers are thought to date from the late sixteenth century or early seventeenth century. Note the splendid gilt-bronze fireplace, elegant paintwork and beautiful tiles from the peak of Iznik production. The exterior walls facing the **Courtyard of the Favourites** are also tiled. Apartments flanking this courtyard are thought to have housed some of the sultan's favourite girls. Look over the balustrade at the disused pool and garden below, and other floors of the harem not open to the public. From here the '**Golden Road**' leads back to the main gate and exit from the harem via **Birdcage Gate** (*Kuşhane Kapısı*) into the Third Court.

EUNUCHS

Eunuchs played an important role in the courts of the Middle East, as guardians of the harem and officers in the administration, for at least 2,000 years before the Ottoman conquest of Constantinople. Castration is forbidden in the Qur'an and was unknown to the Turks until they took over the Byzantine Empire and adopted Byzantine customs. Like the Byzantine emperors, the Ottoman sultans developed an elaborate court ceremonial, practised royal seclusion, established a harem and also employed eunuchs. Their white eunuchs came mainly from Georgia and Circassia, the black eunuchs from Nubia and Abyssinia. After the boys had been castrated, an operation performed by Christians, those that survived were transported to the slave market in Constantinople, which was by the Covered Bazaar in the city centre. Youths bought for the palace were educated in the Palace School along with the pages, and assigned tasks in the inner service or the harem. It was the duty of the white eunuchs to supervise activities in the *selamlık*, while the black eunuchs were responsible for all harem affairs.

The Chief White Eunuch (*Kapı Ağa*), a formidable figure, acted as the sultan's personal advisor, Head of the Palace School, Gatekeeper-in-Chief, Head of the Infirmary and general master of ceremonies for the inner palace. Other head eunuchs were in charge of the Treasury, payments and accounts and the kitchens, while the remaining white eunuchs, who numbered between twenty and thirty, assisted their superiors. At first the status of the white eunuchs was higher than that of the black eunuchs, but in 1591 Murat III divested them of many of their powers, and thenceforth the black eunuchs reigned supreme.

From the seventeenth century there were normally several hundred black eunuchs in the harem, whose quarters were beside the long corridor inside the Carriage Gate. Black eunuchs were given pet names such as Hyacinth, Narcissus, Tulip, Goldfinch or Emerald, which contrasted with their often grotesque appearance. Despite careful inspection by the seraglio doctors, it seems a few eunuchs retained some sexual potency even after emasculation especially if the testicles but not the penis had been removed. Rumours circulated of bored odalisques finding pleasure with the black eunuchs, who not only satisfied their desires but also indulged them with precious gifts.

The Chief Black Eunuch (*Kızlar Ağa*), one of the most powerful and feared officials in the Ottoman Empire, had a luxurious

The *Kızlar Ağa*

apartment just inside the Birdcage Gate of the harem. He controlled entrance to and discipline within the harem, and was responsible for organizing the education of the young princes. He managed the harem finances as well as the endowments of the imperial mosques and the holy cities of Mecca and Medina. He was a member of the Privy Council, confidential messenger between the sultan and Grand Vizier, and the only person in the empire who could approach the sultan at any time of day or night. His influence and his wealth were enormous. The Chief Black Eunuch enjoyed the position of second man in the empire for over 300 years, until Sultan Abdül Hamit was deposed in 1908 and the harem with its attendant eunuchs finally abolished.

THE THIRD COURT

Just inside the Gate of Felicity, the **Throne Room** was the focal point of palace business and ceremonial. Here foreign ambassadors, clothed in special kaftans, were presented to the sultan, and here he received his Grand Viziers and other ministers, who reported on transactions in Council which needed the royal assent. Rigid protocol was observed. Access to the Audience Chamber was strictly controlled by the white eunuchs whose quarters were on either side of the Gate. Holding them tightly by the arm, the eunuchs led visitors into the sultan's presence and made sure they performed the compulsory prostrations. They might then be allowed to kiss his hand, which rested on his knee, or the hem of his kaftan. After the reign of Süleyman the Magnificent the sultan usually received ambassadors in silence, which increased his aura of majesty. Indeed, silence pervaded the inner courtyards – several of the sultan's attendants were mutes, ministers only spoke on official matters in his presence, the palace pages literally tiptoed around and a special sign language was developed for communication.

Everyone left the presence of the sultan walking backwards.

The original throne room probably dates from the fifteenth century, though it has undergone several restorations since. It is a splendid pavilion with unusually broad eaves supported on antique marble columns. Above the wooden door is a *bismillah* (prayer) dating from 1723, and it is flanked by superb green and yellow Iznik tile panels (sixteenth century), crowned by the *tuğra* of Abdül Mecit (1856). Right of the door is a charming gilt marble fountain from Süleyman's reign. The audience chamber is viewed through the grating of the large window where gifts of foreign monarchs and ambassadors used to be paraded before the sultan. Inside the chamber is a lovely gilt-bronze chimney-piece, a little fountain

Library of Ahmet III

perhaps intended to mask any words the sultan might utter, and the grand imperial throne. The throne, which is not unlike a low four-poster bed, was made in 1596 for Mehmet III.

Though the throne room is quite small and dark, all accounts agree that its decoration was magnificent. In addition to walls studded with jewels, luxurious carpets, even a diamond-encrusted inkstand, there were eight different coverings for the throne, chosen according to the status of the visitor – either velvets embroidered with gold or precious stones, or glittering gold brocades. Cushions and bolsters were equally sumptuous, while the sultan himself wore brocades, furs and satins and a selection of the priceless imperial jewels.

Entrance to the courts beyond the throne room, the sultan's private domain, was restricted to the white eunuchs and palace pages. Part of the Third Court was devoted to the **Palace School**, where the pages were given the best education in the empire. Most were from Christian families, the best of the boys taken from their homes in the annual *devşirme* (levy), and then converted to Islam. All of course were the sultan's slaves. School rules were strict and any infringement was punished with a severe beating. Forty of the top pages served in the Privy Chamber, with individual responsibilities such as shaving the sultan or clipping his nails. This was the most prestigious of the different divisions or 'chambers' of the school, which had dormitories, classrooms, baths and a mosque. Most of the school buildings were destroyed or damaged by fire in the nineteenth century. On completion of their education the students went to the army, the provinces or were given court appointments. Forty-eight Grand Viziers were trained in the Topkapı Palace School.

Behind the throne room, **Ahmet III's library**, an elegant marble pavilion completed in 1719, stands alone in the centre of the Third Court. A painted and gilded fountain with a fancy crest graces the portico façade. Inside, the books were kept in cupboards with glass doors while sofas in the three bays provided ample reading room. Panels of fine seventeenth-century tiles cover the upper walls and the inlaid wooden shutters are exquisite. It is not clear whether this library was exclusively for the sultan or also used by the palace school. In any case, many of the palace books are now housed in the red brick 'New Library', formerly the **Palace School Mosque**, which juts out into the court on the harem side (open only to readers).

On the opposite side of the court a series of rooms house some of Topkapı's most precious museum exhibits. The **Dormitory of the Expeditionary Force**, part of the Palace School, originally accommodated the pages who laundered the royal costumes for campaigns and ran the military band. Now it displays some of the imperial costume collection. Note the many talismanic shirts and caps made of fine white cotton and covered with charms and Qur'anic verses believed to protect the wearer from enemies and misfortune. Mehmet the Conqueror's garments and sword are on show, and Süleyman the Magnificent's turban and long-sleeved ceremonial velvet kaftan. Süleyman often wore 'cloth of gold', which was reserved for the sultan and made only by looms which were 'on contract' to the palace. At times so much gold and silver went into the making of thread that the

Library of Ahmet III – fountain

mint almost ran out! Mahmut II, who abolished the Janissary corps in 1826 and undertook Westernizing reforms, adopted a more European style of dress and took to wearing the fez instead of the turban. A decree of 1829 banned the old costumes for all except the clergy, which enraged the conservatives. His grandson Abdül Hamit II's pyjamas are quite special, made of silk, lined with cashmere and sewn in Paris!

At a lower level, the rooms known as the **Conqueror's Kiosk**, in a prime position overlooking the Sea of Marmara, were used by Mehmet and later sultans as a royal reception suite. At that time the **Imperial Treasury** was in the vaults below, but from the seventeenth century the upper rooms were also used to store treasures. Today some of the fabulous palace treasures are appropriately on display in these rooms. **Room 1** contains several splendid imperial thrones. Mehmet Ağa, architect of the Blue Mosque, fashioned Sultan Ahmet I's royal seat, which is inlaid with precious stones and mother-of-pearl. Murat IV used the mid-sixteenth-century portable ebony throne with ivory and mother-of-pearl inlay during his Baghdad campaign while Nadir Shah of Iran sent the elaborate throne and footstool plated with gold and set with precious stones in enamel as a gift to Mahmut I. It was made in Mughal India where Nadir Shah had acquired it as booty. The mid-eighteenth-century gold ceremonial throne was last used at the accession of Mehmet VI on 4 July 1918. Also displayed in this room are the great sword of Süleyman the Magnificent, a jewelled bowcase and quiver, archers' rings and glittering rock crystal flasks and writing boxes. **Room 2** displays gifts and spoils of war from Iran, Egypt, India and Russia. Reliquaries claim to contain the arm and occipital of John the Baptist; there are pieces of jade encrusted in jewels and European, Ottoman and Iranian medals, including the Order of the Garter which Queen Victoria presented to Abdül Aziz in 1876. **Room 3** is dominated by two huge solid gold candlesticks studded with several thousand diamonds, each weighing 48kg. Originally a gift from Sultan Abdül Mecit to Muhammad's tomb in Medina, they were sent back to Istanbul during the First World War. Other cases contain Qur'an bindings and vessels of jewel-encrusted jade, zinc and rock crystal. **Room 4** is mainly devoted to diamonds and emeralds. Mehmet IV's mother, Turhan, gave him the dagger with a solid emerald handle in 1663, while Mahmut I sent the famous Topkapı dagger, which has three huge emeralds on the sides and one at the top that conceals a watch, to Nadir Shah of Iran. As the Shah was killed in a revolt before it had even reached him, the dagger was brought back to Istanbul. The fabulous 'Spoonmaker's Diamond', at 86 carats the fifth largest in the world, is surrounded by 49 brilliants and belonged to Mehmet IV. Also on display in this room is the ceremonial sword with which each new sultan was girded on accession to the throne. It was reputed to belong to Osman Gazi, the first of the Ottoman line. Other cases contain Mustafa III's splendid suit of armour, delicate ivory ornaments and a gold cradle, of traditional Turkish style, with an opening below in which to place the chamber pot.

Alongside the Treasury is the office of the Museum Directorate, formerly the **'Chamber of the Pantry'**, to which up to 100 pages were attached, responsible for supervising the sultan's food. Across the passage leading to the Fourth Court was the **'Chamber of the Treasury'**, where several dozen pages, supervised by one of the white eunuchs, looked after the imperial treasure, made payments and kept accounts. This hall is often closed, but has been used to display a selection of the Topkapı's renowned collection of Turkish and Persian miniatures and manuscripts. Exhibits have included splendid illuminated Qur'ans in different calligraphic scripts and Safavid Persian drawings and miniatures.

Alongside the red brick library on the harem side of the court is the former **Privy Chamber**, which now displays portraits of various sultans. Among the earlier portraits are several attributed to the school of

Veronese sent to Murad III by the doge of Venice. There are a number of works by Kapıdağlı, court painter to Selim III, and an interesting series of twenty-eight sultans, painted in gouache between 1804 and 1806. Note that sultans from Mahmut II onwards wear the fez rather than the turban.

Pages from the Privy Chamber were appointed custodians of the imperial collection of sacred relics, housed in the adjacent **Pavilion of the Holy Mantle**. The Prophet's robe and other relics were brought to the palace by Selim I after his conquest of Egypt in 1517 and only displayed to the sultan, his family and high palace officials. In 1962 the pavilion was opened to the public; as its contents are highly revered it is often crowded with devout Muslims. Behind the elegant porch is a suite of domed rooms which contain, apart from the relics, a charming little fountain and some beautiful tilework. In the room to the right of the entrance hall a reader intones verses of the Qur'an; from here you can look through to the golden case containing the Holy Mantle, the Prophet's swords and bow, the sacred banners and a magnificent silver throne. Other exhibits in the pavilion include Moses' baton, Abraham's saucepan, the sword of David, a footprint of Muhammad in marble, dust from his tomb, one of his teeth and several hairs from his beard.

From the Pavilion of the Holy Mantle there is access through a columned portico to a lovely marble terrace which overlooks the Golden Horn. Opposite the pavilion the **Revan Kiosk** was built in 1635 as a *çilehane* or religious retreat, to commemorate Murat IV's capture of Revan (Erivan) from the Persians. Murat led his army personally in this victorious campaign, the first sultan since Süleyman to do so. On the colonnade side the kiosk is faced with marble and inside it is revetted with fine Iznik tiles. Alongside, the marble pool and fountain were redesigned by Murat's brother and successor, generally known as Mad Ibrahim. Ibrahim, who had been confined to the Cage

OTTOMAN PAINTING

Ottoman painting offers an interesting variety of portraits and miniatures, inspired largely by Safavid Persian art but more vigorous and earthy in style. As their major patron was the sultan, the principal subjects of the Ottoman artists were the sultan himself, his military campaigns and life in the seraglio. Illustrated annals recording the career of individual sultans were compiled from the reign of Süleyman onwards by the best of the court painters. The pages of the *Süleymanname* (annals of Süleyman) depict the sultan riding into battle, besieging brightly-coloured cities, hunting with his courtiers, receiving his admiral Barbarossa and walking in his garden as an old man.

Many of the outstanding paintings of Süleyman's reign were executed by the former sea captain Haydar Reis, known as Nigari. Other albums, of calligraphy and paintings or drawings were made for presentation on accessions, on the great feasts of the Muslim year or on return from successful campaigns. The most famous later Ottoman illustrated manuscript was the *Book of Festivals* (Surname), compiled to commemorate the circumcision festivities of Ahmet III's four sons in 1721. One elaborate scene, spread over sixteen double pages, depicts the princes escorted from the archery ground above the Golden Horn to the Topkapı Palace where the circumcisions were performed.

The Ottomans also demonstrated an interest in topographical representation and cartography, inspired by European maps and sea charts. Corsair admiral Piri Reis presented a world map to Selim I in Egypt in 1517 and the splendid *Book of the Sea* (Kitab-i Bahriye), which contains 215 coloured plates, to Süleyman in 1525. Many illustrated copies were made in Istanbul of the sixteenth-century Persian *Conquest of the Two Sanctuaries* (Futuh al-Haramayn) depicting the stations of the pilgrimage to Mecca and Medina. Court painting reached its peak under Murat III (1574–95) who commissioned a six-volume illustrated copy of the *Life of the Prophet*. Four volumes and 814 illustrations survive in the Topkapı Palace collection, many of them masterpieces of the Ottoman classical style.

for twenty-two of his first twenty-four years, was mentally unstable and quite unfit to rule. He indulged in epic orgies in the harem and during romps on the terrace often threw his favourites, buffoons, mutes and dwarfs into the pool for amusement. At the southern end of the marble terrace Ibrahim added the **Circumcision Chamber** (closed) where thenceforth all the young princes were circumcised. Inside and out it is covered with tiles of different periods. Note the lovely panels on the outer wall depicting mythical animals, birds and flowers.

Along the terrace Ibrahim also erected the gilded bronze bower, called the **Iftariye**, because there during Ramadan he took his *iftar*, the meal which breaks the fast after sunset. From here there are magnificent views of the old city and the Golden Horn. At the corner of the terrace the **Baghdad Kiosk** is the epitome of an Ottoman pleasure dome, grand but intimate. It was built in 1639 after Murat IV's reconquest of Baghdad, a success achieved at the expense of 100,000 Turkish soldiers. Marble columns support the broad eaves and antique marbles revet the lower walls. Inside the decoration is superb. Golden stars spangle the dome and over the sofas in the four alcoves there are gilded and painted ceilings. Fine tiles cover the walls and the back of shelves and cupboards, and the doors are beautifully inlaid with mother-of-pearl.

Steps lead down from the terrace to the gardens of the **Fourth Court**, where Ahmet III staged his famous tulip festivals at the time of the first full moon in April. Vases of tulips were ranged on shelves with lamps of coloured glass, cages of song birds hung from the trees, tortoises with candles on their backs wandered through the flowers while musicians and dancers entertained the sultan and his harem (see p. 208). During his festivals Ahmet may have relaxed in the **Sofa Pavilion**, which was redecorated in rococo style in the 1750s. Tucked away below the pavilion terrace is Murat IV's stone throne where the Sultan sat watching the sporting activities of his pages.

In the Fourth Court there is one more kiosk, the **Mecidiye**, with its wardrobe chamber (now a book-shop), the last buildings in the palace, erected around 1840 for Abdül Mecit I. Western in style, it heralds the Dolmabahçe Palace. The ground floor is sometimes used for special functions, while the lower floor accomodates the Konyalı Restaurant. There is a self-service café on the terrace, an ideal place to relax and enjoy the view of the Bosphorus at the end of a visit to Topkapı.

THE ISTANBUL ARCHAEOLOGICAL MUSEUMS

From the First Court of Topkapı a road leads downhill to the Archaeological Museums in the lower gardens of the palace, a complex which comprises the Museum of the Ancient Orient, the Tiled Kiosk and the Archaeological Museum (open 9 am–5 pm, except Monday). Through the gate on the left the **Museum of the Ancient Orient** contains important finds from the ancient civilizations of Anatolia, Mesopotamia and Egypt. There are beautiful coloured glazed brick reliefs of animals from the Processional Way and Ishtar Gate of Nebuchadnezzar's Babylon (sixth century BC), and objects from Nebu-chadnezzar's own 'palace museum', including a statue of a governor of Mari on the Middle Euphrates (c. 2000 BC). The earliest known political treaty, written on a large clay tablet, was drawn up in 1269 between the Egyptian pharoah Ramses II and the Hittite king Hattusili III after their armies had fought a battle at Kadesh in southern Syria which ended in stalemate. It is in Akkadian cuneiform, the diplomatic lingua franca of the time. Several basalt statues and stele exemplify the 'naive' style popular in south-east Anatolia during the neo-Hittite period (tenth–eighth century BC).

Beyond the tea garden is the **Çinili Kiosk** or 'Tiled Kiosk' (closed at the time of writing), built by Mehmet II in 1472 as a pleasure pavilion. Here the Conqueror enjoyed watching animals from his menagerie, supervising his pages as they played games on the terrace and being entertained by his harem women. The two-storey kiosk, which has an elegant colonnaded portico, is revetted inside and outside with fine tiles. Note the beautiful dedicatory inscription in *cuerda seca* technique above and near the door. A superb collection of ceramics is on display inside; this includes Seljuk pottery and eight-pointed star tiles showing birds and animals, beautiful Iznik blue and white, blue and turquoise and polychrome wares, Kütahya ceramics with delicate floral motifs and stylized figures, and Çanakkale plates decorated with schematic mosques, sailing boats and animals.

Sarcophagus of the Weeping Women

Across the courtyard the **Archaeological Museum** exhibits one of the most important collections of antiquities in Turkey. It was originally established in 1891 to house a group of six fourth-century BC sarcophagi from the royal necropolis at Sidon in Lebanon. These are on the ground floor in galleries to the left of the entrance. Most famous is the late fourth-century BC **'Alexander Sarcophagus'**, one of the jewels of Hellenistic art, commissioned by Abdalonymos, king of Sidon, who owed his throne to Alexander the Great. One of the long sides depicts a battle scene between the Greeks, wearing short tunics, and the Persians, wearing long trousers and long-sleeved overgarments. Alexander is on his horse at the far left, distinguished by the pelt of the Nemean lion on his head. The hunting scene on the other long side also depicts Alexander, identified by a diadem, though only the indentation in the hair now survives. The Persian in front of Alexander may be Abdalonymos, and the other mounted Greek could be Alexander's close friend and general, Hephaestion. The short sides of the sarcophagus also show battle and hunting scenes.

Also from Sidon are the **'Sarcophagus of the Weeping Women'** depicting eighteen elegantly-draped women in different poses of mourning, the **'Lycian Sarcophagus'** which has a tall lid shaped like Lycian funerary monuments and the **'Satrap Sarcophagus'** showing scenes in the life of a bearded Oriental ruler. An Egyptian-style sarcophagus contained the mummy of Tabnit, king of Sidon, which is on display alongside and there are two anthropoid marble sarcophagi of a type popular in Phoenicia in the fifth–fourth century BC. Rooms beyond the 'Sidon rooms' are currently closed to the public.

On the other side of the ground floor is an excellent display of **classical sculpture** in chronological order – *kouroi* and *korai* (youths and maidens) of the Archaic period, a lion from the Mausoleum at Halicarnassus (one of the Seven Wonders of the World), Greek funerary reliefs, Hellenistic sculpture including three busts and one statue of Alexander the Great, sculpture from Magnesia on the Meander and from Tralles including a stylish caryatid, a portrait gallery of Roman emperors, a reclining Oceanus from Ephesus, Athena attacking two Titans (part of the battle between the gods and the giants) from Aphrodisias and opulent Roman imperial sculpture including a highly elaborate Tyche from Prusias ad Hypium, an indolent Silenus from Nablus and a huge Zeus from Gaza.

An exhibition called **'Bithynia, Thrace and Byzantium'** (days and times of opening vary) occupies the back rooms on the ground floor. For Thrace and Bithynia there are good sections on daily life, burial traditions and beliefs, including the 'heroic horseman' cult.

The bristling bronze boar from near Edirne is quite special and there is a nice reconstruction of a Thracian tumulus (46 BC). Many interesting objects are on show in the Byzantium section. Two decorated and inscribed pedestals once bore statues of the renowned charioteer Porphyrius and stood in the Hippodrome. Porphyrius is shown in his quadriga while the inscriptions praise his victories and give the names of his horses. From the church of Constantine Lips there is an exquisite St Eudocia of coloured stone and glass inlaid in marble. A green breccia door lintel decorated with crosses and monograms comes from the same church. Part of a slab sarcophagus from St John of Studius depicts Christ's entry into Jerusalem.

On the first floor the exhibition **'Istanbul through the Ages'** (days and times of opening vary) is fascinating. There are prehistoric and Greek pottery fragments, Hellenistic funerary stele, inscriptions from the Land and Sea Walls, sculpture fragments from

Funerary stele

the Golden Gate and a most impressive relief of Nike which decorated the Balat Gate. The head of one of the snakes from the bronze column in the Hippodrome is here, and a piece of relief sculpture from the Baths of Zeuxippus. An important pre-iconoclastic mosaic from Kalenderhane (late sixth century/early seventh century) depicts the Virgin and Child with St Simeon, while later frescoes of St Francis (thirteenth century) from the same church are the only works of art found *in situ* from the period of the Latin occupation. Crosses, inlay and sculpture from St Polyeuktos, sculpture fragments and architectural pieces from Constantine Lips, fragments of painted window glass from St Saviour in Chora and the Pantocrator, and a capital from St Mary Pammakaristos give some insight into the decoration of Constantinople's fine churches. Note also the great fourteenth-century bronze bell from the Galata Tower and a section of the chain which was used to close off the Golden Horn.

On the second floor the exhibition of **'Anatolia and Troy through the Ages'** (closed at the time of writing) displays models and finds from the different periods at Troy, and a selection of objects from a wide span of Anatolian cultures, including nicely painted Chalcolithic pottery, cuneiform tablets from the Hittite capital Boghazköy and the contents of a Phrygian burial chamber at Gordion.

The third floor is devoted to objects from **Neighbouring cultures in Cyprus, Syria and Palestine** (closed at the time of writing). Among the exhibits are archaic statues from Cyprus, lion and bull consoles from the Temple of Jupiter at Baalbek, an inscription from the Temple of Jerusalem and an excellent collection of Palmyrene funerary portraits.

Life in the Ottoman city

In 1453, when Constantinople fell to the Ottoman Turks, much of the once great city was already abandoned and in ruins. Mehmet immediately set about the daunting task of restoring prosperity and creating his own grand Islamic capital. First and foremost Constantinople had to be repopulated. When the carrot of free land and housing did not work, the Conqueror resorted to coercion. Officers sent out to the provinces bearing imperial firmans forced ordinary families, merchants and artisans to move to the new capital. The Ottoman élite were commanded to build mansions, baths, inns, markets, workshops and mosques. Mehmet's policy worked. By the end of his reign Istanbul was prosperous and populous, and had begun to display its new Islamic identity.

Mosques, markets and *hammam*s (baths) define the essence of an Islamic city. Sultan Mehmet founded his monumental imperial mosque complex on the Fourth Hill, over the ruins of the church of the Holy Apostles and built his first palace, the Eski (Old) Saray, in the area where the University now stands. Nearby, at the heart of Istanbul's principal market quarter, he established the **Old Bedesten**, a securely-gated domed trading hall for precious goods. The rents went to the endowment which supported St Sophia. All typical Islamic markets have such an interior 'strong-room', surrounded by a network of covered streets and several *han*s, for the warehousing and manufacture of goods and the lodging of merchants. In addition every market district always had at least one *hammam*.

Under Mehmet and his successors Istanbul's bazaar developed and expanded to become one of the most impressive market complexes in the Islamic world. Süleyman the Magnificent added the twenty-domed **Sandal Bedesten**, named after a fine silk satin made in Bursa, for the trade in silks, which was a state monopoly. By the nineteenth century the labyrinth of shopping

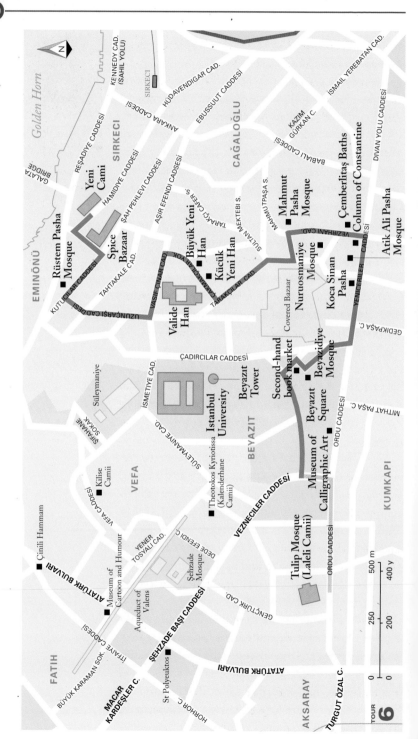

alleys around the two *bedesten*s, each alley named after a particular trade, such as slipper-makers, mirror-makers, quiltmakers or goldsmiths, had been roofed with vaulted arcades, and the entire complex became known as the *Kapalı Çarşı*, or '**Covered Bazaar**'. It covered forty hectares, and was enclosed by a thick wall with eighteen gates which were locked at night. Under one roof were over 4,000 brightly painted shops and stalls as well as workshops, mosques, courtyards and fountains. Twenty-one *han*s surrounded the bazaar, both within the gates and outside, and open street markets filled the warren of lanes down to the Golden Horn.

Ottoman insignia, Covered Bazaar

Business started at about 8.30 am after prayers for the sultan and an injunction against cheating and hoarding and the gates were generally locked at around 6 pm. Istanbul's grand shopping mall, which also functioned as bank and stock exchange, greeted customers with a rush of colours, sounds and smells. Shopkeepers sat cross-legged in their cubicles, reading or smoking water-pipes, their wares displayed on benches in front, veiled and cloaked women accompanied by servants and eunuchs rummaged through the merchandise and haggled for the best prices, porters staggered under heavy loads, shouting 'Guarda! Guarda!', caravan leaders drove their horses and camels through the crowds, and carts and carriages clattered past, making a deafening noise. Crowded and cosmopolitan, the bazaar was at the centre of the city's commercial life and vast amounts of wealth changed hands there. All the city's merchants, whether Muslim, Jewish, Greek or Armenian, would meet in the bazaar to discuss trade and conclude business deals.

Despite the valuables stored and sold there, the Covered Bazaar was relatively crime-free and any theft was severely punished. Market guards patrolled the streets at night and the two *bedesten*s, repositories of the costliest goods, had their own special guards and porters. Several times a week the Chief Inspector of Weights and Measures and his staff went around the

PLAN OF THE COVERED BAZAAR

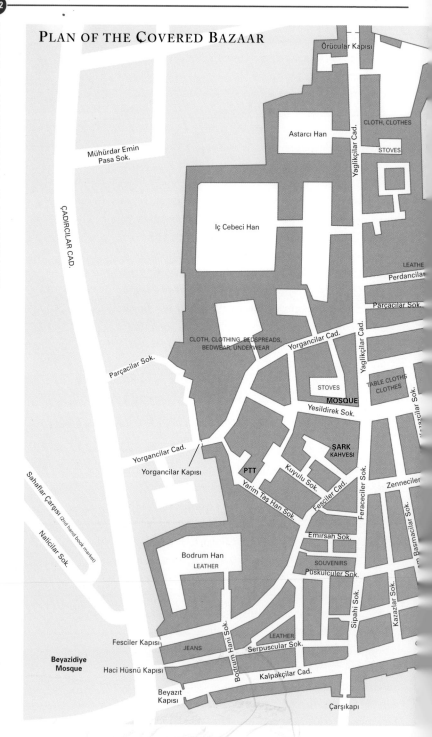

Örücular Kapısı

Mühürdar Emin
Pasa Sok.

ÇADIRCILAR CAD.

Astarcı Han

Yaglıkçılar Cad.

CLOTH, CLOTHES

STOVES

Iç Cebeci Han

LEATHE
Perdancılar

Parçacılar Sok.

CLOTH, CLOTHING, BEDSPREADS,
BEDWEAR, UNDERWEAR

Yorgancilar Cad.

Yaglıkçılar Cad.

Parçacılar Sok.

STOVES

TABLE CLOTHS
CLOTHES

Kazazcılar Sok.

MOSQUE
Yesildirek Sok.

ŞARK
KAHVESI

Yorgancilar Cad.

Yorgancilar Kapısı

PTT

Kuyulu Sok.

Fesciler Cad.

Feraceciler Sok.

Zenneciler

Basmacılar Sok.

Yarim Taş Han Sok.

Sahaflar Çarşısı (2nd hand book market)

Nalicilar Sok.

Emirsah Sok.

Bodrum Han
LEATHER

SOUVENIRS
Püskülculer Sok.

Sipahi Sok.

Kazazlar Sok.

Fesciler Kapısı

JEANS

Bodrum Hanı Sok.

LEATHER
Serpuscular Sok.

Beyazidiye
Mosque

Haci Hüsnü Kapısı

Kalpakçılar Cad.

Beyazıt
Kapısı

Çarşıkapı

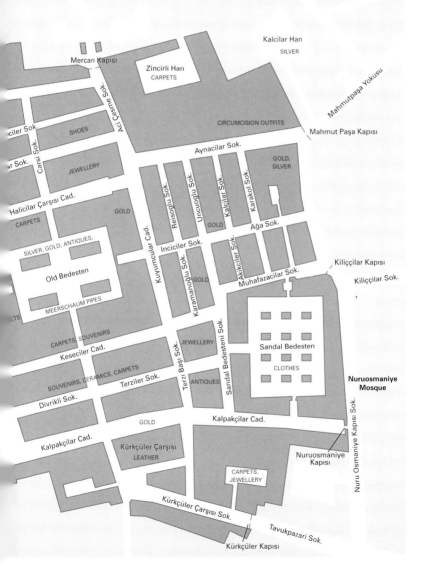

markets of Istanbul to ensure trade regulations were complied with. Any shopkeeper found guilty of short measure was given a harsh beating on the soles of his feet, so that he hobbled around for days after, his guilt plain for all to see.

Though it has been restored and rebuilt several times after fires and earthquakes, the Covered Bazaar has kept much of its original character. Many of the old trades have vanished, and tourist shops proliferate, but the streets and gates retain their evocative names and the warren of alleys still confuses and excites. Shops selling the same kinds of goods still cluster together, their displays colourful and enticing, and khans little-changed for centuries hide down incongruous looking alleys. Cafés and tea-houses offer drinks, snacks and a place to relax and watch the constant ebb and flow of locals and tourists. Try the crowded Şark Kahvesi (Eastern Coffee House), one of the institutions of the bazaar and near the small traders' mosque, for a genuine old-fashioned ambience.

At the heart of the market the **Old Bedesten**, with its four gates and fifteen domes, specializes in silver, gold and antiques. Erdün Collection at No. 34–39 has a fantastic display of antique and new glass and ceramic lamps, and Ismail Çelebi at No. 92–93 sells beautifully crafted genuine meerschaum pipes with amberoid stems. Around the Old Bedesten are the specialist carpet dealers; if you want a carpet be prepared to bargain hard, drink numerous glasses of tea and have your credit card ready. Today the **Sandal Bedesten** no longer stocks silks and satins but sells mainly shirts and T-shirts, 'genuine copies' of designer brands, which are often a real bargain. In front of the Sandal Bedesten the bazaar's main street, lined with glittering gold shops, runs east-west between the Nuruosmaniye and Beyazıt Gates, and behind the *bedesten* by the Kiliççilar (swordmakers) and Mahmut Pasha Gates are the gold dealers, crowded into a few small alleys and negotiating noisily on mobile phones.

Leather goods are concentrated in the south-western quarter of the bazaar around the Fesçiler (fez-makers) and Yorgancılar (quiltmakers) Gates and also opposite the Sandal Bedesten, near the Kürkçüler (furriers) Gate. Traders in many of the streets around the central area of the market sell ceramics, hammered copper and brass, onyx and other souvenirs. The northern part, which is much less touristy, is devoted to clothes, haberdashery, glitzy fabrics, bed linens, tablecloths and towels. Striped *hammam* towels, as used in Turkish baths, are on sale at Eğin Pazarı just by the Örücüler (darners) Gate. Appropriately there is a *hammam* (men only) just outside the gate to the left.

Iç Cebeci Han, the largest in the bazaar, greets the visitor with the rhythmic sound of copper hammering from the workshops upstairs. All sorts of copper objects are on sale, including crescent-topped finials for mosque domes and huge candlesticks. In the north-east corner by the Mercan (coral) Gate the pretty **Zincirli Han** has a tree-shaded, cobbled courtyard with a flower bed and fountain. Silversmiths are still at work in the **Kalcılar (silversmiths) Han** outside the bazaar by the Mahmut Pasha Gate. Straight out of glowing furnaces, the molten silver is poured into moulds to make ingots, and in cramped ateliers the metal is beaten, stamped and chased. On sale are ornate silver bowls, trays, candlesticks, tea and coffee services which cater more to Turkish than Western taste.

The **Mahmut Pasha Mosque** is a few hundred metres along Kiliççilar Sok., a picturesque old market street. Completed in 1464, this mosque is one of the oldest Ottoman foundations in Istanbul. Mahmut Pasha, Mehmet II's Grand Vizier, was an able statesman and accomplished poet, who complied with the sultan's command to build monuments in his newly-conquered city. Mahmut's mosque has been much modified since the fifteenth century, in particular the original fine columns of the portico have been encased within ugly stone piers. Beyond the portico is a narthex, unusual in a mosque, with different styles of decoration in the vaults. Steps lead up to the main hall which is twin-domed and flanked by narrow barrel-vaulted passages communicating with side chambers used originally as *tabhanes* or hospices where travellers might lodge free for three days. This is a feature peculiar to early Ottoman mosques. In the mosque garden, **Mahmut Pasha's tall, octagonal *türbe***, dated 1473, is also unusual. Inside it is plain, but the exterior is covered with turquoise and deep blue glazed bricks forming geometric patterns. The *hammam* attached to Mahmut Pasha's *külliye*, a short distance away on Mahmut Pasha Yokuşu, is an impressive building which has been restored and converted into a shopping mall.

Adjacent to the bazaar, south of Mahmut Pasha, is the more prominent and quite distinctive **Nuru-osmaniye Mosque**, begun by Mahmut I in 1748 and completed by Osman III in 1755 (hence the name, which means 'light of Osman'). As the earliest surviving major monument in the new Turkish baroque style, inspired by European architecture, the Nuruosmaniye is a landmark. It is raised on a high plinth, and the four great arches supporting the dome with its ring of curved buttresses distinguish the mosque from afar. In front is an unusual D-shaped court, which is rather redundant as the main access is up flights of steps from the sides. The spacious prayer hall is a simple square with a projecting *mihrab* relieved by a band of elegant calligraphy in low relief which runs around the cornice above the galleries. Around the mosque is a busy, irregular-shaped courtyard shaded by trees which encloses a number of ancillary buildings including the *medrese* and library, both still in use. A covered gallery spanning the courtyard leads to the sultan's loge. Opposite the impressive west gate to the mosque precinct is the **Nuruosmaniye Gate** to the Covered Bazaar, the most interesting and elaborate of all the market gates, splendidly decorated with the sultan's *tuğra* and the imperial coat of arms.

South of the Nuruosmaniye a square surrounds the much-battered **Column of Constantine**, called **Çemberlitaş** (the 'hooped stone') by the locals because of the rusty hoops clamped around it. On the east side of the square is the **Çemberlitaş** *hammam* (see below), a fine sixteenth-century Turkish bath commissioned in 1584 by the Valide Sultan Nur Banu, mother of Murat III (open every day 6 am–midnight).

HAMMAMS

*Hammam*s, with their familiar smoking chimneys and glass-studded domes, played a vital role in the social life of all Islamic towns and cities. As cleanliness is a religious obligation for Muslims every district had its communal bathhouse consisting of a number of domed marble rooms: a disrobing room with a fountain and various cold and hot rooms for bathing and massage. In Istanbul alone there were about 150 *hammam*s, many with separate sections for men and women. Women were particularly addicted to *hammam* culture – they arrived with their hairbrushes, henna, kohl, choice morsels of food, sewing and embroidery. Bath attendants provided towels and clogs, and then soaped, scrubbed, rinsed and massaged their clients. Using sugar syrup and strips of linen they depilated the bather's body so that the skin was soft and smooth, and coloured her hair with different shades of henna. Reclining on sofas in the disrobing room the women drank tea, coffee or sherbert and nibbled on titbits while their servants braided their hair and everyone exchanged the latest gossip. In the *hammam* many a mother found a suitable bride for her son, and a few days before the wedding the bride's mother hosted a *hammam* party where the bride-to-be was given all the latest beauty treatments and everyone was entertained with music, dancing and bawdy stories.

West of Çemberlitaş along the main road is another early Ottoman mosque, built in 1497 for **Atik Ali Pasha**, a slave and eunuch who became Beyazıt II's Grand Vizier. It is a bright and spacious building with a single dome supported on stalactite pendentives over the main hall and a semi-dome above the raised *mihrab*. While in other fifteenth century mosques the domed side units are separate chambers, in Atik Ali Pasha arches open these up to the prayer hall. Just beyond Atik Ali Pasha the **Koca Sinan Pasha** complex was built in 1595 by Davut Ağa, Sinan's pupil and successor. Koca Sinan Pasha, who also earned the epithet Yemeni Fatıh, 'Conqueror of the Yemen', was Grand Vizier under Murat III and Mehmet III. He is buried with his wife in a sixteen-sided *türbe* built of pink and grey-white stone with a stalactite cornice (9.30 am–4.30 pm, closed Monday). Koca Sinan's *medrese* is now a 'Traditional Mystic Water Pipe and Tea Garden'! Next door, the **Çorlulu Ali Pasha medrese**, built in the early eighteenth century for Ahmet III's Grand Vizier, has also become a tea house-cum-shopping mall.

Above: **Outside Beyazidiye Mosque**

Top: **Shoeshine boy**

Past here is the bustle of the Beyazıt bus station and the outdoor clothes market around the **Çarşıkapı** (market gate) of the Covered Bazaar. From the market steps lead up to the Beyazidiye Mosque and **Beyazıt Square**, the ancient Forum Tauri, which is lively, noisy and crowded with stalls and hawkers. Here you can buy books, cassettes, CDs, clothes or slices of water melon. Alarm clocks ring for your attention, a row of shoeshiners sit behind their decorated boxes with shiny brass-topped bottles of shoe creams, and water sellers jangle their urns. Headscarved women sit on low stools selling corn to scatter to the pigeons.

Since Mehmet the Conqueror's original mosque was destroyed in the earthquake of 1766, the **Beyazidiye**, which takes up most of the eastern side of the square, has been the oldest imperial mosque complex in Istanbul. It was built between 1501 and 1506 by Beyazıt II, who was very different from his warrior father Mehmet, preferring palace life to the battlefield. This earned him the sobriquet of 'Sedentary Sultan'. Beyazıt was a great patron of architecture, and his mosque marks the beginning of the Ottoman classical style. It is an imposing building with a majestic outer façade in finely finished stone and two tall, widely spaced minarets, said to be the furthest apart in Islam. Three grand gateways with stalactite vaulting, and gilt and green inscriptions designed by the master of Ottoman calligraphy, Şeyh Hamdallah, lead into the attractive outer courtyard. In the centre is a lovely fountain with an elaborate metal grille and a broad low dome resting on antique columns. Around the court twenty more antique columns of verd antique, porphyry and granite support an elegant arcade with alternating red-and-white or black-and-white voussoirs in the arches.

Access to the prayer chamber, which covers the same area as the court (a plan repeated in the Blue Mosque), is through a grandiose portal. Inside, the dome is supported on four piers and flanked by two semi-domes, a design which creates the maximum of space and was inspired by the great Byzantine cathedral of St Sophia which Beyazıt's father Mehmet had converted into a mosque. Later, Sinan used and improved on the same concept in many of his

Istanbul University

mosques. A curiosity of the Beyazidiye is the long corridor on the west side, where two wings extend from the side aisles. Some scholars believe that these were *tabhanes* or hospices for travellers, and were originally closed off from the main chamber.

Beyazıt died in 1512, on his way to retirement in Thrace after his son Selim I had forced him to abdicate. His *türbe* is in the garden behind his mosque, a pleasing octagonal building of pink and grey-white limestone, verd antique and reddish marble. A porch with deep overhanging eaves has been added and the painting inside, black on white with landscape vignettes, is also later. One of Beyazıt's many daughters, Seljuk Sultan, also has a mausoleum in the garden.

On the west side of Beyazıt Square, the *medrese* which was attached to the mosque is now a **Museum of Calligraphic Art**, well worth a visit (open 9 am–4 pm, except Sunday and Monday). Rooms ranged around a pretty garden with a fountain display illuminated books and manuscripts and some exquisite examples of the different calligraphic scripts. From this side of the square you can look down on the huge and dilapidated **Beyazıt** *hammam* (closed), which faces the main road. The ostentatious main gate to **Istanbul University**, built in the mid-nineteenth century, dominates the north of Beyazıt Square. In the University grounds is the tall **Beyazıt Tower** (closed), one of Istanbul's most prominent landmarks. It was built in 1828 to replace an earlier wooden tower and was used for fire-watching.

A large and shady tea garden occupies the square north of the Beyazidiye. By the north minaret of the mosque is the entrance to the **second-hand book market (Sahaflar Çarşışı)**, which also sells new books and prints. Though a nice place to browse, you are unlikely to get a bargain; indeed, under the Ottomans second-hand booksellers acquired such a reputation for meanness that the expression 'worse than a second-hand bookseller' was coined! Leave the book market down steps at the end, turn right and you come to the **Fesçiler (fez-makers) Gate** of the Covered Bazaar, which bears a calligraphic inscription. Just beyond are the small **Hacı Hüsnü Gate** and the **Beyazıt Gate**, embellished with the sultan's *tuğra*.

Outside the Covered Bazaar a fascinating maze of market streets, with shops, stalls, itinerant peddlars and old Ottoman *han*s, leads downhill to the Golden Horn. The finest of the *han*s are on Cakmaçılar Yokusu. On the south side of the street the **Küçük Yeni Han** (Small New Han) and **Büyük Yeni Han** (Big New Han) were both commissioned by Mustafa III in the 1760s and belong to the Ottoman baroque style. Particularly striking is the zig-zag façade of the upper rooms which project outwards on corbels over the street. The main feature of the Küçük Yeni Han is the small mosque on its roof, which was probably also used by the merchants of the Büyük Yeni Han next door. This was once one of the city's most important *han*s, with over 150 cells on three storeys.

THE TULIP MOSQUE

From Beyazıt Square enthusiasts of the baroque may like to walk down to the Laleli Camii, or 'Tulip Mosque' at Aksaray. Mustafa III's imperial mosque (1759–63) is a creation of Mehmet Tahir Ağa, greatest of the Turkish baroque architects, and is a jewel of the period. Raised on a high vaulted terrace which forms a semi-subterranean shopping arcade, the tall and graceful mosque is a striking landmark. Its façade is enlivened with windows and open arcades, curved buttresses surround the low dome, the minarets are crowned with pointed finials on a bulbous base and pepperpot turrets abound.

The main feature of the mosque interior is the subtle use of different coloured marbles. Panels of grey-black, yellow, red, verd antique and brown marble revet the lower walls, and delicate medallions of *opus sectile* with a raised central boss ornament the west wall gallery. Eight marble columns support the arches of the dome, the *mihrab* and *minber* are fashioned of colourful marbles, while the Qur'an chair, wooden shutters and main door are high-quality inlaid wood. Mustafa III is buried in a *türbe* at the gateway of the Laleli complex on Ortu Cad. together with his unfortunate son Selim III. The latter's attempts to reform the empire led to a Janissary revolt, his abdication and finally his murder in the music room of the Topkapı Palace harem. Selim is remembered for his poetry and music, still appreciated in Turkey today.

Across the road the grand **Valide Han** was built by the indomitable Valide Sultan Kösem in 1651 on the site of the former palace of Cerrah Mehmet Pasha. Cerrah Mehmet was a surgeon (*cerrah*) who had circumcised Mehmet III when he was crown prince and who later became his Grand Vizier. From the street pass through an arched entrance to the small outer courtyard, and then into the huge main court which has a new mosque in the centre. There is also a lower court entered from the far left corner which incorporates a Byzantine tower in the outer wall. Manufacture of textiles is the speciality of the Valide Han; for a small *baksheesh* young lads will show you the way up to the roof with its forest of wonky chimneys, where you can enjoy fantastic views of the Nuruosmaniye Mosque, the Bosphorus Bridge and across the Golden Horn to Pera and Galata.

Uzunçarşı Cad. ('Long market street') follows the course of the Makros Embolos, an earlier Byzantine colonnaded avenue, downhill to **Tahtakale**, or 'Wooden Castle'. This is a fascinating and functional part of the market area which sells a multiplicity of wooden objects and other household articles. Wooden stools, spoons, rolling pins, coat hangers, walking sticks, backgammon and chess sets, stepladders, bread-oven paddles – you can find almost everything in Tahtakale. Musical instruments are also made here. Number 242 Uzunçarşı Cad. has a nice collection of *saz* (traditional Turkish stringed instrument) and *zurnas* (a wind instrument with a double reed which resembles an oboe – see p. 169). Next to the vendors of wooden articles are the ironmongers, with garden tools, sieves, balloon whisks, braziers. Nearby, copper and brass merchants sell lengths of chain, cow bells, coffee mills, pestles and mortars for grinding spices.

On a high terrace amid the warren of market streets is the **Rüstem Pasha Mosque** (see p. 98), famous for its glorious tilework, which can be entered up steps from Hasırcılar Cad. At the end of the same street a delicious aroma of ground coffee pervades the air. Here is the famous Kurukahveci Mehmet Efendı, purveyors of fine Turkish coffee and also of *salep*, a traditional drink made from ground orchid root. In this area of the market you can find olives, pickles, dried fruit and nuts, spices, cheeses, fresh fruit and vegetables.

Detail of tile from Rüstem Pasha Mosque

Kurukahveci Mehmet Efendı is opposite one of the entrances to the covered **Egyptian Market (Mısır Çarşışı)** popularly known as the **Spice Bazaar**, the revenues from which went to the Yeni Camii (New Mosque) alongside. The Egyptian Market, so named because most of its goods came by sea from Egypt

Spices – market near Egyptian Bazaar

in the annual 'Cairo caravan', is a striking L-shaped barrel-vaulted arcade with eighty-six shops and with chambers over the end gateways. Formerly, the commercial judges sat in these gatechambers to determine and enforce the maximum prices for goods and make sure no one had a monopoly of any commodity. Pandeli's restaurant, which now occupies the rooms over the main entrance facing the Golden Horn, has a brilliantly tiled interior and has long been a favourite of locals and tourists.

Inside, the Spice Bazaar is a feast for the senses. The spice shops have colourful heaps of paprika, peppercorns, cumin, turmeric, nutmeg, cinnamon, aniseed and henna. There are boxes full of dried fruits and nuts, and strings of dried aubergines, courgettes and peppers hanging alongside loofahs and natural sponges. Perfumeries-cum-pharmacies sell essential

**Chestnuts –
market near
Egyptian Bazaar**

oils and soaps, camomile, sage and linden blossom for teas and traditional herbal remedies. Other vendors offer halva, honeycomb, *lokum* (Turkish delight) and 'Sultan's aphrodisiac', and there are shops which specialize in *pastırma* and in caviar from Russia and Azerbaijan.

Outside the Spice Market, behind the Yeni Cami, is a shady tea garden, a pleasant spot to sit and relax for a while (ask the price first or you may be over-charged). Alongside is the market for pets and flowers, where among livestock, pet foods, plants, seeds and bulbs you may come across large jars of wriggling black leeches, traditionally believed to cure certain ailments when applied to the body to suck the blood. From here it is well worth a short detour of about 100m along Hamidiye Cad., to discover one of Istanbul's oldest and best Turkish delight shops, Hacı Bekir, founded in 1777.

Strikingly positioned by the Golden Horn, and visible from afar across the water, the **Yeni Cami** is the fourth largest mosque in Istanbul. Its name is an abbreviation of Yeni Valide Cami (New Mosque of the sultan's mother). Valide Sultan Safiye, mother of Mehmet III, commissioned the mosque in 1598; the architect was Davut Ağa, successor to Sinan. At this time the area by the waterfront was home to the Karaites, an unorthodox Jewish sect who were expelled to make room for the mosque complex. It was a difficult location, being close to the water, and to ensure firm foundations the workmen had to build a series of bridges on stone piers reinforced with iron. Safiye was a clever woman and the real power behind the throne during Mehmet's reign. She even corresponded with Elizabeth I of England, who sent her a magnificent coach as a present.

However, when Mehmet died in 1603, her grandson Ahmet I banished Safiye to the Old Saray and construction of her mosque was abandoned. It was finally completed in 1663, by another Valide Sultan, Hadice Turhan, mother of Mehmet IV, and under the direction of a new architect, Mustafa Ağa. As Hadice Turhan was anxious to monitor the progress of her mosque, Mustafa Ağa's first job was to build her a large pavilion as a *pied-à-terre*. This novel feature comprises a suite of rooms approached by a long ramp from where there is a door into the royal loge inside the mosque.

The Yeni Cami is a fine building, raised on a terrace and set in a spacious square with the inevitable pigeons and itinerant tradesmen. The three flights of steps up to the mosque make convenient seating for local people and passers-by. On the north and south sides of the building are elegant two-storey arcades, and in front is the usual courtyard surrounded by a colonnaded portico. In the centre is an octagonal *şadırvan*. Beneath the porch, the outer wall of the mosque is decorated with tiles, and two splendid

Yeni Cami and the Galata Bridge

verd antique columns frame the main entrance. Inside, the prayer hall is light and spacious. Four great piers, spanned by arches with four squinches between, support the dome, which is flanked by two semi-domes. The lower walls are revetted with tiles up to the stalactite cornice and the upper part is painted. Though the tilework is inferior quality, for Iznik was past its apogee, the general effect is pleasing. Behind the Yeni Cami, near the Egyptian Market, is the *türbe* of the second foundress, Hadice Turhan, who died in 1682, leaving to posterity the last great mosque of the classical age, a landmark by the Golden Horn.

Mosques, mansions and mausolea (around the Hippodrome)

In the years after the Conquest, Constantinople was given a facelift as the Ottomans redesigned the old city centre and built new monuments over the ruins of Byzantium. On the promontory they created the pavilions and gardens of Topkapı Palace, and imperial mausolea clustered around the great cathedral of St Sophia, which was converted into a mosque and endowed with four minarets. Ottoman dignitaries erected stylish mansions around the Hippodrome (Atmeydan in Turkish). Undoubtedly the most impressive edifice to rise alongside the Hippodrome, where once stood the Great Palace of Byzantium, was the Ahmediye or **mosque of Sultan Ahmet I**. This is the largest in Istanbul, popularly known as the **Blue Mosque** (closed during prayer times). Its size, its location and its six minarets (unique in Turkey) made the Blue Mosque one of the city's landmarks, visible to all vessels sailing in from the south.

Ahmet's reign did not have a particularly auspicious beginning. Soon after the young prince came to the throne in 1603, at the age of fourteen, he contracted smallpox and nearly died. Undeterred, he developed such a passion for hunting and the pleasures of the harem that it caused a scandal. When in 1606 he had to sign the humiliating Peace Treaty of Zsitva-Torok and recognize the Hapsburg emperor as his equal, Ahmet decided it was time to build a mosque to placate God. Whereas earlier sultans had paid for their mosques with the booty of conquest, Ahmet had to use money from the seriously depleted treasury, which his viziers and the religious leaders were strongly against. But the young sultan was determined; all the buildings along the east side of the Atmeydan were pulled down, including the mansion of former Grand Vizier Sokullu Mehmet Pasha, and in 1609

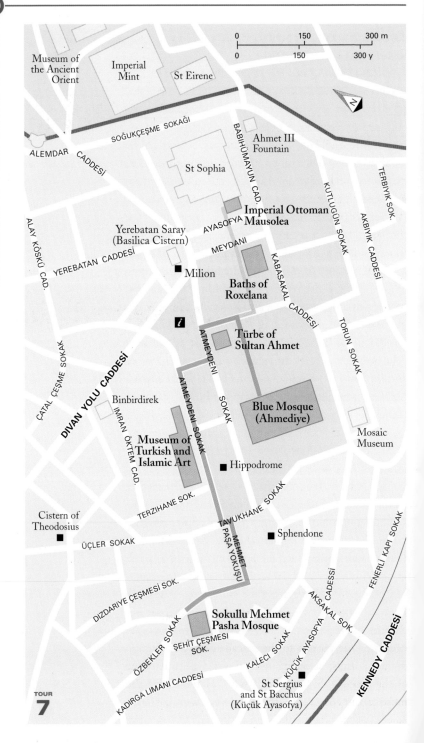

Museum of
the Ancient
Orient

Imperial
Mint

St Eirene

0   150   300 m
0   150   300 y

N

SOĞUKÇEŞME SOKAĞI

ALEMDAR   CADDESI

BABIHÜMAYUN CAD.

Ahmet III
Fountain

St Sophia

TERBIYIK SOK.

AYASOFYA

Imperial Ottoman
Mausolea

ALAY KÖŞKÜ CAD.

Yerebatan Saray
(Basilica Cistern)

MEYDANI

KUTLUGÜN SOKAK

AKBIYIK CADDESI

YEREBATAN CADDESI

Milion

Baths of
Roxelana

KABASAKAL CADDESI

i

Türbe of
Sultan Ahmet

ATMEYDANI

TORUN SOKAK

ÇATAL ÇEŞME SOKAK

DIVAN YOLU CADDESI

Binbirdirek

ATMEYDANI SOKAK

SOKAK

Blue Mosque
(Ahmediye)

Mosaic
Museum

IMRAN ÖKTEM CAD.

Museum of
Turkish and
Islamic Art

Hippodrome

TERZIHANE SOK.

TAVUKHANE SOKAK

Cistern of
Theodosius

ÜÇLER SOKAK

MEHMET PAŞA YOKUŞU

Sphendone

FENERLI KAPI SOKAK

DIZDARIYE ÇEŞMESI SOK.

ÖZBEKLER SOKAK

Sokullu Mehmet
Pasha Mosque

ŞEHIT ÇEŞMESI
SOK.

AKSAKAL SOK.

AKSAKAL CADDESI

KÜÇÜK AYASOFYA SOKAK

KALECI SOKAK

KENNEDY CADDESI

KADIRGA LIMANI CADDESI

St Sergius
and St Bacchus
(Küçük Ayasofya)

Ahmet symbolically cut the first turf for the mosque foundations.

Work was entrusted to the imperial architect Mehmet Ağa, who was also a skilled artisan in mother-of-pearl, and it is said that Sultan Ahmet was so enthusiastic about his project that he often laboured beside the builders. Eight volumes in the palace archives record the construction of the mosque and the vast supplies of stone, marble and tiles. Accounts were drawn up every month and signed by the sultan. Ahmet personally approached the Venetians to acquire the best coloured glass for the windows. In 1617, though the mosque complex was not quite finished, there was a grand opening ceremony and Sultan Ahmet prayed there for the first time. However, he had little opportunity to enjoy his masterpiece, for he died in November aged only twenty-seven, and was buried in the large *türbe* in the precincts. Mehmet Ağa, architect of this last great classical mosque, passed away a few years after his master. Though his project had encountered initial opposition, Sultan Ahmet's mosque was a great success. Most of his successors on the imperial throne chose the Ahmediye for their Friday prayers and today it remains Istanbul's most popular mosque.

Like all grand imperial mosques, the Ahmediye was the centrepiece of a complex comprising the sultan's mausoleum, a college, primary school, asylum, hospice, kitchens and bazaar. The main façade faces the Hippodrome, where a grand gate with a calligraphic inscription above leads into a spacious arcaded court-yard which covers the same area as the mosque itself. In the centre is an octagonal fountain. Stand at the courtyard gate for a lovely view upwards over the domes of the portico to the cascade of corner domes, domed turrets, semi-domes and great central dome of the mosque. Six elegant fluted minarets frame the mosque and courtyard – the pair to the west have two balconies, the others have three.

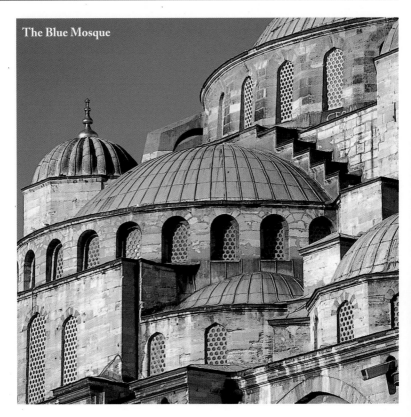

The Blue Mosque

Arcades along the outer walls of the courtyard shelter ablution fountains, and rather grander arcading extends along the sides of the mosque. Today's tourist entrance is beneath the south arcade. Inside, the impression is more of light and space than of elegance. Four massive, cumbersome circular piers with convex fluting, aptly dubbed 'elephant feet', support the central dome, which is 43m high and flanked by four semi-domes to make a quatrefoil plan. At 47m square the prayer hall is somewhat smaller than the Süleymaniye. Arcaded galleries run along three sides. Light floods in through the 260 windows, but unfortunately the original fine Venetian glass has been replaced by modern glass of no merit. Gone also are the gold-plated lamps hung with ostrich eggs, lustres and crystal balls.

The popular name 'Blue Mosque' derives from the predominantly blue decoration inside. Apart from the modern blue carpet, over-elaborate and mainly blue painting covers 75 per cent of the interior and totally detracts from the fine tilework revetting the lower walls and galleries. Ahmet I, who had an absolute passion for tiles, diverted the entire production of

Iznik to his mosque, until he literally exhausted the potteries. Over 20,000 tiles grace the walls of the Ahmediye, and although not all are top quality, some of the panels are superb. The best are in the galleries (not accessible), where flamboyant designs of slim cypress trees, fruits and rambling leaves and flowers almost herald the baroque. Apart from the tiles, the inlaid wooden doors and carved marble *mihrab* and pulpit are also high-quality craftsmanship.

Outside the mosque, at the north-west corner, a ramp leads up to the **royal pavilion**, connected by a corridor to the imperial box. Today the pavilion houses a **carpet museum** (9 am–noon, 1 pm–4.30 pm, except Sunday) which displays a variety of old Turkish rugs and carpets, including Konya, Uşak and Caucasian. They come either from mosques or the warehouse which stores pious donations. Down a few steps beneath the royal pavilion the restored bazaar street, now devoted entirely to tourist shops, was part of the original *külliye* (pious foundation) of Sultan Ahmet's mosque. It bears the unusual name of Kabasakal Cad. or 'Bushy Beard Street'. Rent from the shops went towards the upkeep of the mosque and its dependencies.

Every evening the Blue Mosque and St Sophia are illuminated and look almost ethereal as the seagulls circle overhead. There are regular sound-and-light performances (free, check board for times and languages); rows of benches are ranged in the gardens north of the mosque. Nearby are the *medrese* (closed) and **Sultan Ahmet's mausoleum** (9.30 am–4.30 pm). Osman II employed his father's architect, Mehmet Ağa, to design the tomb, which was completed in 1620 and decorated with Iznik tiles of the period. Inside, Sultan Ahmet I is buried alongside his sons Osman II and Murat IV and Murat's mother, the Valide Sultan Kösem Mahpeyker.

Osman came to the throne in February 1618, only thirteen years old, after his mad uncle Mustafa had been declared unfit to rule and confined to the Cage in Topkapı. Osman quickly managed to alienate both the

army and people, who revolted in 1622 and unceremo-
niously dragged the sultan in a cart to the notorious
prison of Yedikule by the Land Walls. There he was
tortured and strangled, the first Ottoman sultan to be
assassinated by his own subjects. Mad Mustafa was
brought out of the Cage for a while, but after sixteen
chaotic months he was replaced by his nephew Murat
and retired to the Old Saray. As Murat was only
fourteen, his mother Kösem, who had been Ahmet's
favourite, became regent as well as Valide Sultan.

Kösem was a clever woman with a good power
base. She had married her four daughters to viziers and
powerful Pashas and did the same with the daughters
of her son. Though the treasury was empty she wisely
melted down some of the palace gold and silver to pay
the troops and forestall insurrection. When he reached
manhood Murat, who was a good soldier, though also
a cruel and violent alcoholic, had two of his brothers
killed but Kösem managed to save Ibrahim and thus
preserve the Ottoman line. Cirrhosis of the liver finally
killed Murat in 1640, after a brutal though successful
reign. Kösem remained in power through the eight-year
reign of the crazy and debauched Ibrahim and became
Büyük Valide or Queen Grandmother under his son
Mehmet IV. Her many charitable works won her the
love of the people but in the end her frank criticism of
the viziers led to her downfall. A plot was hatched and
in 1651, while trying to flee, she was discovered hiding
in a clothes cupboard in the harem and murdered after
a violent and bloody struggle.

Mustafa and Ibrahim, two mad sultans, are buried
side by side in the former **baptistery of St Sophia**
across the square (closed). Mustafa finally died in 1639,
sixteen years after he had been deposed for the second
time. Mad Ibrahim, cosseted by Kösem, who was
desperate he should sire a son, was provided with so
many concubines, aphrodisiacs and pornographic tracts
that he became an insatiable monster. Eventually even
his own mother turned against him; he was persuaded

to abdicate and was strangled in the harem by the chief executioner. Despite his decadence Ibrahim was popular with the people, elegies were composed on his death and his tomb received regular women visitors, for, they said, he loved women so much!

There are three other **imperial Ottoman mausolea** in the garden of St Sophia, designed by different architects (all closed). Selim II's *türbe*, a work of Sinan, is revetted with beautiful Iznik tiles. Selim, nicknamed 'the Sot', was Süleyman the Magnificent's son and successor. He was a pleasant enough character, though much addicted to women and wine. He died in the harem in December 1574 after a fall in his bath while drunk. Selim is buried alongside his favourite Nurbanu, plus three of his daughters and five of his sons. The latter were strangled according to Ottoman custom when their elder brother Murat III came to the throne. Some of Murat's children are also buried in Selim's *türbe*, because he had so many that they would not all fit in his own mausoleum, which is beside that of his father. Murat shares his *türbe* (designed by Sinan's successor, Davut Ağa) with more of his children, his favourite Safiye, and four concubines.

Murat's successor Mehmet III executed his nineteen younger brothers when he came to the throne in 1575, but this was the last instance of systematic fratricide on accession. Thenceforth a sultan's brothers were usually confined to the *Kafes* or Cage in the harem. Mehmet, who grew very obese, died of a heart attack in 1603. He is buried in a mausoleum designed by Dalgic Ahmet Ağa alongside his favourite Handan, several of his children and some of his sisters who died of plague. A small *türbe* attached to Murat III's mausoleum contains the catafalques of five infant princes, sons of Murat IV, who succumbed to another of the plagues that regularly swept through the city.

In 1556 Sinan was commissioned to build a *hammam* to serve St Sophia, in the name of **Haseki Hürrem Sultan**, beloved wife of Süleyman the

Magnificent, better known in the West as Roxelana. The fine double *hammam*, which replaced the Byzantine Zeuxippus baths, still standing in 1536, was the largest he ever built. It has recently been restored and serves as a carpet sales centre (9 am–5 pm, except Tuesday). Today, its elegant domes can be seen across the park between St Sophia and the Blue Mosque, but in the sixteenth century the area was crowded with houses and criss-crossed with alleyways. There are two almost identical sections for men and women, comprising a disrobing room (larger for the men), a triple domed cool room and an octagonal hot room with marble basins and a central marble slab. The men's entrance faces St Sophia across the square while the women slipped in through a more modest doorway down steps at the opposite end.

Of the grand mansions and palaces which once lined the Atmeydan, only part of the **palace of Ibrahim Pasha** still stands, a massive stone building opposite the Blue Mosque which now houses the **Museum of Turkish and Islamic Art** (9 am–4.30 pm, except Monday). Ibrahim Pasha, Süleyman's second Grand Vizier, was also one of the sultan's closest friends. The young Greek boy, who was captured by pirates and then sold, showed such flair that he was sent to the palace school and presented as a gift to Süleyman before he became sultan. On Süleyman's accession in 1520 Ibrahim was appointed Head of the Privy Chamber and the privy purse paid for his palace on the Hippodrome, probably the grandest private residence ever built in the Ottoman dominions.

In 1523 he was made Grand Vizier and the following year there were lavish celebrations in the Hippodrome to mark his marriage. Magnificent tents were erected, wrestlers, buffoons and mounted archers entertained the sultan, and firework displays lit up the night sky. Ibrahim Pasha made his entrance preceded by traditional Turkish '*nahils*', artificial wax palm trees hung with mirrors, precious stones, fruits and flowers which were symbols of fertility and virility. To Süleyman, his friend and master, Ibrahim presented ten slaves carrying gold vessels, rich fabrics and furs, together with horses, camels and a huge diamond bought from the Venetians. Ibrahim started something of a trend, for in 1530 Süleyman also used the Hippodrome for even more extravagant celebrations on the occasion of the circumcision of his sons, Mustafa, Mehmet and Selim. Ibrahim stood beside the sultan in the magnificent royal tent, while they watched jugglers and tightrope walkers and listened to poems composed for the occasion. On the eighteenth day of festivities the princes were brought from the Old Saray and circumcised in Ibrahim Pasha's mansion, an honour indeed for the powerful Grand Vizier.

Ibrahim was not only a skilled administrator but also an able military strategist, Commander-in-Chief of several successful campaigns. With each success his arrogance increased and may in part have contributed to his downfall. Possibly instigated by Roxelana, rumours circulated that Ibrahim wanted to share in the sultan's power. On 15 March 1536 Ibrahim dined with Süleyman as usual, then retired to an adjacent room. He was strangled while he slept and his body dumped outside the palace. All his wealth and possessions, including his mansion, were confiscated by the state.

After Ibrahim's death his palace was used for a while by other viziers, then as a barracks, a residence for foreign ambassadors, the Land Registry, a clothing factory and a prison. Today it houses over 40,000 items which represent different periods and genres of Turkish and Islamic art. The collection includes Seljuk, Mamluk, Timurid, Persian and Ottoman metalwork, glassware, ceramics, woodwork and stone carving. Also on display are lovely manuscripts and miniatures dating from the seventh century through to the twentieth century, and some fine examples of Ottoman calligraphy and writing materials. Writing sets comprised scissors, calligraphers' knives, *maktas* (grooved tablets for cutting and nibbing reed pens) and *divits* (pencases). *Divits* had a pen compartment and an inkwell, containing a wad of raw silk which prevented the ink spilling and ensured just the right amount of ink was taken up by the pen (see opposite).

Several rooms in the museum are devoted to a magnificent display of Turkish carpets. There are some fine Seljuk pieces and a range of sixteenth–eighteenth-century Ottoman carpets from the workshops at Uşak, Konya and Bergamo, some of which are an impressive size. Turkish carpets were popular in Europe in the fifteenth and sixteenth centuries (Cardinal Wolsey was the proud owner of sixty of them!) and appear in many contemporary paintings. Certain designs are even known by the name of the European artists who included them in their works. These early Anatolian rugs show geometric and floral patterns, and the predominant colour is a deep, rich red. In 'Bellini-style' prayer rugs, which appear in several paintings by Giovanni and Gentile Bellini, the lower end of the *mihrab* niche is keyhole-shaped. A good example is shown in Gentile Bellini's 'Virgin and Child Enthroned' which hangs in the National Gallery, London. 'Holbein' carpets are named after the carpet draped over the table in Hans Holbein's portrait of Georg Gisze, now in Berlin. Lorenzo Lotto also gave his name to certain early Turkish carpets he included in his paintings, as did Hans Memling. A fine example can be seen in Memling's 'Virgin and Child' in London's National Gallery.

On a lower floor the museum has an excellent ethnographic section which shows kilims and looms, a yurt, an Anatolian black nomad tent, the interior of a village home, and daily life in an Istanbul house at the beginning of the twentieth century. Across the courtyard is a small café and there is a lovely view of the Hippodrome and the Blue Mosque from the courtyard terrace.

On the steep hillside below the southern end of the Hippodrome is the very fine **mosque of Sokullu**

CALLIGRAPHY

The art of calligraphy has always been esteemed in the Islamic world because of its connection with the transcription of the Qur'an and traditions of the Prophet Muhammad (*hadith*). Şeyh Hamdallah (1436–1520), the founder of Ottoman calligraphy, who adopted and adapted the canonical 'six scripts' of the thirteenth-century Baghdad calligrapher Yakut al-Mustasimi, was greatly admired by Sultan Beyazıt II. It was said that while Hamdallah drew, Beyazıt held his inkpot. Hamdallah also had a reputation as an athlete, and swam the Bosphorus holding his writing implements between his teeth! Hamdallah belonged to the class of outstanding calligraphers who not only wrote beautiful Qur'ans but also designed monumental inscriptions. Two later artists of the same calibre were Ahmet Karahisarı, famous for his Qur'ans and specimen alphabets, and his adopted son Hasan Çelebi who was responsible for the monumental inscriptions of the Süleymaniye.

However, most professional calligraphers were employed either as copyists in the palace studio or as scribes in the Chancery, writing documents of state. Firmans and other imperial decrees, though functional, were exquisitely beautiful, a suitable reflection of the sultan's majesty. They were written in the elegant *divani* script as refined by Hamdallah, which curved up towards the left margin. At the top was the *tuğra*, the highly distinctive Ottoman imperial monogram, comprising the sultan's name and patronymics, his title 'han' and the epithet 'ever victorious'. The *tuğra* demonstrated that the document emanated from the sultan himself. Broad pen strokes lay the basic lines of the monogram on the page, while between them is often a delicate web of decoration, which may extend around the *tuğra* to enclose it in a cone or triangle.

Many calligraphers were also skilled in the art of illumination. Illumination was usually concentrated on frontispieces, opening pages and section headings. Arabesques, flowers, feathery leaves, cloud scrolls and palmettes are delicately painted in gold, lapis blue and carmine to create masterpieces of the illuminator's art.

The Blue Mosque

Mehmet Pasha, one of Sinan's minor masterpieces. Sokullu Mehmet was born in Bosnia, graduated from the palace school as Falconer Royal and rose up through the ranks to become Grand Admiral, Viceroy of Europe, third and second vizier and finally Grand Vizier, a post which he held for fifteen years (1564–79) and under three sultans, Süleyman, Selim II and Murat III. A tall man with a black beard and hawk nose, Sokullu Mehmet was one of the Ottoman Empire's finest statesmen. When Süleyman died in his tent during a campaign in Hungary, Sokullu Mehmet astutely concealed the event until Süleyman's son Selim was able to join up with the army and personally announce his father's death. Selim gave Sokullu Mehmet full charge of the government while he devoted his time to the pleasures of the harem. When Selim died in 1574, Nurbanu, his favourite, contrived with Sokullu Mehmet to conceal the death by keeping the sultan's corpse in an icebox until their son Murat returned from Manisa and was proclaimed sultan. Sokullu Mehmet served Murat well for five years, until he was assassinated at a meeting of the Divan by a disaffected soldier. He left behind four palaces in

Istanbul, one palace in Edirne and 18 million gold piastres.

Sinan completed Sokullu Mehmet's mosque, which was commissioned by the Grand Vizier and his wife, Ismihan Sultan, the daughter of Selim II, in 1571. It was a challenging site on which to build. Mosque and courtyard are raised on a platform which is approached by a covered, domed staircase from the street level below. Ascending the steps you see first the domed *şadırvan* with its broad eaves, then the domed portico and above that the dome of the mosque itself. Around the courtyard are the sixteen cells of the mosque's *medrese* which is still fully functioning. On either side of the porch there are two lateral gateways to the courtyard with a room for a müezzin above each one. Behind the mosque the cemetery, which is cut back into the hillside, has some fine examples of Ottoman gravestones.

In the porch, before you enter the mosque, note the handsome panels of blue tiles with white inscriptions above the windows and side doors. Inside, the mosque is refined and peaceful, a simple rectangular chamber roofed by a high dome on pendentives. Its genius lies in the judicious use of the finest tilework ever produced by the Iznik potteries. Superb tiles, floral and calligraphic, cover the *mihrab* wall and pendentives and there are inscriptive panels above the windows at casement and gallery level. Unusually, the conical roof of the *minber* is also tiled. Much of the rest is stonework, with sensitive stencilling in the dome and semi-domes and fine paintwork on the ceilings under the galleries and above the entrance door, some of it original. The original window glass has been replaced but is unobtrusive. A unique feature of Sokullu Mehmet's mosque are the four pieces of black stone from the Ka'ba in Mecca which are framed in brass and inset above the main doorway and *mihrab* and into the canopy and gate of the *minber*. They were a gift to Sokullu Mehmet Pasha after he had sponsored restoration of parts of the sanctuary at Mecca.

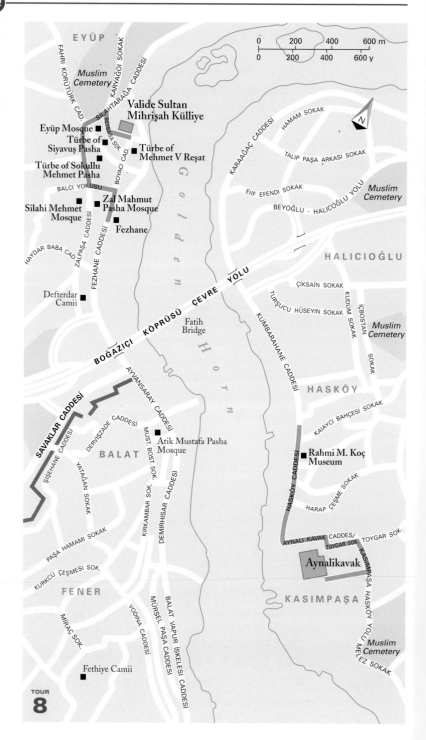

EYÜP

FAHRI KORÜTÜRK CAD.

Muslim Cemetery

SILAHTARAĞOI SOKAK

SILAHTARAĞA CADDESİ

Valide Sultan Mihrişah Külliye

Eyüp Mosque

BEBBEA SOK.

Türbe of Siyavuş Paşa

BOYACI CAD.

Türbe of Mehmet V Reşat

Türbe of Sokullu Mehmet Paşa

BALCI YOKUSU

Zal Mahmut Paşa Mosque

Silahi Mehmet Mosque

ZALPAŞA CADDESİ

Fezhane

HAYDAR BABA CAD.

FEZHANE CADDESİ

Defterdar Camii

KARAAĞAÇ CADDESİ

HAMAM SOKAK

TALIP PAŞA ARKASI SOKAK

EIIF EFENDI SOKAK

Muslim Cemetery

BEYOĞLU - HALICOĞLU YOLU

HALICIOĞLU

Golden

ÇIKSAIN SOKAK

BOGAZIÇI KÖPRÜSÜ ÇEVRE YOLU

TURŞUCU HÜSEYIN SOKAK

KUDÜM SOKAK

İÇBOSTAN

Muslim Cemetery

Fatih Bridge

KUMBARAHANE CADDESİ

HASKÖY

SOKAK

Horn

AYVANSARAY CADDESİ

SAVAKLAR CADDESİ

KAIAYCI BAHÇESİ SOKAK

ŞİŞEHANE CADDESİ

DERVIŞZADE CADDESİ

MUST. BOST. SOK.

Atik Mustafa Paşa Mosque

BALAT

HASKÖY CADDESİ

Rahmi M. Koç Museum

YATAĞAN SOKAK

KIRKAMBAR SOK.

DEMIRHISAR CADDESİ

ÇEŞME SOKAK

HARAP ÇEŞME SOKAK

PAŞA HAMAMI SOKAK

AYNALI KAVAK CADDES/

TOYGAR SOK.

KASIMPAŞA HASKÖY YOLU

TOYGAR SOK.

KURKÇÜ ÇEŞMESI SOK.

FENER

Aynalikavak

KASIMPAŞA

MIRAÇ SOK.

VODINA CADDESİ

BALAT VAPUR ISKELESI CADDESİ

MÜRSEL PAŞA CADDESİ

Muslim Cemetery

MELEZ SOKAK

Fethiye Camii

0   200   400   600 m
0   200   400   600 y

N

Eyüp and the Golden Horn

TOUR 8

The **Golden Horn**, a curved waterway which cuts a swathe between the Old City and Pera-Galata, has always played a key role in the life and commerce of Istanbul. Today, three bridges cross the Horn, all post-1900, but plans to build a permanent link between the two parts of the city date back to the sixteenth century. Nothing happened, however, until 1836, when a pontoon bridge was opened in the same spot as the modern Atatürk Bridge. It is the **Galata Bridge** which has always been the hub of city life; the first wooden bridge was constructed in 1845, and the modern bridge (1992) is the fifth in the series. Colourful accounts describe the jostling, noisy, cosmopolitan crowds on the Galata Bridge in the nineteenth century. Greeks, Albanians, Arabs, Kurds and Armenians in national costume, Turks in traditional gowns and turbans or in more western-style dress, Europeans in the latest fashions, all going to and fro, on foot, on horseback or in carriages. There were beggars waiting for alms, porters straining under heavy loads, soldiers in smart uniforms.

After 1889 many Europeans arrived in Istanbul at **Sirkeçi Station**, terminus of the Orient Express, thence to be transported across the bridge to the hotels

Fatıh Camii and Atatürk Bridge over the Golden Horn

and residences of Pera. Sirkeçi's flamboyant pink and white façade is hard to miss – a meal in the station's Orient Express restaurant gives a flavour of past times. In the commercial district around Sirkeçi there are a number of interesting buildings of the era; the main post office along Mevlana Cad. is a grand turn-of-the-century edifice and **Flora Han** on the same street is in discreet Art Nouveau style.

Halic, or 'estuary', as the Turks call the **Golden Horn**, is about 7.5km long and runs into the Bosphorus where it joins the Sea of Marmara. There are occasional boat services that ply the Horn, but as attempts to clean the stinking and polluted waters have so far been unsuccessful, boat travel is not recommended. It is hard to believe that the two rivers, Alibey and Kağıthane, which flow into the upper reaches, were once known as the **'Sweet Waters of Europe'**. Formerly, the woods and meadows there were a favourite place for excursions, crowded with tents and revellers. In the early eighteenth century Ahmet III built a pleasure palace in the Kağıthane valley, with gardens modelled on Versailles. Marble embankments were constructed along the river to channel the waters into pools and cascades, and soon over 200 colourful villas and pavilions for the Ottoman élite appeared on the banks. In spring and summer, right up to the early twentieth century, hundreds of gaily-painted caiques moored at the 'Sweet Waters of Europe', while their families sat beneath the trees picnicking and hawkers plied their wares. At dusk, when everyone returned home, the Golden Horn was at times so jammed with boats they could hardly move their oars.

WEST BANK

One of Islam's holiest shrines is at **Eyüp** on the west bank of the Golden Horn, a short distance outside the walls of the old city. The district is named after Ayyub (Job) Ansari, companion and standard-bearer of the Prophet Muhammad, who is said to have been killed during the first Arab siege of Constantinople in 674–8. His tomb came to be venerated by the Byzantines, who believed that Ayyub had the power to bring rain in time of drought. Perhaps by the fifteenth century the tomb had fallen into disrepair, for there is a story that Mehmet II, while besieging Constantinople, organized a search for it; this effort was rewarded when Akşemsettin, the Şeyh-ül-Islam, had a vision that the tomb was below his prayer mat. Ayyub was Constantinople's direct link to the Prophet Muhammad, and after the Conquest Sultan Mehmet built a mosque complex around the tomb which became highly revered and attracted believers from far and wide. Later sultans came to Eyüp to be invested with the sword of Osman, the founder of the Ottoman dynasty, the equivalent of Britain's coronation ceremony.

Eyüp today is a lively place, thronging with visitors, where shopkeepers and stallholders do a busy trade. Young boys in fancy white and gold circumcision outfits have their photos taken by proud parents, and pigeons swoop down on handfuls of corn. There are a few restaurants around the main square.

Below: **Boy in circumcision outfit, Eyüp**

Bottom: **Herbal medicine shop, Eyüp**

In the centre of Eyüp is the **mosque**, completely rebuilt by Selim III in 1800 after Mehmet's original building had fallen into disrepair. Only the west minaret is older, added by Ahmet III in the eighteenth century; the east minaret was rebuilt in 1822 in the same style. From the square, two baroque gateways open into the irregular outer courtyard, pleasantly shaded by two huge plane trees and spanned by a covered bridge which leads to the mosque loge. In the inner courtyard there is another ancient plane tree on a platform surrounded by a railing with finials in the form of dervish caps. At the corners are four small fountains. This platform was the stage where, with due pomp and ceremony, the sultans were girt with the dragon-handled sword of Osman, generally by the Grand Master of the Mevlevi dervishes whose main lodge was in Galata. After the investiture, the sultan led a long and colourful procession through the streets of Istanbul.

A stately portico runs around three sides of the court, and above the mosque door is the dedicatory inscription and *tuğra* of Selim, a design repeated in the *mihrab*. Inside, the prayer hall is spacious and peaceful, with galleries on three sides supported on slim, elegant columns. Decoration, predominantly blue, white and gold, is restrained and there is a handsome central chandelier. Women may pray in a separate hall alongside. Most of the visitors to **Ayyub's tomb** on the other side of the courtyard are women, always attracted to the cult of saints, and you may have to queue for a few minutes as everyone files in. Inside and outside, the walls of the shrine are covered with tiles of different periods, some of them very beautiful – note the particularly fine cypress trees. A niche in the wall contains a footprint of Muhammad in marble, and Ayyub Ansari's sarcophagus, covered with a green cloth, is fenced by an elaborate silver screen.

Around the mosque are ancillary buildings, cemeteries and mausolea. Eyüp has always been a popular place for burial; on the hillside above is one of the largest cemeteries in Turkey, an impressive sight with thousands of tombstones, crowned with turbans, fezzes and flowers, among the cypress trees. Access is up steps and a steep path off the street behind the mosque precincts. For the energetic a leisurely stroll up through the tombs is pleasant and invigorating and from the heights there are lovely views over Eyüp and the Golden Horn.

Along the streets between the mosque and the Golden Horn lies the baroque *külliye* of **Valide Sultan Mihrişah**, mother of Selim III. This charitable foundation, built in 1796, comprises an *imaret* (kitchen), *mekteb* (Qur'an school), *türbe* (mausoleum) and *sebil* (drinking water tank). Mihrişah is buried in the white marble *türbe*, with two of Selim's sisters and one of his wives. From the handsome gate in the *külliye* wall a path leads to the *imaret*, one of few such kitchens still in use, which every morning serves food to several hundred poor people. It is scrupulously clean and the cooking pots are huge! Passers-by could once obtain water and sherbert from the elaborate *sebil* on the corner by the street. Just along this road across from the *sebil*, by the Golden Horn is the *türbe* of **Mehmet V Reşat** (1909–19), the only Ottoman sultan buried at Eyüp.

There are other mausolea and graveyards along the road that runs diagonally from the main square past the mosque towards the Golden Horn. On the left, the classical *türbe* of **Siyavuş Pasha**, brother and Grand Vizier of Murat III, boasts superb polychrome Iznik tiled panels above the windows and either side of the doorway, depicting vases of flowers and charming mosque lamps. Splashes of vivid tomato red are also used in the calligraphic band around the walls. Across the street the *türbe* of **Sokullu Mehmet Pasha**, Grand Vizier under three sultans, was built by Sinan in 1574. Note the judicious choice of different marbles and the handsome tile inscription below the dome.

Continue to the simple stone and brick mosque known as **Kizil Mescit** (late sixteenth century) and along Zalpasha Cad. past the *türbe* of **Nakkaş Hasan Pasha** to the **Silahi Mehmet Mosque** with its curious hexagonal minaret. Opposite, the **Zal Mahmut Pasha Mosque**, built on a slope, is an unusual work of Sinan, constructed of alternate courses of stone and brick. Inside there are some nice floral tiles around the *mihrab* and a calligraphic band above the windows. A *medrese* runs around three sides of the upper courtyard from which steps go down to the lovely *türbe* garden, where there is a second *medrese*, now used by the Eyüp Sultan Mehter, a military band. From the garden, take the gate through to the main road opposite the huge pink **Fezhane**, the former fez factory.

EAST BANK

In Hasköy on the east bank of the Golden Horn (best accessed by bus or dolmuş from Taksim Square) there are two places worth a visit, Aynalıkavak Kasrı and Rahmi M. Koç Museum.

Aynalıkavak (open 9 am–4 pm, except Monday and Thursday), a cream-coloured pavilion in a walled garden, was built at the beginning of the nineteenth century by Selim III, on a hillside overlooking the Golden Horn. A high industrial building now obstructs the view across the water. The little palace comprises a series of elaborately decorated rooms on one floor over a basement. Of particular note are the Bohemian crystal chandelier and original straw matting in the domed reception hall, verses by Selim III in gold on a blue band in the dining room, and damascene furniture with mother-of-pearl inlay in a room across the hall. Stairs go down to the basement where there is an exhibition of traditional musical instruments.

The **Rahmi M. Koç Museum** (open 10 am–5 pm, except Monday) houses a fascinating collection of instruments and machines from the Industrial Revolution

MUSIC

Turkish music draws its inspiration from different Islamic cultures and uses an interesting variety of instruments. For classical music the main instruments were the spike fiddle (*kemençe*), psaltery (*kanun*), flute (*ney*), and different lutes (*ud, saz*). Also popular was the zither, played with drumsticks (*santur*). Mevlevi dervishes developed their own style and repertoire, using flutes, kettledrums, fiddles and long-necked lutes (*tanbur*), which they played during the prayer service and Islamic festivals. Music was also played in Ottoman hospitals, for its therapeutic value. Spectacular sounds were produced by the army bands (*mehter*), who performed on ceremonial occasions and following the afternoon prayer. The imperial *mehter*, composed of ninety musicians, woke the palace every morning for the dawn prayer with a reveille of fifes (*zurna*), trumpets (*boru*), cymbals (*zil*), different kettledrums (*nakkare, kös*), larger drums (*davul*), and ornamental standards with bells (*cevgan*), known as 'jingling Johnnys'.

and after in the old nineteenth-century foundry, which used to cast anchors for the ships in the Ottoman Naval dockyard downstream. Later the building was used as a warehouse to store alcohol. On exhibition are a superb collection of model engines, scientific, navigational and communication instruments, cycles and motorbikes (including a penny-farthing and a 1913 Royal Enfield with a wicker side-car), various models of ships, aircraft, trains and cars and the wreckage of an American B-24D Liberator aircraft known as 'Hadley's Harem'. Most of the ships' engines on display were made in Britain for Turkish vessels. Next to the museum the tastefully decorated Café du Levant serves drinks and food.

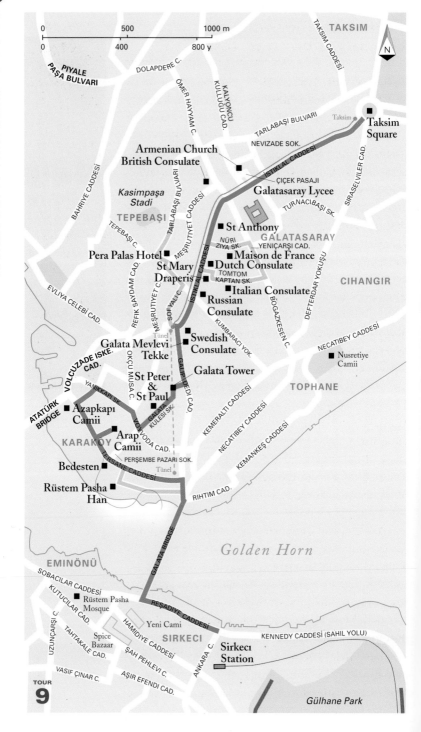

| 0 | 500 | 1000 m |
| 0 | 400 | 800 y |

TAKSIM

PIYALE PAŞA BULVARI

DOLAPDERE C.

ÖMER HAYYAM C.

KALYONCU KULLUĞU CAD.

TAKSİM CADDESİ

TARLABAŞI BULVARI

Taksim

NEVİZADE SOK.

Taksim Square

SİRASELVİLER CAD.

Armenian Church
British Consulate

İSTİKLAL CADDESİ

ÇİÇEK PASAJI

Galatasaray Lycee

BAHRİYE CADDESİ

Kasimpaşa Stadi

TEPEBAŞI

TEPEBAŞI C.

TARLABAŞI BULVARI

MEŞRUTİYET CADDESİ

TUR.NACIBAŞI SK.

St Anthony

GALATASARAY

NÜRİ ZİYA SK.

YENİÇARŞI CAD.

Pera Palas Hotel

Maison de France

Dutch Consulate

St Mary Draperis

TOMTOM KAPTAN SK.

CİHANGİR

REFİK SAYDAM CAD.

MEŞRUTİYET C.

İSTİKLAL CADDESİ

SOFYALI C.

Italian Consulate

Russian Consulate

DEFTERDAR YOKUŞU

BOĞAZKESEN C.

EVLİYA ÇELEBİ CAD.

KUMBARACI YOK.

Tünel

Swedish Consulate

NECATİBEY CADDESİ

Galata Mevlevi Tekke

Nusretiye Camii

VOLCUZADE İSKE. CAD.

OKCU MUSA C.

GALİP DEDE CAD.

Galata Tower

TOPHANE

YANIKKAPI SK.

St Peter & St Paul

KEMERALTI CADDESİ

ATATÜRK BRIDGE

Azapkapı Camii

VOYVODA CAD.

GALATA KULESİ SK.

NECATİBEY CADDESİ

KARAKÖY

Arap Camii

KEMANKEŞ CADDESİ

TERSANE CADDESİ

Bedesten

PERŞEMBE PAZARI SOK.

Tünel

Rüstem Pasha Han

RIHTIM CAD.

Golden Horn

GALATA BRIDGE

EMİNÖNÜ

SOBACILAR CADDESİ

KUTUCULAR CAD.

Rüstem Pasha Mosque

REŞADİYE CADDESİ

C.

UZUNÇARŞI CAD.

TAHTAKALE CAD.

Spice Bazaar

Yeni Cami

HAMİDİYE CADDESİ

ŞAH PEHLEVİ C.

SİRKECİ

KENNEDY CADDESİ (SAHİL YOLU)

Sirkeci Station

VASIF ÇINAR C.

AŞIR EFENDİ CAD.

ANKARA C.

Gülhane Park

Galata to Sirkeci: the Europeans in Istanbul

Across the Golden Horn lies the part of town now known as Karaköy and Beyoğlu, formerly the European quarter of Galata and Pera where the Genoese traders first established a toehold in the twelfth century and managed to maintain a presence even after the Conquest. Long before that it was called Sycae from the Greek word for fig trees, and was an official district of the early Byzantine town, although there is nothing to be seen of this period. Post-Conquest, the Ottoman sultans preferred to keep the Europeans at arm's length, and other nationalities joined the Genoese across the Golden Horn. In the steep and narrow streets of Galata and Pera an exotic blend of traders, spies, soldiers, diplomats and dragomen mingled. In the early eighteenth century Lady Mary Wortley Montagu, the wife of the British Ambassador, wrote 'I live in a place that very well represents the Tower of Babel; in Pera they speak Turkish, Greek, Hebrew, Armenian, Arabic, Persian, Russian, Slavonian, Wallachian, German, Dutch, French, English, Italian, Hungarian; and, what is worse, there is ten of these languages spoke in my own family.' Churches were plentiful, as was the variety of Christian sects, many of which still worship there today, albeit in much reduced numbers.

As Pera developed apace in the nineteenth century, the foremost European powers vied with each other to build the most impressive embassies high up the slopes, and then rebuild them as fast as fires destroyed them. A number remain as consulates (the embassies are now in Ankara). The Golden Horn was bridged in 1845 as the Ottoman sultans succumbed to European influences – Sultan Abdül Mecit built Dolmabahçe Palace and moved across the water, abandoning the Topkapı in 1856. Shortly after this, the whole area was cleaned up, streets were widened and the notorious brothels moved

Tram along Istiklal Cad.

from the main thoroughfares. By the late nineteenth century almost a quarter of the population of the city lived here, the large majority being Christian.

Beyoğlu provides a welcome change to the tourists and persistent carpet sellers of Sultanahmet. The former *Grande rue de Pera*, Istiklal Cad., is still a busy shopping street – though supposedly pedestrian, beware of the old trams and the surprising number of vehicles which find their way onto it. Look up at the façades above the shop fronts; many date from the street's heyday at the turn of the century and there is some fine, if weathered, art nouveau architecture to be seen on a stroll here, stopping for Inci's famed profiteroles or to sample Hacı Bekir's delicious Turkish delight (in business since 1777!) before continuing past the grand consulates. Most date to the nineteenth century; fire was a scourge in the city and frequently devastated large swathes, sweeping easily through the narrow streets of wooden houses. Çiçek Pasajı may now be on the tourist beat, but take a walk down the colourful market in Sahne Sok. to Nevizade Sok. for some of the best *meyhane* food in town, where diners are mainly Turks not tourists.

With your back to the bustle of Taksim Square look at the octagonal building on the right of Istiklal Cad. which has given its name to the square: this is the **Taksim** (water distribution centre). The little birdhouses either side of the window above the entrance are a feature of many older Istanbul buildings. Further along on this side is the **old French Consulate**, not to be confused with the present consulate (see below). Built in 1719, it was at one point a plague hospital and now serves as the Institut Français. There is a fairly expensive, but clean *hammam* down Turnacıbaşı Sok. just before the elaborate wrought iron gates of **Galatasaray Lycée** (or *lisesi* in Turkish) where the street bends to the left. The lycée began life as a palace school for pages established in 1481 under Beyazıt II. It was reformed in the nineteenth century at a time of strong French influence and has since educated many famous Turks, from politicians to poets.

Look across the street and right for the elaborate facade of Çiçek Pasajı. Once the flower sellers' street and now devoted entirely to restaurants, it began life in 1874 as the *Cité de Pera*, a complex built by a Greek that had shops below and an apartment above. The **Armenian church of the Holy Trinity (Üç Horon)** is hidden away behind stout doors off neighbouring Sahne Sok., but you may go in for a look around.

On the corner of nearby Mesrutiyet Cad. is the **British Consulate, Pera House**. A terrible fire destroyed the British, French and Dutch Embassies in 1831 – the Russian Embassy had gone only the week before. Only in 1844 did work begin on its replacement, on a plot of land granted by the grateful sultan following British assistance in ridding Egypt of the French. Pera House was designed by Thomas Smith, a disciple of Charles Barry (architect of the Houses of Parliament), for the Great Elchi or Ambassador, Lord Stratford de Redcliffe. Among other difficulties the British had to compete for stone and masons with the sultan, who was building Dolmabahçe Palace, and the embassy was not completed for over ten years. The imposing building has an inner court and fine grounds – a reminder of the heyday of the *Vignes de Pera,* when from its woods and fields there were wonderful views of the Bosphorus and Istanbul, for which you must nowadays climb the heights of the Galata Tower. Some idea of the splendours of diplomatic life in Pera can be gained from a description by Lady Hornby of a fancy-dress ball held at the embassy in the mid-nineteenth century which even the sultan attended:

> Every costume in the known world was to be met with: Queens and shepherdesses, Emperors and caiquejees ... The flash of diamonds was something wonderful, especially among the Armenians and Greeks ... I am quite charmed by the sultan [Abdul Mecit], so different to most of the Pashas by whom he is surrounded ... They are forever paying visits to the refreshment room, and drink vast quantities of champagne, of which they pretend not to know the exact genus and slyly call it 'eau gazeuse'.

On a sadder note, a recent bomb attack has damaged part of the complex and, tragically, caused numerous casulties to both bystanders and consulate staff.

Back on Istiklal Cad., the red brick of the Franciscan **church of St Anthony** makes a bold statement for a church in an Islamic city. Through the arch there is a pretty courtyard, although the church itself, dating from 1912, has not much to recommend it. For browsers there is a good bookshop in what was once a gatehouse of the **Dutch Embassy**. The consulate itself can be glimpsed through the gates; the Fossati brothers (who also restored St Sophia) built it in the early 1850s to replace one burnt, like the British Embassy, in the disastrous fire of 1831.

To see two of the finest former embassies, those of France and Italy, turn left into Nüru Ziya Sok. and descend steeply towards the yellow gatehouse of the **Maison de France**, an elegant two-storey square block built in 1839–41 with a chapel in its grounds. In 1535 France was the first country to receive the so-called capitulations, granting trading privileges and considerable autonomy over its own subjects in the city. It was for long the foremost foreign power here; with a shared concern for the might of Austria, the union of the 'lily and the crescent' was a strong one. Continue on to the end of the street and right into Yeniçarşı Sok. As the street descends past picturesque old wooden houses there is a good view of Topkapı. Turn right again into Tomtom Kaptan Sok. and up towards the **Italian Consulate**, opposite the back entrance to the Maison de France. This is one of the oldest surviving embassies with something of a chequered history. Originally the palace of the Venetian bailo (ambassador) it took its present shape in the mid-seventeenth century. With the demise of the Venetian Republic it changed hands several times, falling to both France and Austria before being finally reclaimed by Italy.

For visits to the Franciscan church of **St Mary Draperis** (1789), which celebrates Mass in Italian or Spanish, check the times on the notice-board outside. After the beautiful art nouveau Mudo Shop (401 Istiklal Cad.), on the same side is the grandiose neo-classical facade of the **Russian Consulate**. Built in 1837–45 by Guiseppe Fossati, a Swiss architect who had previously worked in St Petersburg, its rooms include a large ballroom and anteroom with a ceiling decorated with scenes of nineteenth-century St Petersburg. Just before the Swedish Consulate look at No. 475, the first art nouveau building in the area. Named the **Botter House** after its original occupant, a Dutchman who was tailor to Abdül Mecit II, it has seen better days, but the extravagant wrought iron is wonderful. The **Swedish Consulate** was built in 1870 by an Austrian architect. Opposite is the ugly bulk of the **Narmanlı Han**; the Russian Embassy until the 1840s, it is run down and now houses a large population of stray cats. In the eighteenth century the Ottomans favoured Sweden as a counterbalance to the ever-present threat of Russia, covetously eyeing Constantinople from across the Black Sea.

A short distance on we come to the end of the *Grande rue de Pera* with the entrance to **Tünel**, the little funicular railway built in 1875 to ferry people up the hill. It rises over 60m on its 0.5km journey and originally had separate compartments for men and women. Tickets are cheap and the trains run frequently throughout the day.

Opposite Tünel Station a pleasant detour takes you through a little arcade to Sofyalı Sok., with its little shops and art galleries. Stop at Çep Sanat Galerisi on an alley corner for tea or a beer or for a more substantial meal, try Refik's, just down the street (with a great range of meze, it specializes in Black Sea dishes). Vines cross the street overhead, there are few cars and in summer tables for *al fresco* dining line the street. Continue on turning left into Asmalı Sok., which brings you to Meşrutiyet Cad. and the former **American Embassy** ahead on the left, the legendary Pera Palas Hotel on the right. Unlike the European embassies which sprang up in Pera from as early as the tenth century, but more commonly in the sixteenth and seventeenth centuries, it was not until 1907 that the United States established a firm presence with the purchase of the Palazzo Corpi, built for a Genoese shipowner and decorated with the finest materials shipped from Italy.

The **Pera Palas Hotel** is a must for visitors, if only to step inside for a moment and admire its wonderful wrought iron lift-cage and lift (with seats), elaborate Moorish ballroom and overhead domes. Room 101, where Atatürk once stayed, houses an Atatürk Museum; all the bedrooms are named after the rich and famous who once stayed here. Built by the French architect Vallaury in 1892–5, it marks the advent of the railway in 1889. Indeed, Agatha Christie is supposed to have written *Murder on the Orient Express* here. At the end of Istiklal Cad. on the left is Galip Dede Cad. It is well worth a visit to the dervish *tekke* (lodge), **Galata Mevlevi**

Tekke (open 9.30 am–4.30 pm, closed Tuesdays), just a few minutes' walk down here (see p. 179).

Performances are given three Sundays a month (buy tickets in advance); although the audience is made up of tourists and the whirring of cameras is a distraction, the rite is performed gracefully and simply in the pretty octagonal *semahane* (dancing-room) of the mid-nineteenth century *tekke* after a short explanation of its significance as a form of prayer. The whirling, anticlockwise dance is accompanied by the haunting Sufi music and chant, which rises to a crescendo before the dancers finally sink to their knees. Lutes, pipes and drums line the walls of the *semahane*, which was built in 1766 and restored after a fire in the nineteenth century. Upstairs are screened rooms from where visitors once watched the rite.

Galata Tower

The complex houses the *türbe* of Şeyh Galip Dede immediately on the left of the entrance, and a little graveyard where many headstones bear the distinctive elongated dervish fez (wrapped with ribbon at the bottom in the case of the masters of the sect). Follow the stone path to the railings around the tomb of the French Count Bonneval, alias Kumbaracı (Bombardier) Ahmed Pasha. A convert to Islam, he was employed to modernize the army in the mid-eighteenth century.

Galip Dede Sok. itself is full of shops selling a wealth of musical instruments, both ancient and modern, and leads down to the **Galata Tower** (open daily 8 am–9 pm). Built in 1348 with walls almost 4m thick, this tower marked the extent of Genoese fortifications up the hill. The Genoese were probably in Galata from as early as the twelfth century. Although they were not supposed to fortify the area, they promptly enclosed it with a wall and towers and were subsequently allowed considerable autonomy. Not much remains of the walls, but one of the original gates is still in use lower down the hill. Fierce trade rivals of the Venetians, the Genoese lost favour during the Latin occupation when the Venetians sided with the Fourth Crusade (see p. 10) and prospered. Their turn came, however, with the return of the Greeks in 1261, and they wisely allowed Mehmet the Conqueror to haul his boats overland to the Golden Horn during the siege of Constantinople. The tower offers stunning views of the famous Istanbul skyline – the light is best in the morning and evening. There is a lift to the seventh floor, from where stairs ascend to the eleventh, past the expensive restaurant. In the square behind the tower note the pretty little eighteenth-century fountain against the wall.

From the tower descend Galata Kulesi Sok., passing the **Church of St Peter and St Paul** on the right, and turn right into Voyvoda Cad., the nineteenth-century banking street where some grandiose façades are still to be seen. The old **Genoese Podesta** (seat of government) is located on a corner here, from where steps lead to the old **Han of St Peter**, birthplace of André Chénier, whose death on the guillotine just two days before Robespierre's fall robbed France of a brilliant young poet. His father was French Consul here. From the Podesta building **Perşembe Pazarı Sok.** descends, lined with picturesque houses and a few old *han*s whose upper stories zigzag decoratively above the street. Continue along Voyvoda Cad. to **Yanık Kapı Sok.** (Burnt Gate) which forks left to the sole remaining gate and short section of ruined wall of the Genoese quarter. Much of the wall was destroyed in the nineteenth century as Galata developed. A plaque on the far side of the gate bears the cross of

DERVISHES

Mevlana was a thirteenth-century mystic and founder of the Mevlevi sect, better known as the Whirling Dervishes. An offshoot of Sufism, itself a mystical Islamic sect, the dervish movement sought to achieve communion with God through music, dance and chant. They venerated the memory of their 'friends of God' (comparable to Christian saints) and made pilgrimages to their tombs. Some of the mosques in Istanbul have 'dervish wings' attached as accommodation for itinerant dervishes. There were many different dervish brotherhoods, including the Howling Dervishes who inflicted injuries on themselves in their ecstasy. Beyazıt II is reputed to have been a Sufi, while the Janissaries had close links with the Bektashi sect (see p. 106). The Mevlevi sect was established in Istanbul in the fifteenth century. In the nineteenth century there were over 300 dervish lodges in the city, but their conservatism and links with Shi'ism made them suspect and they were abolished in 1925 when Turkey became a secular state.

St George for Genoa and the arms of the Doria, one of the most prominent Genoese families.

Now descend to **Azap Kapı Camii**, built by Sinan in 1577–8 for the Grand Vizier, Sokullu Mehmet Pasha. Look first at the nearby fountain, a beautiful example of eighteenth-century baroque. A typical *sebil*, its elaborate stone bas-relief decoration includes fruit trees and floral motifs. Tucked into a noisy corner between the Atatürk Bridge, the Golden Horn and Tersane Cad., pass the unusual free-standing minaret to enter the mosque up steps on the far corner. Inside four domes and four semi-domes support the main dome. Although the traffic thunders by outside one can at least still see out onto the Golden Horn, and with the building of a waterside park it is now possible to return alongside the Golden Horn to the Galata Bridge in relative peace.

Alternatively, follow Tersane Cad. to visit **Arap Camii**, a mosque with a long and varied history. Initially a thirteenth-century church, it was later given over to Moors fleeing from sixteenth-century Spain, hence its name – the mosque of the Arabs. Its tower of stone, brick and wood is visible down a side street to the left, where there is an entrance to the mosque, or you can walk round to the pleasant courtyard on the other side, shaded by huge lime and plane trees. Outside, the brick and stone courses alternate, while the plain interior is immediately recognizable as a basilica-plan church with a pretty wooden ceiling.

Continuing along Tersane Cad., note the *bedesten* across the way with its distinctive nine domes. The **Fatıh Hırdavatçılar Çarşışı** (Ironmongers' Market) dates back to the days of Mehmet the Conqueror (Fatıh) – the ground floor arches have been bricked in and little shops selling machinery and tools fill the side aisles. This is still the ironmongers' area; plunge down the side streets towards the Golden Horn to experience the modern day bazaar. Here there is also an old *han* which is worth a quick visit. The **Rüstem Pasha Han** (built by Sinan in the mid-sixteenth century) is still a working *han*. On entering, look left to see the upended Corinthian capital which has been pressed into service as part of a water pump. It probably came from a church, which was torn down when the *han* was built.

From here it is only a short distance back to the Galata Bridge. One final glimpse of nineteenth-century Istanbul lies across the bridge: Sirkeci Station was built by a German architect in 1889 as the terminus of the Orient Express. It is a curious blend of neo-classical and oriental architecture, an example of the influences of the East on a Western imagination.

The Asian shore:
Üsküdar and Kadiköy

TOUR

10

On a hot day in Istanbul, the ferry-ride across
to the Asian suburbs of the city is one of the
nicest ways to cool off. The views of Topkapı Palace
across the sparkling water are superb while in the other
direction the palaces of Dolmabahçe and the Çirağan
are visible up the Bosphorus. Coming in to the landing
stage at Üsküdar past the little tower of Kız Kulesi on
its rocky outcrop, the mosques, minarets and fishermen
along the waterfront make a most attractive scene.
Üsküdar and Kadiköy may nowadays count as suburbs,
but in ancient times they were towns in their own
right, called Chrysopolis and Chalcedon respectively.
The former was founded by the Athenians in the
late fifth century BC while besieging Byzantium during
the Peloponnesian War. The seventh century BC
settlement of Chalcedon (modern Kadiköy) actually
predates the founding of Byzantium; for some reason
its Greek settlers ignored the advantages of the site
at Byzantium, which gave them the embarrassing
reputation in history as coming from the land of the
blind. As the Persian Megabazus said, according to
Herodotus, 'if they had had any eyes, they would never
have chosen an inferior site, when a much finer one
lay ready to hand'.

In 324 the emperor Constantine resoundingly
defeated his rival Licinius near Chrysopolis. At the
end of the road from Asia, these towns witnessed the
passage of many an invading army – the Persian
emperor Darius crossed the Bosphorus on a bridge
of boats near here, and his son Xerxes also passed
through in 481 BC. Following a revolt in his absence
the Roman emperor Valens used the stones from
the walls of Chalcedon to build his aqueduct in
Byzantium, which still stands. The martyred St
Euphemia met her death in Chalcedon in the early
fourth century and her relics remained here until the

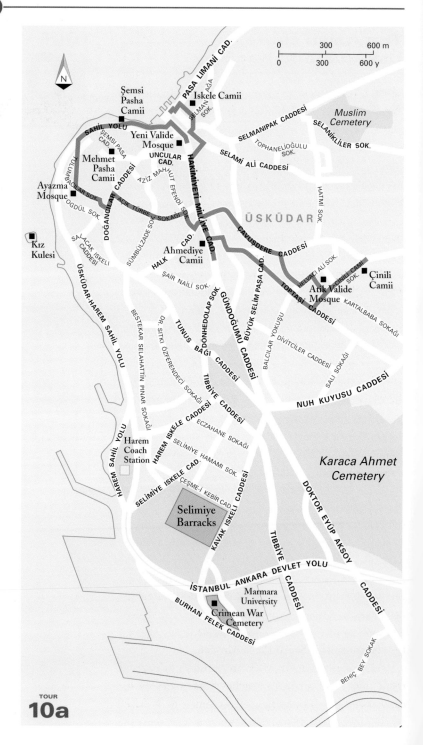

0   300   600 m
0   300   600 y

Şemsi Pasha Camii

İskele Camii

PAŞA LİMANI CAD.

SELMAN AĞA SOK.

SELMANİPAK CADDESİ

SELANİKLİLER SOK.

Muslim Cemetery

SAHİL YOLU

ŞEMSİ PAŞA CAD.

Yeni Valide Mosque

Mehmet Pasha Camii

UNCULAR CAD.

TOPHANELİOĞLU SOK.

SELAMİ ALİ CADDESİ

HAKİMİYETİ MİLLİYE CAD.

AZİZ MAHMUT EFENDİ SOK.

AÇIK TÜRBE SOKAĞI

DOĞANCILAR CADDESİ

Ayazma Mosque

OĞDÜL SOK.

KULÜMBAÇILAR SOK.

ÜSKÜDAR

HATMİ SOK.

ÇAVUŞDERE CADDESİ

Kız Kulesi

ÜSKÜDAR-HAREM SAHİL YOLU

SA AÇAK İSKELE CADDESİ

SÜMBÜLZADE SOK.

Ahmediye Camii

HALK CAD.

GÜNDOĞUMU CADDESİ

ŞAİR NAİLİ SOK.

BÜYÜK SELİM PAŞA CAD.

TOPTAŞI CADDESİ

HELVACI ALİ SOK.

ÇİNİLİ CAMİ SOK.

Çinili Camii

Atik Valide Mosque

KARTALBABA SOKAĞI

DÖNHEDOLAP SOK.

DR. SITKI ÖZFERENDECİ SOKAĞI

BESTEKAR SELAHATTİN PINAR SOKAĞI

TUNUS BAĞI CADDESİ

BALCILAR YOKUŞU

DİVİTÇİLER CADDESİ

SALİ SOKAĞI

NUH KUYUSU CADDESİ

TİBBİYE CADDESİ

HAREM SAHİL YOLU

HAREM İSKELE CADDESİ

ECZAHANE SOKAĞI

Karaca Ahmet Cemetery

Harem Coach Station

SELİMİYE HAMAMI SOK.

SELİMİYE İSKELE CAD.

ÇEŞME-İ KEBİR CAD.

KAVAK İSKELE CADDESİ

Selimiye Barracks

DOKTOR EYÜP AKSOY CADDESİ

TİBBİYE CADDESİ

İSTANBUL ANKARA DEVLET YOLU

Marmara University

Crimean War Cemetery

BURHAN FELEK CADDESİ

BEHİÇ BEY SOKAK

seventh century, when for safety they were moved to a martyrium in Constantinople. The Fourth Crusade sailed here before invading Constantinople, and in his contemporary account of the siege of Constantinople, Geoffrey de Villehardouin describes the palace of the emperor Alexius at Chalcedon, which he says was 'one of the most beautiful and enchanting that ever eye could see'. He also mentions a second palace at Scutari – the name Üsküdar derives from the twelfth-century Scutarion Palace which once stood here. Under the Ottomans, the sultan's army was mustered each year in Üsküdar if he was going to war in Asia; he would ride out with the Banner of the Prophet and the Sword of Omar, and it was from Üsküdar that the annual pilgrimage set off for Mecca. When the reforming sultan Selim III decided to train a new army, it was trained on the Asian side and later housed in the enormous Selimiye barracks. The 'Scutari' barracks became famous to the British during the Crimean War, when Florence Nightingale nursed British soldiers there (see p. 190).

Coming in towards the shore, the ferry passes the rock with a little tower known in Turkish as **Kız Kulesi** (the Maiden's Tower, from a Turkish tale about a young girl who was shut up here to protect her from a prophecy that she would die of a snake bite. Inevitably, the snake found its way to her and the prophecy was fulfilled). It was also erroneously called Leander's Tower, after the Greek myth of Leander, who swam the Hellespont from Abydos to his lover Hero's tower at Sestos and eventually drowned in the winter storms. The mosque which stands so prominently on the ridge behind is the baroque Ayazma Camii – to the right of the landing stage is the charming little Şemsi Pasha Mosque.

Most sights on this walk are mosques. Between them they cover a range of architectural styles, from early post-Conquest, to classical Ottoman to Turkish baroque. While it is best to avoid being inside a mosque for the noon prayers, if this is unavoidable one should be as discreet as possible. However, smaller mosques may only be open at prayer times, in which case immediately before or after is the best bet.

Opposite the landing stage at Üsküdar is the **Iskele Camii** – built by Sinan for the princess Mihrimah, daughter of Süleyman the Magnificent. As you cross the road towards the mosque, pause for a moment to look at the lovely eighteenth-century fountain of Ahmet III, the 'Tulip King' where the basins at its four corners are still in working order. Climb up to the mosque courtyard: it has an unusually deep portico roof extending from the portico proper with its five domes. Though striking, this makes the courtyard and *şadırvan* feel rather dark and cramped, for the central gable projects over the latter. The dome is supported by three semi-domes inside, but is missing one at the seaward side, which has a gallery. Stained glass decorates the roundels, lunettes and upper windows, and there is a marble *mihrab*. Nearly twenty years later, Sinan was to improve on this first effort for the princess when he built her the beautiful Mihrimah Camii at Edirne Kapı in the city walls.

Up a stepped street behind the mosque is the former *mektep*, which now houses a childrens' library. If the day is hot, try an ice cream at Mado, a chain of excellent ice cream parlours. You may like to try a glass of *boza* – famous as the fermented millet drink of the Janissaries, it is a glutinous, pale yellow drink comparable to scented semolina. This may not sound all that appetizing, but the nineteenth-century Vefa Boza shop in Istanbul (see p. 92) is well worth a visit.

Now stroll through the colourful market on Karacaoğlan Sok. before embarking on the fifteen minute hike uphill to the **Atik Valide Mosque**, one of Sinan's last commissions and the highlight of any trip to Üsküdar. (Alternatively, bus number 12C will take you up the hill.) The Atik Valide ('old queen mother', to differentiate between the Yeni or 'New' Valide, whose

Fish market

mosque is described later in this chapter) was one of the most famous of all queen mothers – Nurbanu, mother of Murat III. Of mixed Venetian and Greek blood, she was captured on a Greek island in her youth and sent by Barbarossa to the harem where she had the good fortune to catch the eye of Selim II, Süleyman's son. Selim, known as 'the Sot', left the running of his government to his Grand Vizier and retreated to the harem. Thus began an era known in Ottoman history as the Sultanate of the Women, when queen mothers and wives or favourites gained ascendancy over the sultans, whom they often sought to distract through the pleasures of the flesh. When Selim died, Nurbanu kept his body concealed in an icebox until her son Murat had returned to the capital. She then found herself with a rival in the form of Murat's wife Safiye, but managed to keep control and continued to wield great power until her death in 1583, when her grieving son commissioned Sinan to build this mosque.

Enter the precinct on the corner of Valide and Çinili Camii Sok. and walk down the path to the courtyard past the graveyard on the right. Like the Iskele Camii, there is a huge overhanging porch roof to the mosque, but here there is plenty of space for it. The delightful cloistered courtyard with its cypresses and two very ancient plane trees has a domed *şadırvan*. On the north side steps lead down to the *medrese* courtyard with a sweet little fountain. Oddly, the *dershane* projects into the street running along this side, where it is raised on arches. Around the mosque courtyard red and white stone voussoirs decorate the arches, which sport large rosettes in the spandrels. Boldly swirling blue and white calligraphic panels adorn the mosque wall and a fine marble entrance decorated with *muqarnas* leads into the mosque. Four piers bear the weight of the dome, with an intermediary column on each side. The galleries were a later addition, as is apparent from the arrangement. Some of the old painted decoration remains on the ceilings under these galleries. However, the fame of the Atik Valide is attributable to its beautiful tiles; flanking the *mihrab* niche are beautiful bright panels of vases and a variety of flowers including carnations and lilies. The red glaze which is the hallmark of this period of Iznik tiles (see p. 101) is laid on thickly, but dark blue, turquoise and green and white complement it. A wide inscribed band runs around the top and there are more faience panels over the windows of this wall.

Tile from Atik Valide Mosque

A ten-minute walk from here is the seventeenth-century **Çinili Camii** ('Tiled Mosque') – to reach it, turn left out of the mosque gate and head along Çinili Camii Sok. If it is closed, the caretaker should be around to open it up. Walk up the steps to a portico with a very low roof to be greeted by a stunning array of tiles which cover this little mosque, both on the external and the internal walls up to 3m high. Inside, in the lunettes of the windows there are inscribed panels, the rest is floral decoration with an inscription running around the top. The *mihrab* is tiled and even the *minber* has a tiled hat! In structure the mosque is a simple dome with pendentives and a gallery at the back. The Çinili Mosque was built for the Valide Sultan Kösem, wife of Ahmet I, the builder of the Blue Mosque. Like Nurbanu, she was born a Christian, having been captured on a Greek island and sold into slavery. Two of her sons became sultan and she exercised great power over them, involving herself in intrigue and power struggles until eventually she was killed by the Chief Black Eunuch in 1651.

After returning to the Atik Valide Mosque, continue into Atik Valide Imaret Sok. noting the chimneys of the *külliye* kitchen behind the wall on the right. On the way to the Ayazma Mosque look out for the sweet little brick and stone mosque complex of the **Ahmediye Camii**. Raised on a platform above street level and now housing a qur'anic school, there are now two *dershanes* (one in a chamber over one of the entrances), one of which used to be the library. Running around two sides of the courtyard, the *medrese* serves to link these two buildings. The mosque itself is tiny; its single dome projects from the square and is supported by four quarter-domes in the corners. A modern gallery has been added at the back.

The **Ayazma Mosque** was built for his mother in the late 1750s by Mustafa III, who also built Laleli Mosque (see p. 142). Like the Nuruosmaniye, which was built shortly before, its dome rests on the projecting arches, which rise from the building. Steps lead up to the terrace on which the Ayazma Mosque stands, and slender columns support two shallow doors under the portico. On the left is a two-storey library or loge and below is the cistern which gives this mosque its name (an *ayazma* is a holy fountain). The structure is simple: a dome raised high on arches and set within a square, and a single gallery at the back borne on slender arcaded columns. The chandeliers are rather overwhelming and, despite the amount of light from the windows below the arches, there is a sense of clutter. Fine carving decorates the *minber* and *mihrab*, the latter unfortunately painted a boarding-house brown. Note the scalloped top, which here replaces the more classsical *muqarnas*. Behind the mosque are two more entrance gates, one on either side. A typically baroque feature of the exterior are the bird-houses. While these may also be seen on the Üsküdar Yeni Camii and Laleli Mosque, the architect of the Ayazma Mosque obviously had a penchant for them as there no fewer than nine, some extremely elaborate, on the gates, outer walls and the walls of the mosque itself.

From here either cut down to the sea road for a spot of lunch or head down Tulumbacılar Sok. to the seafront, noting the undulating red and white dome of **Mehmet Pasha Camii** which peeps attractively over the rooftops. Built in 1471, the influence of late Byzantine church architecture on the recently arrived Ottomans is most marked in this mosque, perhaps appropriately, since the Mehmet in question was a Greek convert to Islam, who rose to become Fatih's vizier. Unfortunately the mosque itself has not much to recommend it, having been mostly whitewashed and modernized. The founder's *türbe* lies in the garden behind.

One mosque definitely worth a visit is the nearby **Şemsi Pasha Camii**, small in size, but long on charm. Built by Sinan in 1580 for a Grand Vizier, it stands on the waterfront, a pretty little portico around two sides of the tiny courtyard, with the light from the sea flooding the small, single chamber of the mosque. The flattish dome, resting on four quarter-domes, is nicely proportioned and the whole constitutes a very pleasing, if simple, structure. Unusually, the founder's *türbe* is actually attached to the mosque on the sea side. The *medrese*, which takes up two sides of the courtyard, is now a library.

Finally we turn to the **Yeni Valide Camii**. Built in the early seventeenth century, it has a curious *türbe* adjacent to the main road – a wire grill open to the elements. The porticoed courtyard is fairly plain, apart from an ornate *şadırvan* (built in the early eighteenth century by Ahmet III for his mother, it marks the transition from the more sober classical style to Ottoman baroque). Over the main entrance to the outer courtyard is the *mektep*, its brick and stone courses a contrast to the sober stone elsewhere. Before entering the inner courtyard, note the birdhouses high on the left corner of this wall; the one on the left is particularly sophisticated with its two minarets. The interior is restrained, however; a wide, flat dome is borne on arches with semi-domes in the corners. Galleries on either side are supported on slender pillars and there is a further gallery at the back. Tiles of blue rosettes on a pale turquoise background surround the grey marble *mihrab*.

Mosque bird-house

Eight calligraphic roundels decorate the spandrels.

The bright yellow *dolmuşes* ('shared' taxis or minibuses) in the square outside the Yeni Camii run between Üsküdar and Kadıköy via Karaca Ahmet Cemetery. To reach the **Selimiye Barracks** it may, however be easier to take a taxi. Prior permission is necessary in order to visit the building. All that needs to be done is to fax a request through to the barracks (tel/fax 0216 3331009) a couple of days before the intended visit, giving your hotel name and contact number. The main entrance is on the busy road which runs below the barracks. Soldiers at the gate will phone ahead for someone from the Protocol section to escort you to the **Florence Nightingale Museum**.

ISTANBUL: A TRAVELLER'S GUIDE

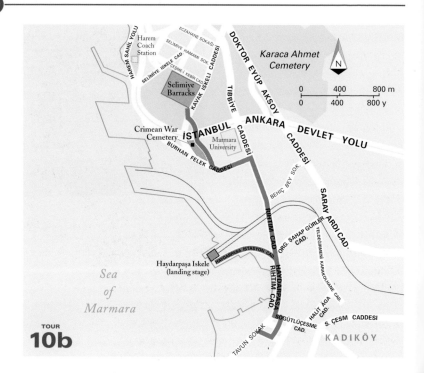

TOUR
10b

FLORENCE NIGHTINGALE

The woman who was responsible for turning nursing into a proper profession was born in Florence in 1820. Unusually for the time, her father gave her a classical education, which he may have rued when his strong-minded daughter went on to decline a marriage proposal from Lord Houghton. At the age of seventeen she had had some sort of a mystical experience which she believed was a calling from God. Despite the rather dubious reputation of the nursing profession in Victorian Britain (one has only to think of Dickens' gin-swigging Mrs Gamp, whose company it was difficult to enjoy 'without becoming conscious of a smell of spirits') she was from early on interested in nursing and braved her parents' disapproval to receive training in Germany. This was, however, agreed only after she had refused Lord Houghton and effectively removed herself from the marriage market.

Her chance to have a real impact on the hospital system came with the outbreak of the Crimean War in 1854. Through family connections, Florence was invited to tackle the appalling conditions prevailing in the military hospitals there. She arrived in Scutari in November of that year with a party of thirty-eight nurses. It was not a warm welcome. Most army officers resented what they saw as meddling in their business and the Army Barracks hospital was in a scandalous state: wards were filthy, there was almost no linen, men were operated on in the wards and for the 1,000 men in her charge, there were a mere twenty chamber pots. By enforcing stricter hygiene a startling reduction in mortality from wounds was achieved – it fell from 42 per cent to 2 per cent.

In 1860 she founded the Nightingale School for Nurses at St Thomas' Hospital in London. The school was the first to provide nurses with a proper professional training. Her book *Notes on Nursing* became a classic and is still in print today. Although her health was undermined by the rigours of her life, Florence Nightingale lived to the age of ninety.

While in recent years there have been some criticisms of her achievements, there is no denying that she was largely responsible for ensuring that nursing, a far from respectable profession earlier in the century, was established on firm ground by the time of her death. She had understood that for this to happen, nursing qualifications were essential: 'I would also say to all young ladies who are called to my particular vocation, qualify yourself for it as a man does for his work.' In so doing she and other nurses struck a blow for womens' rights, by asserting their right to both an education and a livelihood. Her drive and commitment were astounding and her fame well deserved; the image of the 'Lady of the Lamp' is one which remains with us today.

The first barracks were built of wood and burnt down shortly after. They were rebuilt in stone by Mahmut II and are of impressive dimensions: 276 x 200m and with 3,000 windows. The oldest wing faces the sea. The barracks now house the Turkish First Army. The Florence Nightingale Museum, a small collection of exhibits, includes some letters written from Scutari ('never let us be ashamed of the name of nurse', she writes in one) and various engravings of the barracks. It occupies two floors of the tower furthest from the main gate. On the first floor there is also a collection of guns, cannon and swords.

Perhaps more interesting than the museum, and a poignant reminder of the deaths from disease in the hospital prior to Florence Nightingale's reform, is a visit to the **Crimean War Cemetery**. A short walk from here in a peaceful garden on the hillside, the cemetery is well tended. It also contains the graves of British citizens resident in Constantinople and of soldiers who died in other, later battles. The first section, well shaded by large trees, contains the Crimean monument 'raised by Queen Victoria and her people' in honour of the officers and men who died in the war. It is striking to note, as one wanders around these graves, quite how many died of infection and diseases such as cholera. Balaclava, Sebastopol, Inkerman: the famous names can all be read on these gravestones. Near to the monument, a long, flat stone with a Latin inscription is that of Edward Barton (d. 1597), Queen Elizabeth I's ambassador to Constantinople. Wander further into the next section, where residents of Constantinople are buried and there are more soldiers' graves from Gallipoli and the Middle East. The gardener may unlock the back gate for you, which brings you out nearer to Kadiköy.

Down below, beyond the busy docks, looms the bulk of **Haydarpaşa Station**. Sadly, for all the eastern destinations from here, the trains are so slow that most people prefer to take a bus from the nearby Harem bus station. The railway station is, however, of some

Crimean War Cemetery

IN MEMORY OF
EDMUND SIDNEY WASON ESQ M D
ASSISTANT SURGEON 13 REG LIGHT INF
ONLY SON OF EDMUND SIDNEY WASON ESQ
LATE OF MERTON HALL WIGTONSHIRE WHO DIE
IN THE HOSPITAL AT SCUTARI WHILST ACTIVE
AND FAITHFULLY DISCHARGING HIS TO
ARDUOUS PROFESSIONAL DUTIES
FEBRUARY 8
1855

interest. Apart from the charming *iskele* (landing stage), still in use, the ponderous European style in which it is built, in marked contrast to the oriental style Sirkeçı Station on the European side, is a symbol of German interests in Turkey in the early twentieth century. From here a short stroll takes you to busy Kadiköy, where you can either take the ferry home or stroll around the pedestrian streets of Kadiköy centre, stopping for coffee and cake at Baylan Patisserie. There are also a few churches here (one is Armenian), and on Tuesdays and Fridays there is a bustling market some distance away. The return trip on the ferry gives good views of both the Barracks and the large mass of the Marmara University Medical Faculty (Haydarpaşa Lisesi) nearby, built in the late nineteenth century to house the Military Medical Academy.

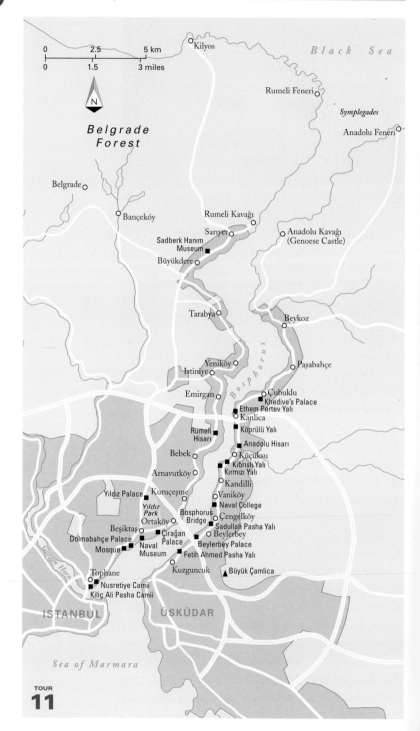

The Bosphorus

TOUR
11

'Those waves, we follow'd on till the dark Euxine roll'd
Upon the blue Symplegades'
Byron: *Childe Harold's Pilgrimage*

A long time before palaces and parks graced the Bosphorus and roads ran up and down both sides of the straits, the Greeks had chosen them as the setting for some potent myths. Here it was that Io, one of Zeus' unfortunate lovers, roamed in the guise of a cow, vainly attempting to escape the wrath of Hera. The jealous goddess sent a gadfly to torment poor Io, who crossed the straits, thus giving them the name Bosphorus, 'the ford of the cow'. Jason and his Argonauts rowed up them to the Black Sea on their quest for the Golden Fleece – here they braved the clashing rocks known as the Symplegades, following a dove between the perilous rocks. The dove lost some tail feathers and the *Argo* her stern mascot, but thanks to the intervention of Athena they made it through and the rocks henceforth remained apart.

Despite development and the encroachment of greater Istanbul, the Bosphorus has kept its beauty; there is still much woodland, the water sparkles and in summertime gangs of little boys bathe in the cold water. In the village squares are fountains, often shaded by great plane trees and, many losses notwithstanding, there are still plenty of the charming old wooden waterfront houses known as *yalıs*, where people once came to spend their summers away from the heat and dust of the city. Armenians, Greeks, Jews, Turks and Westerners once lived in these *yalıs*; indeed, though there are far fewer foreigners here than formerly, a number of villages do still have functioning churches and synagogues. The sultans too looked up the Bosphorus, and built splendid extravaganzas at various points along both sides of the straits, continuing, despite the straitened circumstances of the empire to the late nineteenth century. In summer, there would be night-time concerts on the water at full moon, when a procession of boats full of the most affluent families would follow a caique full of musicians up to Bebek Bay, stopping at *yalıs* along the way. During the reign of Ahmet III, the gardens of the Bosphorus *yalıs* and palaces were filled with tulips, so much the fashion that this is known as the Tulip Period (see p. 208). A number of nineteenth-century Ottoman palaces may still be visited; guides, not all of whom speak English, accompany visitors around them. These palaces are open 9.30 am–5 pm, closed Mondays and Thursdays.

For the best view of the waterfront palaces, pavilions, mosques and mansions along the Bosphorus take the boat trip which stops at Beşiktaş, Istinye and Sarıyer on the European shore. There are also landing stages at Ortaköy, Bebek and Yeniköy which operate morning and evening commuter services while from Bebek some boats cross during the day to the Asian side. Alternatively buses and *dolmuşes* run regularly along the European shore.

BOSPHORUS (EUROPEAN SIDE)

The **Tophane** or 'Cannon House' district on the lower Bosphorus is named after the great Ottoman gun foundry built there soon after the Conquest. On the hillside the domes and chimneys of a later (early nineteenth century) foundry (now part of Mimar Sinan University) still dominate the skyline. Below, the flamboyant eighteenth-century **Tophane Fountain** has a series of low relief panels bearing floral decoration, fruit trees and date palms, sheltered by broad eaves. Across the street the **Tophane Mosque** was commissioned by Kiliç ('the sword') Ali Pasha, Ottoman High Admiral. It is one of Sinan's latest works, built in 1580, and seems to be modelled on St Sophia. In front there is a pleasant, shady, irregular-shaped courtyard and double porch, with an intricate calligraphic panel over the door. The mosque interior is spacious, with fine

YALIS

Yalıs (derived from the Greek word for seashore) developed along the Bosphorus from the late seventeenth century onwards, showing a range of styles from grandiose to simple. Plain beginnings gradually turned into full-blown baroque, then turn-of-the-century 'cosmopolitan' style and, later, Art Nouveau. Houses were built on the water's edge and indeed over it (the bay window or *cumba* is typical, as was the deep red colour known as 'Ottoman rose' with which they were initially painted – later on, pastel colours were used in a sign of growing European influence). The interior was traditionally cruciform in plan, harking back to the Turks' Central Asian origins and first houses. The design of the Çinili Kiosk, the oldest kiosk in the Topkapı Palace, was also influential. Smaller rooms led off the central *sofa*, the gathering place, which often had a fountain, carpets and divans – chairs and tables came later along with other European fashions. As elsewhere, houses were divided into male and female sections; since women required privacy, shutters were important, not just to keep out the summer heat. This separation persisted into the twentieth century. Sadly, fire, damp and neglect have seen the demise of many of the older *yalıs*, though recently a number have been restored. Nowadays the Bosphorus is busy with cargo boats, tankers and ferries ploughing up and down the narrow straits, but only a hundred years ago little rowing boats called caiques were everywhere to be seen. Their size was an indication of status, and so the sultan's caique was the largest, crewed by twenty-six oarsmen and escorted by a number of other caiques. The Naval Museum at Beşiktaş displays various caiques, including one owned and rowed by Atatürk. A steam ferry service was started in the mid-nineteenth century, signalling the end of an era.

Iznik tiles in the *mihrab* though surprisingly garish stained glass windows. Of the ancillary buildings the *hammam* is still in use (men only).

Not far away is Mahmut II's imperial mosque, completed in 1826 and named **Nusretiye**, ('victory') to commemorate his victory over the Janissaries. Its Armenian architect, Kirkor Balian, was the founder of a dynasty of royal architects, several of whom studied in Paris. The Balian family introduced elaborate European styles into Ottoman architecture and created most of the flamboyant imperial buildings of the nineteenth century. Nusretiye Camii is in exuberant baroque style, light inside, with a high dome and a pair of slender minarets on pepperpot bases.

Dolmabahçe Palace (guided tours only, closed Mondays and Thursdays), 'palace of the filled-in garden', is on the site of a small bay which was filled in and transformed into a pleasure park in the seventeenth century. The ostentatious nineteenth-century palace which now dominates the lower Bosphorus shore between Kabataş and Beşiktaş was the brainchild of Sultan Abdül Mecit I and architects Karabet and Nikoğos Balian. Abdül Mecit came to the throne in 1838, a

Main entrance gates, Dolmabahçe Palace

frail and sickly young man of sixteen who developed a passion for women and managed to sire forty-three children during his twenty-two-year reign. For the new sultan, the Topkapı Palace was too old-fashioned. European styles were in vogue and Abdül Mecit had money to spend (though his excesses virtually ruined the empire), so around 1846 he commissioned a vast new residence. Ten years later, in July 1856, a sumptuous banquet celebrated the completion of Dolmabahçe and the defeat of Russia in the Crimean War.

Access to the palace and gardens is through the elaborate Administrative Gate, which bears the sultan's *tuğra* in black and gold. In front is the ornate 37m-high clock tower, another Balian creation, as is the waterfront **Dolmabahçe Mosque**, pleasant and light inside, built for Abdül Mecit's mother, the Valide Bezmialem.

Dolmabahçe Mosque

Dolmabahçe is designed to face the water. Along the shore an elegant wrought iron railing, crested with lanterns, fronts a marble promenade. Behind is the majestic 284m-long white façade of the palace, comprising the traditional state rooms (*selamlık*) and residential wing (*haremlık*) which flank the largest throne hall in the world, twice the height of the rest of the building. Within are over 300 lavishly decorated rooms containing a profusion of Oriental and French porcelain, European clocks, silk drapes and Hereke carpets, Bohemian and Baccarat crystal candelabras and chandeliers, gilded radiators and mirrors. A grand crystal staircase sweeps up to the state rooms on the first floor where the sultan received and entertained foreign dignitaries. Sultan Abdül Mecit, his father Mahmut II and his half-brother, the powerful 18-stone Abdül Aziz, hang together in the palace portrait gallery alongside Queen Victoria, Prince Albert and other European monarchs. It was Queen Victoria who presented the sultan with the most extravagant crystal chandelier in the palace, which weighs 4.5 tons and hangs from the ceiling of the most ostentatious room, the ceremonial throne hall. Fifty-six fluted columns supporting the upper gallery and the 36m-high dome, which is painted blue and gold with *trompe l'oeil* windows, huge silver and crystal candelabras and the 120m sq. Hereke carpet contrive to make this the epitome of Dolmabahçe's wild exuberance. Steps lead down to the terrace and waterfront gate, where guests arrived in their caiques and launches for the sparkling receptions and banquets of the late Ottoman Empire.

Beyond Dolmabahçe Palace is Beşiktaş, a popular suburb with a lively market and some nice *meyhanes*. A row of renovated terraced houses on Spor Cad. used to house some of the staff of the Dolmabahçe. By Beşiktaş landing stage is the Deniz Müzesi or **Naval Museum** (open 9 am–12.30 pm and 1.30 pm–5 pm except Wednesday and Thursday), housed in two separate buildings with a garden between. On the waterfront, in a former hangar, is the Caiques Gallery, with a fascinating display of the beautiful imperial rowing barges which used to ferry the sultan and his harem along the Bosphorus and the Golden Horn. The garden and main museum contain an impressive collection of naval equipment and model ships. One room is devoted to Hayrettin Pasha, known to the West as Barbarossa or 'Redbeard', whose statue is in the square outside. Hayrettin was a Barbary pirate who became Ottoman High Admiral in 1533. Barbarossa's octagonal *türbe* (usually closed) is an early work of Sinan, as is the mosque across the road, which he designed for another Ottoman admiral, Sinan Pasha, brother of Grand Vizier Rüstem Pasha.

Barely twenty years after the completion of Dolmabahçe, the impoverished Ottoman Empire had to bear the expense of another grandiose Bosphorus residence. **Çirağan Palace**, which again bears the stamp of the Balian family, is now a luxury hotel with a modern wing (we recommend a drink on the waterfront terrace). The palace was built for Abdül Mecit's brother and successor Abdül Aziz, a man of considerable bulk whose favourite activities were wrestling and spending money. The first sultan to tour Europe, Abdül Aziz was royally received by various monarchs including Queen Victoria, who invested

Çirağan Palace, from the seaside

him with the Order of the Garter and entertained him to a fireworks display at the Crystal Palace. In May 1876 Abdül Aziz was deposed in favour of his nephew Murat, and confined to an annexe of the Çirağan, where he committed suicide by slashing his wrists with scissors. Murat, a mentally unstable alcoholic, was deposed in August 1876 by his brother Abdül Hamit and also imprisoned in Çirağan, where he died in 1905. In 1910 a dreadful fire totally gutted the palace which remained a blackened shell until its recent reconstruction.

While Murat and his family wasted away in Çirağan Palace, Abdül Hamit II moved from Dolmabahçe to **Yıldız**, on the hillside above Çirağan. Yıldız Palace was a collection of kiosks, pavilions, workshops and even a zoo, amidst woods and lovely gardens, all surrounded by a high wall patrolled by guards and fierce dogs. Within the complex the sultan founded a porcelain factory which manufactured the fashionably ornate Yıldız plates and vases. At Yıldız, during the twilight days of the Ottoman Empire, Abdül Hamit held a more Western-style court, while nationalism slowly corroded his power beyond the palace walls. On 27 April 1909, less than a year after the 'Young Turk' revolution, a deputation came to Yıldız to inform the sultan he was deposed and two days later he left for exile from Sirkeçi Station.

For today's visitors to Yıldız, there are two sections with separate entrances, the Palace Museum and Yıldız Park. From the Bosphorus road the museum is a steep climb up Barbarossa Boulevard and Eski Yıldız Cad., past the Ertuğrul Tekke mosque complex (note the interesting art nouveau *türbe*) and Conrad Hotel. The first of the palace buildings are the ornate stone clock tower and the pink and white Balian mosque, the Hamidiye, where Abdül Hamit, keen to promote Islam, performed his Friday prayers. Up the hill to the right is the **Palace Museum** entrance (open 9.30 am–4.30 pm, except Monday). Abdül Hamit was a skilled carpenter, and his former workshop now displays wooden furniture, Yıldız porcelain and some of the sultan's personal effects, including his ceremonial uniform and his carriage. The small City Museum alongside exhibits mainly ceramics and glassware. On one side of the first courtyard is the largest of the palace buildings, the Büyük Mabeyn (closed). This was built by Abdül Aziz and used to house the sultan's advisors and secretaries. His officers were quartered in the low building with wooden shutters opposite. In the second courtyard, opposite the conservatory, is Abdül Hamit's private residence, the Küçük Mabeyn (also closed), designed by the fashionable Ligurian architect Raimondo D'Aronco.

Beyond is the charming **Yıldız Palace Theatre and Museum of Stage Arts**, which displays a collection of theatrical costumes. Sultan Abdül Hamit used to entertain his family, harem and important guests to performances of his favourite plays and operas in the beautifully restored little theatre with its star-studded ceiling. Sometimes he changed the plot himself to make a 'happy ending'! Kaiser Wilhelm II once sat in the royal box, and among those who performed here was the famous actress Sarah Bernhardt.

Yıldız Park entrance is on the main Bosphorus road, opposite the high walls of Çirağan Palace. If you are walking, it is quite a steep hike up to the other pavilions and kiosks of Yıldız. **Şale Kiosk** (guided tours only), built in the so-called 'Swiss Chalet' style, contains a plethora of over-ornate furnishings and decoration. Via bedchambers with enormous beds, a large central dining room with damascene inlaid doors and a florid bathroom, the tour culminates in a huge conference hall endowed with Baccarat crystal chandeliers and an enormous Hereke carpet. Five minutes away, the **Malta Kiosk** has been converted into a restaurant (open 9 am–11 pm) where you can relax on the shady terrace and look across the Bosphorus. On the other side of the park the smaller pink and white **Çadir Kiosk**, which also has a pleasant terrace with Bosphorus views, sells drinks, sandwiches, cakes and ice cream. Like the Büyük Mabeyn, these two kiosks were built in 1871 under Abdül Aziz.

Ortaköy is one of the trendiest and most popular of the Bosphorus 'villages'. Bars, cafés, *mantı* houses, restaurants, craft shops and fashion boutiques compete in the narrow streets between the main road and the pretty waterside square. Try Café First Class for cheesecake and coffee and Mado's for delicious ice cream. At the weekends from around 11 am there is a lively outdoor flea market selling clothes, jewellery, books, tapes, CDs and bric-à-brac.

Ortaköy Mosque, on a small promontory lapped by the waters of the Bosphorus, was built just after the Dolmabahçe Palace by the same architects. Even on a dull day it is lovely and light inside, with two storeys of tall windows in the great dome arches. Recently the interior of the dome has been repainted in the pompous *trompe l'oeil* style of the time. Fluffy clouds float through a blue sky behind pillared balconies draped with curtains.

As a contrasting backdrop to the mosque, the graceful **Bosphorus Bridge**, completed in 1972, spans the straits some 200 feet above the water. Beyond the bridge, **Kuruçeşme**, another favourite haunt of Istanbul's smart set, is followed by **Arnavutköy**, the 'Albanian village', which boasts a pretty row of waterside *yalıs* by the landing stage. Around Akıntı Burnu ('Current Headland'), where the Bosphorus runs deep and its currents meet, is the calm bay of **Bebek**. Since the eighteenth century this has been one of the most popular Bosphorus villages. The elegant white art nouveau mansion by the waterfront was designed by Raimondo d'Aronco in 1902 for the last khedive of Egypt. It is now the Egyptian Consulate. Bebek, which means 'baby' in Turkish, is named after one of the Conqueror's henchmen, Bebek Çelebi, whom Sultan Mehmet made responsible for security

**Ortaköy
Mosque**

while the Ottoman army was building Rumeli Hisarı.
Çelebi had a house and garden here, where he lived
while the castle was under construction.

Rumeli Hisarı (Open 9 am–4 pm, except Wednesday), the 'Fortress of Europe', was built with speed and
vision between April and August 1452 as the forward
base for Mehmet's attack on Constantinople and is an
impressive feat of Ottoman military engineering. For
his fortress, Mehmet chose a spur where the straits are
narrowest, opposite Anadolu Hisarı (the 'Fortress of
Asia'), the castle built by his great grandfather Beyazıt
I. Timber from the nearby forests, stone from Anatolia

Rumeli Hisarı fortress

and stones and columns from abandoned churches were used to build the great walls and towers which stretch along the waterfront and climb up the hillside. When the castle was complete, it was garrisoned with Janissaries and armed with cannon to close the Bosphorus to hostile shipping and effectively cut off Constantinople from the Black Sea. After the fall of Constantinople Rumeli Hisarı was used as a prison, and since its restoration in 1953 it has been a museum. On some summer evenings there are concerts in the small open air theatre which has been built over the cistern and castle mosque, leaving just a stump of the minaret standing.

Entrance to the fortress is through the barbican to the right of the formidable waterfront tower, built by Mehmet's Grand Vizier Halil Pasha, who was beheaded soon after the conquest of Constantinople for treasonable correspondence with the Byzantines. In the castle grounds is a collection of Ottoman cannon, but the main interest lies in the well-preserved curtain walls, three to five metres thick. These you can climb in places to reach the sentry walk, though there is no continuous circuit. Karaküle ('the Black Tower') to the north and Gülküle ('the Rose Tower') to the south, built by two other viziers, are both closed to the public. From the heights of Rumeli Hisarı there are fabulous views of the Bosphorus, crossed here by Fatih Mehmet Bridge, and of Anadolu Hisarı on the Asian side.

On the hill behind Rumeli Hisarı is the **University of the Bosphorus**, founded in 1971 to replace Robert College, a nineteenth century American establishment which for many years was Turkey's most prestigious educational institution.

Rumeli Hisarı village, which has a few cafés and restaurants, is between the fortress and **Fatih Mehmet Bridge**. It was probably here, at the narrowest point of the straits, that the very first bridge crossed the Bosphorus, a bridge of boats which Mandrokles of Samos built in the late sixth century BC so that his overlord Darius, king of Persia, could pass into Europe with his army and march against the Scythians.

Emirgan has a pleasant pedestrian street with lots of cafés and an eighteenth-century part-wooden mosque in baroque style. The Sabancı Museum (open 10.00 am–6.00 pm weekdays, 11.00 am–5.00 pm weekends, closed Mondays), a collection of Ottoman calligraphy and nineteenth- to twentieth-century Turkish art housed in an elegant family mansion is worth a visit. On the hill above the village are the Emirgan woods, a park with several Ottoman kiosks and tulip gardens, best visited during the April Tulip Festival (see p. 208).

Emirgan's kiosks are brightly painted in different colours. Pembe Kiosk (the 'Pink Kiosk') serves drinks and sandwiches in summer, Beyaz Kiosk (the 'White Kiosk') is currently only open for Government functions, but the café in Sarı Kiosk (the 'Yellow Kiosk') is open all year round.

TULIPS

No bloom was ever prized by the Ottomans more than the tulip, indigenous to Anatolia and the Turkish homelands of Central Asia. The flower was considered special not just for its beauty but because its Turkish name *lale* resembles 'Allah'. By the sixteenth century the sultans had developed a passion for tulips and sent their officials to scour the empire for different varieties, which were judged by the Chief Florist and given official names. 'Rose Arrow', 'Beloved's Face' and 'Glitter of Prosperity' graced the imperial gardens. Turkish tulips with their characteristic pointed petals became one of the loveliest motifs in the decorative arts. Baron de Busbecq, who became Hapsburg

ambassador to the Ottoman court in 1555, sent the first bulbs from Turkey to the Low Countries and was thus indirectly responsible for the establishment of the Dutch tulip trade. In the seventeenth century tulip mania was rife in Europe, where collectors paid fortunes for rare bulbs. Turkish tulip frenzy peaked in the eighteenth century when Ahmet III's Tulip Fête in the seraglio gardens outshone all other festivals. During his reign, which is known as *Lale Devri*, or the 'Tulip Age', the tulip also became a popular image in Turkish poetry.

After Emirgan is the deep bay of **Istiniye**, a fishing village with a lively and colourful fish market along the quay. At **Yeniköy**, known as Neapolis in the Byzantine era (both names mean 'New Town'), there are some very handsome waterfront *yalıs* beyond the landing stage. Take a break at Zeynel ice cream and pudding salon for Turkish milk puddings. Specialities include *tavuk göğsü* (milk pudding with chicken and cinnamon), *muhallebi* (white pudding with corn starch, rose water and icing sugar) and *keşkül* (vanilla blancmange). Zeynel also sells *salep* (made from orchid root) and *boza*, both traditional winter drinks.

Tarabya, Byzantine Therapia ('healing'), was a popular resort for both the Greeks and Ottomans, celebrated for its healthy climate and elegantly curved bay. Now its charm is marred by a large and ugly modern building which dominates the north entrance to the bay. European ambassadors built their summer residences and moored their boats along the shore near Tarabya, which on balmy summer evenings was a colourful international pageant. Along the promenade, young ladies exhibited their charms, financiers negotiated business deals and diplomats discussed the latest sports tournaments and embassy balls. Today, the former British summer embassy accomodates officials from the consulate while in the grounds there is a bar and social club for ex-pats.

Between the large bay of **Büyükdere** and the next village, **Sarıyer**, the **Sadberk Hanım Museum** is one of the highlights of the Bosphorus. It is open 10 am–5 pm (October to March) or 10.30 am–6 pm (April to September) except Wednesdays. Two lovely nineteenth-century Bosphorus mansions house the collections of Sadberk Hanım, late wife of the wealthy industrialist Vehbi Koç, and Hüseyin Kocabaş, close friend of the Koç family. In the archaeological section an excellent display of antiquities, with objects from the Anatolian Neolithic to Byzantine periods, is arranged over several floors. Everything is clearly labelled and put into historical context. Neolithic painted pottery, bronze axes and spearheads, clay cuneiform tablets from the archives of Assyrian merchants who traded in Anatolia, Phrygian and Urartian metalwork, Mycenaean and Greek vases, Hellenistic figurines, Roman oil lamps, Byzantine censers and reliquaries, multi-period collections of gold jewellery, antique glassware and coins – it would barely be possible to find a better and more representative collection of 7,000 years of Anatolian history. Equally impressive is the Islamic and Ottoman Art and Ethnographical section, which has wonderful displays of Turkish-Islamic metalwork, Iznik, Kütahya and Çanakkale ceramics, Chinese and European porcelains, Turkish embroideries and costumes.

Sarıyer is a pleasant little town with a lively market, famous for its *börek* (cheese pastries). Many of its inhabitants are fishermen, often to be seen mending their nets. From here a cobbled road goes to Rumeli Kavağı, last stop on the Bosphorus. Though the Byzantine and Genoese castle, counterpart of Anadolu Kavağı on the Asian side (the two castles used to exact lucrative tolls from ships plying the Bosphorus), disappeared long ago, visitors come to Rumeli Kavağı for its fish restaurants, where mussels are a delicacy, and lovely views towards the Black Sea.

To visit the Asian side either take a ferry to Üsküdar and then a 15A or 15E bus to Anadolu Kavağı, or the Bosphorus boat trip from Eminönü. This departs from Pier 1 three times daily (signed Boğaz/Bosphorus), makes five stops and allows passengers to get off once and rejoin a later boat. Usually the boat stops at Kanlıca and Anadolu Kavağı on the Asian side. The alternative is to walk part of it; this is easier on the European side where you can walk along the shore for much of the way, although the traffic, especially at peak times, can be a deterrent.

BOSPHORUS (ASIAN SIDE)

From the village of **Anadolu Kavağı** (about one hour on the 15A/15E bus from Üsküdar), allow half an hour to walk up to the **'Genoese' castle** on the hill above. It is in fact earlier in date than the name implies, although the Genoese did occupy it in the fourteenth century. The circuit of the walls is impressively large and from the top there are good views over to the west and to the Black Sea. Within the walls the two round towers of the keep still stand. In the village square down below there are plenty of places for lunch.

The bus now labours over the wooded hill between Anadolu Kavağı and Beykoz. In summertime the bus from Üsküdar is often full of day-trippers who have come to picnic, celebrate circumcisions and visit the hilltop shrine of a local Muslim saint in the woods. **Beykoz** – the name means 'walnut of the prince' (or bey) – is known for its wide-eaved eighteenth-century fountain which stands in the square and more particularly for its fine glass, produced here from the late eighteenth century and now much sought after by collectors. Unfortunately, a large number of industrial buildings have marred what was once a pretty village.

Continuing southwards along the road we come next to the **Paşabahçe Glassworks**, the modern answer to Beykoz glass. There is a shop next to the factory, identifiable by its stack. Bahçe means 'garden' in Turkish and indeed, this was once the site of a seventeenth-century Grand Vizier's palace and grounds. Above the village of Çubuklu, with wonderful views over the Bosphorus, is the **Khedive's Palace**, built in about 1900 by an Italian architect for the last khedive of Egypt, who also owned the art nouveau palace in Bebek on the European side. Deposed by the British in 1914, he managed to keep hold of this palace until he was bankrupted in 1929 (the other was taken over by the Egyptian government for its embassy). Restored by

Ethem Pertev Yalı

the TTOK (the Turkish Touring and Automobile Club), the Khedive's Palace is now operated by the municipality of Istanbul as a hotel and restaurant.

The boat stops at **Kanlıca**, where the local yoghurt for which this little village is famous is brought on board. Served with spoonfuls of icing-sugar, the yoghurt itself is delicious. The mid-sixteenth-century mosque here is actually by Sinan. From this point onwards many of the sights along this route are best seen from the water – indeed, the **Ethem Pertev Yalı** in Kanlıca is visible only from the water. Typical of the turn-of-the-century 'cosmopolitan' style, with a lovely carved wooden balcony and a boathouse underneath, this delightful *yalı* has been sadly neglected and is overgrown with vines.

Just beyond the **Fatıh Mehmet Bridge**, named after Mehmet the Conqueror and opened in 1988, look out for a *yalı*, the modest size and dilapidated appearance of which belies its great historical significance. The **Köprülü Yalı** dates to 1698 and is named after the great family of viziers, which served the Ottoman Empire in the seventeenth and eighteenth centuries. Mehmet Pasha, founder of the dynasty, was an Albanian, recruited into the *devşirme*, or levy of young boys, to be trained for service in the Ottoman government. He finally became Grand Vizier at the age of eighty and proved a very shrewd and able administrator. The *yalı* is named after Amcazade Husein Pasha, a reforming scion of this family who negotiated the terms of the Treaty of Karlowitz, ratified here in 1699. Under this treaty the Ottoman Empire lost many Balkan possessions in the beginning of a long, slow process of decline. Now very dilapidated, the Ottoman rose of this oldest surviving *yalı* is faded to a reddish brown and only the *selamlık*, or male part, remains, jutting out over the water.

Anadolu Hisarı (the Anatolian or Asian Fortress) comes shortly after this. A storybook castle, its towers rise picturesquely above the trees and houses of the village surrounding it. Built by Beyazıt I in the late fourteenth century, this was the first threat posed by the Ottomans to the Byzantine Empire; fortunately for them, Beyazıt was distracted by the arrival of the Mongols and was subsequently captured by Tamerlane in 1402. He died in captivity and it was another half-century before his great-grandson Mehmet II built his fortress at Rumeli Hisarı, thus seizing control of the straits.

Within walking distance of Anadolu Hisarı is the pretty little baroque palace of **Küçüksu**. Nikoğos Balian, third generation son of the family of Armenian architects responsible for so many later imperial mosques and palaces, converted a wooden hunting lodge on the site for Abdül Mecit I in 1856. It is close to the little river once fondly known as the 'Sweet Waters of Asia'; sadly, today 'stinking' would be a better description. From a distance the golden

Küçüksu

Küçüksu, entrance from the Bosphorus

stone and elegant proportions make this a gem on the waterfront; on closer inspection the façade is encrusted with scallops and pendulous wreaths of fruit over every window in an overwhelming display of Turkish baroque. The rear is more sober – indeed, the whole building was so originally, but the sultan protested that it was far too plain for his liking and 'improvements' had to be undertaken to embellish the waterfront façade, from which direction the sultan would approach. A double flight of stairs curves enticingly round a fountain and up to the front entrance, and the wrought iron gate opens on to the waterfront; just to the north is a little fountain, dated to 1796, gift of the Valide Sultan Mihrishah. The interior is full of luxurious Hereke carpets, Bohemian and Venetian glass chandeliers and gilt mouldings.

From the boat the white expanse of the **Kıbrıslı Yalı**, the longest on the Bosphorus at over 60m, cannot be missed. Kıbrıslı means 'Cypriot' and refers to the origins of Kıbrıslı Mehmet Pasha, a Grand Vizier in the time of Mahmut II, who moved here in 1840. Soon after comes the **Kırmızı Yalı**, built in 1790 and painted a deep red, hence the name, meaning 'crimson'. This was the *yalı* of the Ostrorog family, of Polish origins, but prominent in society here in the nineteenth century.

The poet James Elroy Flecker spent a summer in **Kandilli** when posted to the embassy at Constantinople. Beyond the village stands the bulk of the **Naval College**, established by Selim III during initial attempts at military reforms in the early nineteenth century and rebuilt in the mid-nineteenth century. During the Crimean War, Florence Nightingale was in charge of the military hospital here, as well as that of the Selimiye Barracks in Kadiköy where she lived. Reputedly this is also the site of the home for prostitutes founded in the sixth century by Justinian and Theodora, herself of a dubious past. According to Procopius, whose *Secret History* vilified the empress, some preferred death to reform:

> Prostitutes – more than five hundred in all – were rounded up … They were then dispatched to the mainland opposite and confined in the convent known as Repentance in an attempt to force them into a better way of life. However, some of them from time to time threw themselves down from the parapet during the night, and so escaped being transmogrified against their will.

A Grand Vizier of the 'Tulip King', Ahmet III had a palace here; sadly, many *yalıs* have now disappeared, due either to the owners' loss of favour with the sultans and consequent loss of fortune, or to the more general decline towards the end of the empire. **Çengelköy** is a pretty village, renowned for its fish restaurants and worth a lunchtime stop. After this look for the **Sadullah Pasha Yalı**, of which only the harem remains. This brick-red *yalı* dates from 1760, the Turkish baroque period, although it gets its name from a nineteenth-century owner and liberal poet who died in exile in Austria.

Beylerbey Palace, yet another Balian palace, is now dwarfed by the supports of the **Bosphorus Bridge**. The first bridge to span the straits, it opened in 1973 to coincide with the fiftieth anniversary of the Turkish Republic. One and a half kilometres long, it towers over Ortaköy on the European side and Beylerbey Palace on this side. Built in 1860–5 for Sultan Abdül Aziz by Sarkis Balian, brother of the Küçüksu architect, Beylerbey is considerably larger than Küçüksu. Empress Eugenie, who stayed here shortly after the palace was built, had an embarrassing encounter with the sultan's mother. An acquaintance of the empress tells the following story:

> On one occasion, the mother of the Sultan … was to receive the Empress in her palace. All went well till she saw her arrive, on the arm of the sultan, who was to present her. The sight was too much for the outraged feelings of the Queen Mother. The

Beylerbey Palace

sultan, I believe, appeared to be enjoying himself. Stepping forward, she slapped the Empress on the cheek! "This reception", said HM, "naturally alarmed me."

Sultan Abdül Hamit II, who was deposed in 1909, lived here on his return from exile in 1912 until his death in 1918. In typical Ottoman fashion the palace is divided into male and female areas by the large salon at the centre, from which a splendid staircase leads upstairs. There are six large salons and many other extravagantly furnished rooms, but perhaps the most charming features are the lovely little pavilions with flamboyantly ribbed roofs, which stand on the waterfront where the Bosphorus currents race by.

The eighteenth-century **Fetih Ahmed Pasha Yalı** (also known as the Mocan Yalı) at **Kuzguncuk** has three projecting bay windows over the water – the nineteenth-century owner after whom it is named, married a sultan's daughter and attended the coronation of Queen Victoria. The village, with mosque, churches and synagogues, is a reminder that this was once a truly cosmopolitan society. Lady Mary Wortley Montagu enthused to a friend in a letter of 1718 about the Bosphorus palace of a Grand Vizier who had recently died in battle:

> The extent of it is prodigious ... the whole adorned with a profusion of marble, gilding and the most exquisite painting of fruit and flowers ... but no part of it pleased me better than the apartments destined for the *bagnios*. There are two exactly built in the same manner ... the baths, fountains and pavements all in white marble, the roofs gilt and the walls covered with Japan china ... the walls are in the nature of lattices and on the outside of them vines and woodbines planted ... I should go on, but 'tis yet harder to describe a Turkish palace than any other, being built entirely irregular.

Princes' Islands

I n the Sea of Marmara not far from Istanbul lie a cluster of nine islands known collectively as the Princes' Islands. Inhabited even in Roman times, the islands have served as religious retreat, place of exile for unwanted emperors and Patriarchs from Constantinople, and more recently as a summer retreat for those weary of the bustle of the city. Families rent or own houses here and in summertime the morning ferry to Istanbul is full of people setting off to work from their island retreats. In winter the population shrinks drastically, although people do live here all year round. The population until the twentieth century was mainly Greek, with the usual scattering of Armenians, Jews and even some Turks; gradually the latter have increased their numbers, but Greek can still be heard in the streets and there are still Greek and Armenian churches on the inhabited islands.

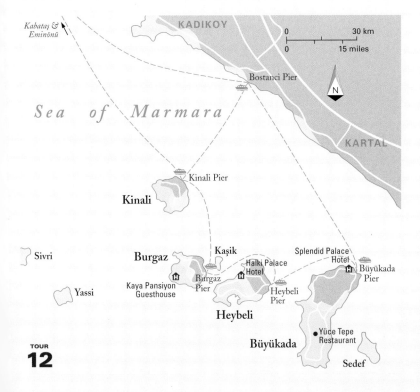

In the Byzantine period there were many monasteries on these islands; due to their isolation these convents and monasteries regularly received exiles from the mainland, some of whom were in a dreadful condition owing to the gruesome Byzantine custom of mutilating contenders to the throne – a fate only marginally better than death, to judge by this account of the blinding of the unfortunate Emperor Romanus IV Diogenes: 'His eyes gouged out and his face and head alive with worms, he lived on a few days in pain … being buried on the island of Proti, where he had built a monastery.' Exiled to Lesbos, (apparently just missing an offer of marriage from Charlemagne, which would have changed the shape of Europe had she held onto her throne) the empress Eirene was buried here on her death. The islands fell to Mehmet the Conqueror shortly before Constantinople – only Prinkipo, the largest, attempted to fight and the fortress there was soon taken. In what was doubtless intended as a salutary lesson to the great city, the population was enslaved and the soldiers all killed. In the nineteenth century, when many *yalıs* were being built up the Bosphorus, it also became fashionable to have a summer house here, especially with the establishment of a regular ferry service.

One of the nicest features of the islands is that there are no cars, transport is by horse-drawn phaeton or bicycle. If hiring a phaeton, look for the list of prices ('tarife') which is usually posted up at the main rank. On Heybeli and Büyükada you can either take the Küçük ('small') Tour or the Büyük ('big') Tour of the island. Bicycles are a good alternative on Büyükada (the largest island), or you may simply stroll along one of the many paths through the woods. Sadly, the Sea of Marmara is now so polluted that it is not advisable to swim in it. The Halki Palace hotel on Heybeli is probably the nicest place to stay, and there is also a guest-house (Kaya Pansiyon) on Burgaz. Büyükada has a few hotels, including the Splendid Palace, once the place to stay and notable in summer for its population of elderly widows who dine on the terrace to watch the world go by!

The cheapest way of getting to the islands is by ferry. These are very frequent in summer, especially on the weekends, leaving from Pier 5 (signed Adalar) where the timetable is also posted. The boat calls at Kınalı, Burgaz, Heybeli and finally reaches Büyükada an hour and a half later. The alternative is the sea bus (a faster, more expensive catamaran) which leaves from Kabataş.

Kınalı, known simply as Proti or 'first' in Greek since it is the closest to the mainland, means 'henna-red' in Turkish – a reference to its red cliffs. Once there were two monasteries and a convent here, later it was known as the Armenian island and there is still an Armenian church here. Nowadays an array of radio masts bristles on the hills above, and the slopes are rather unattractively bare when compared to the other islands. There is nowhere to stay on Kınalı, but large numbers of daytrippers usually disembark here. Various emperors were exiled and died here on Proti, including the unfortunate Romanus IV Diogenes mentioned above – having led his army against the Seljuk Turks at the battle of Manzikert in 1071 and lost disastrously, he then lost his throne, was blinded and died here soon after.

Burgaz (Antigone to the Greeks) is the next stop and is a charming island with a delightful little curving bay and a street of little fish restaurants to the left of the landing stage. Look for the domed church rising above the roofs as the ferry comes in to land; Methodius, Patriarch of Constantinople was reputedly imprisoned here in the ninth century. Along a path southwards through the woods a modern Greek church stands on what was probably the site of the Byzantine monastery of the Transfiguration. A road also runs round to the west side of the island where there is a guest house (the Kaya Pansiyon). Burgaz is still predominantly Greek.

Heybeli

The ferry now passes the island of Kaşık (Spoon) before coming in to the landing stage at **Heybeli**. Formerly known as Halki, this Greek name derives from the copper mines which were once worked here. Heybeli is the second-largest island and a pleasant place to stay is the Halki Palace, a rebuilt wooden Ottoman house with the addition of a swimming pool. The island consists of two hills with a dip between them and from the boat, you can see the buildings of the nineteenth century theological school on the northern hilltop. Previously the site of a Byzantine monastery founded in the ninth century, it now houses a famous library and is within easy walking distance. Another monastery, built shortly before the fall of Constantinople, now lies in the grounds of the Turkish Naval Academy and cannot be visited. Seven Patriarchs of Constantinople are buried here in the churchyard. A walk around the heavily wooded island takes about two hours, but to do it the easy way there are plenty of phaetons for hire.

Büyükada (meaning the Big Island, and known as Prinkipo to the Greeks) is the final port of call and by far the liveliest. The pretty landing stage was built in 1912 and has recently been restored. Justinian founded the convent here in the sixth century and there were also four monasteries. Prinkipo certainly received its share of royal exiles: the infamous empress Eirene took an interest in the convent and, having overseen the blinding of her iconoclast son Constantine to ensure that he could never again be emperor, she sent both him and her daughter into exile here. She was herself buried in the convent on Prinkipo after her death in exile on Lesbos. In 1042 the empress Zoë was exiled here briefly by her adoptive son, but Constantinople erupted in riots at this action and she soon returned to rule together with her sister Theodora before marrying for the third time well into her sixties. Later visitors enjoyed more peaceful times on the island. During the Crimean War, Lady Hornby wrote of the summer days here:

> The Greeks of Constantinople consider Prinkipo as their paradise on earth ... About seven in the morning all the visitors who have not departed for Pera by the early steamer ... are to be seen wending to the little wooden bathing-houses on the shore. Some of these people have returned from an early donkey-ride up the mountain – most from the divan and cup of coffee. Through all the sultry hours, until about four or five o'clock, everybody lies perdu ... scarcely a single caique moving about on the water: only under a large fir-tree opposite our windows a red-capped shepherd fast asleep, with three or four drowsy goats about him.

Prinkipo did, however, continue as a place of exile; Trotsky spent four years here from 1929. Nowadays the town is full of holidaymakers in summer, and the noise of horses' hooves and the jingle of harness is never far away.

It is well worth strolling around the town to look at the fine nineteenth-century mansions. The house which Trotsky stayed in is at 55 Çankaya Cad. and has recently been restored. The Con Pasha Konak opposite is a fine house; Con Pasha was the director of the first scheduled steamboat service connecting the islands with the mainland. Further along this road on the upper side is the Cultural Centre, also housed in a lovely restored building. Here there are concerts in summer and an opportunity for the island's *beau monde* to meet. Nearer to the pier on Nisan Cad. the once-splendid Splendid Palace Hotel is a fine example of faded grandeur. The large domes of the roof cleverly conceal the hotel's water tanks. Take a drink on the terrace to enjoy the view over the Sea of Marmara, in the company of large numbers of elderly ladies who spend their summers here accompanied by daughters or nurses. There are four churches, one Armenian, one Catholic and two Greek Orthodox. For a slightly more energetic tour of the island, hire a bicycle and set off to explore; the far end of Büyükada is both beautiful and very pleasantly quiet after the bustle of town. If cycling anticlockwise, from the far end onwards a long slope downwards means you can freewheel much of the way back to town.

A half hour's walk uphill from the town centre brings you to the Monastery of the Transfiguration (of obscure origins) on the top of Isa Tepe (Isa means Christ), one of the island's two hills. Try ringing the bell, for you may be allowed in to see the nineteenth century church. Once a year, on 6 August, the Patriarch visits this church. At the island's waist is Luna Park, which is as far as the Küçük Tour will take you if you have hired a phaeton. From here a fairly steep path leads up to the church of St George. His name day, 23 April, is a big day when hundreds still flock here, Greeks and Turks alike, tying ribbons on the bushes along the way. In summer this can be a hot and sticky walk, but the presence of a small restaurant at the top where you can get a nice bottle of Imroz wine and a meal makes the journey well worthwhile. (Phone Yüce Tepe Restaurant on 3821333 to check that it is open out of season.) The church is next door and opening hours are posted up; you may be allowed to see inside the monastery building, which is mainly modern. Built on a number of different levels, there is an *ayazma* (holy well) inside and a number of chapels.

From here look for the enormous wooden building on the ridge; built in 1898 by Count Moris Bostari as a hotel, operating permission was refused and it came into the hands of a philanthropist who made an orphanage of it. Now on the point of collapse, it is still an impressive sight and is apparently the largest wooden building in the world. The deserted southern end of the island is lovely countryside with good views over the sea. (If cycling, allow five hours for a leisurely ride with lunch at Yüce Tepe Restaurant).

Other islands at which the ferry does not stop are Yassi, Sedef and Tarsan. Yassi (formerly called Plate, meaning 'flat') has a grim tale. It was here that Adrian Menderes, Turkish Prime Minister from 1950–60, was held during his trial and until his execution in 1961. Sedef (mother-of-pearl, formerly the island of Terebinthos) was also a place of exile, which housed a monastery. It still has houses on it and can be visited by boat. Tarsan also once had a monastery, but it is now uninhabited.

PRACTICAL
MATTERS

Istanbul: basic information

TRAVEL

Spring and autumn are probably the best times to visit Istanbul, but those who don't mind the heat may well prefer summer. With all the water surrounding the city there is often a refreshing breeze to blow the heat away. Winter can be miserable as chilly winds blow down the Bosphorus from the Black Sea.

For Europeans, a visit to the city can be fitted into a long week-end, although there is always more to see in Istanbul and a fortnight could easily be spent soaking up its many sights and sounds.

Istanbul is two hours ahead of the UK, seven hours ahead of New York.

The Turkish Tourist Office is at 170/173 Piccadilly, London WIV 9DD. Tel: 020 7629 7771, Fax: 020 7491 0773.

Turkish Airlines (THY) and British Airways have scheduled daily flights to Istanbul from London. Travel agencies may well have cheaper deals. There are also many charter flights in summer. Visitors may find that a package holiday is cheaper than the cost of arranging a holiday oneself.

VISAS

These can be issued on arrival at the airport. Currently, visitors from most English-speaking countries need visas. Ring your local Turkish consulate, embassy or tourist office for details. Visas cost £10 or $20 and are valid for three months. Passports should be valid for at least six months if a visa is to be issued on arrival.

CURRENCY

The national currency is the Turkish lira. Due to inflation the rate is constantly changing and visitors must learn to grapple with the millions involved even in small transactions. The notes are easily confused so do make sure that you are not inadvertently paying with the wrong note. Traveller's cheques, pounds sterling, euros and US dollars are widely accepted and there are ATM machines where cash may be withdrawn. Banks usually close during lunch-time, but Foreign Exchange centres, which may well offer a better deal for currency, tend to stay open. Rates can vary considerably so shop around.

ARRIVING

A taxi from the airport to the city centre should not cost more than £15; make sure the meter is on before you start. You can check prices at the Information point in the Arrivals Hall. The Turkish Airways shuttle bus (the Havas bus) takes about 30 minutes outside the rush hour and calls at Aksaray and Taksim (it leaves for the airport from outside the THY offices at the Taksim end of Cumhuriyet Cad.).

DISABLED VISITORS
Facilities for the disabled are extremely poor. Wheelchair access to many sites, museums and mosques is difficult if not impossible, although staff are usually very helpful. Check such facilities with hotels before arrival.

WOMEN VISITORS
Women visitors should make sure that they are appropriately dressed before entering mosques: this means no shorts or skimpy tops. A scarf should be taken, though not always required in the biggest mosques, and all visitors must remove their shoes before entering. There are usually racks for shoes. In planning your itinerary for the day try to avoid prayer times; the larger mosques such as the Süleymaniye may well have an area reserved for those at prayer. Please respect these boundaries.

GETTING AROUND ISTANBUL
Many Turks do not speak English. A phrasebook will come in handy and you can also try writing things down for people to read.

Taxis are easy to find and should not be too expensive. Do check that the meter is running once you start. It may also help to have some idea of which direction you should be heading in! If crossing the Bosphorus the toll must be added to the cost.

The **tram** has been one of the success stories of modern Istanbul. It is clean, quick and runs frequently along a route which is useful for tourists. This starts down at Eminönü, running up to Sultanahmet, along Divanyolu Cad. to Aksaray and out along Millet Cad. through the Land Walls to Zeytinburnu. Single tickets can be bought at the *gişe* (ticket kiosk). If you are likely to be using the public transport system frequently then it is worth buying an *akbil*. This is an electronic token for which you pay a deposit and buy a number of units. It can then be topped up at larger *gişes*. The *akbil* can be used on the tram, the metro, Tünel, many buses, and the ferries.

The **metro** currently runs from Aksaray to Esenler bus station, where it forks. It is planned to eventually extend it under the Golden Horn and up through Beyoğlu.

Buses run throughout the city; some are municipal, others belong to private operators. There is a flat-rate charge per journey and on most lines tickets must be bought in advance at a kiosk. Private vendors nearby may also sell tickets at a slightly higher cost.

Dolmuş. This is a shared taxi or minibus which runs along a set route – a card in the window shows the destination. *Dolmuşes* are useful for reaching more distant parts of the city. For example, they run from the city walls into the centre of town (Vezneciler) and along the walls, as well as between Üsküdar and Kadiköy and up the Bosphorus from Taksim.

Trains run from Sirkeci out to the suburbs. If walking the Land Walls, there are frequent trains for Yedikule which take about fifteen minutes. Stations are not well signed so you need to count the stops.

Ferries are still one of the main means of transport and great fun when the weather is good. From Eminönü they run to Üsküdar, Kadiköy, the Princes' Islands (signed Adalar) and up the Bosphorus (signed Boğaz Hatti). Destinations are marked on signs above the pier. From Karaköy on the Galata side they run to Kadiköy, and from Beşiktaş to the Asian shores. There are also tourist boats which go up the Bosphorus from Pier No. 3, stopping at a number of places. You can make one stop along the way and catch another ferry without having to buy another ticket. Unfortunately the pier at Eminönü is thick with ticket touts all trying to sell tickets to tourists, so be prepared for some hassle. There are also some privately operated boats plying the Bosphorus route; prices and service may vary so do be careful. For ordinary ferries the *akbil* may be used, otherwise a jeton may be bought inside the terminal.

Sea buses are catamarans which run summer services from Kabataş to Büyükada on the Princes' Islands. They are more expensive than the ferries.

Accommodation

A wide range of accommodation is available in Istanbul, from hostels to five-star hotels. Sultanahmet is the main tourist district; here you are within walking distance of sites like St Sophia, the Blue Mosque and the Topkapı Palace. Many luxury hotels are located either near Taksim Square within easy reach of the shops, bars and restaurants along Istiklal Cad. or further up the Bosphorus on the European side. For something with a bit more atmosphere, there are now a number of nicely restored old wooden houses operating as hotels, mainly in the Sultanahmet area; these are known as Special Licence hotels. The following is a selection of hotels in the most popular districts in and around Istanbul.

SULTANAHMET

Four Seasons
Tevkifhane Sok. 1
Tel: (0)212 6388200
Fax: (0)212 6388210
Website: www.fourseasons.com/istanbul/
The old prison below St Sophia, beautifully converted, excellent restaurant.

Celal Sultan
Salkımsöğüt Sok. 16
Off Yerebatan Cad.
Tel: (0)212 5209323/24
Fax: (0)212 5229724
E-mail: info@celalsultan.com
Website: www.celalsultan.com
Small but pleasant old house with lovely rooftop terrace views of St Sophia.

Ayasofya Pansiyonları
Soğukçeşme Sok.
Tel: (0)212 5133660
Fax: (0)212 5140213
E-mail: ayapans@escortnet.com.tr
Website: www.ayasofya-pansiyonlari.com
In a street of old houses near Topkapı, these tastefully refurbished houses are on the expensive side but well located.

Amber Hotel
Meydanı Yusuf Askin Sok. 28
Tel: (0)212 5184801
Fax: (0)212 5188119
Several refurbished houses near the railway and the Sea Walls.

Arcadia
Dr. Imren Oktem Cad. I
Off Divan Yohu
Tel: (0)212 5169696
Fax: (0)212 5166118
Converted 19C building with comfortable rooms. Spectacular views of St Sophia and the Blue Mosque from the rooftop restaurant/breakfast room.

Avicenna
Amiral Tafdil Sok. 31/33
Tel: (0)212 5170550
Fax: (0)212 5166555 and 5183964
E-mail: avicenna@superonline.com
Website: www.avicennahotel.com
Old clapboard house with pleasant restaurant looking on to the Sea of Marmara.

Sümengen Obelisk
Amiral Tafdil Sok. 17/19
Tel: (0)212 5177173
Fax: (0)212 5176871
E-mail:
obelisksumengen@superonline.com
Website: www.obelisksumengen.com
Slightly cheaper version of the Avicenna; two converted 19C wooden houses with back rooms and views on to the Sea of Marmara.

Arena Hotel
Üçler Hammam Sok. 13/15
Tel: (0)212 4580364/65
Fax: (0)212 4580366
E-mail: arena@arenahotel.com
Website: www.arenahotel.com
New hotel on the dearer side, below the Hippodrome, with good-sized rooms and pleasant management.

Yeşil Ev
Kabasakal Cad. 5
Tel: (0)212 5176785/6/7/8
Fax: (0)212 5176780
E-mail: yesilevhotel@superonline.com
*In a prime location between the Blue
Mosque and St Sophia. Sets the trend
for Ottoman house conservation; a fine
replica of the original (too dilapidated to
save). Quiet courtyard restaurant.*

Merit Antique
Ordu Cad. 226
Tel: (0)212 5139300
Fax: (0)212 5126390
*Near Laleli Mosque. Early 20C blocks
with roofed-over courtyards, now a
luxury hotel. Rather expensive.*

Ibrahim Pasha Hotel
Terzihane Sok. 5
Tel: (0)212 5180394
Fax: (0)212 5184457
E-mail: pasha@ibm.net
Website: www.ibrahimpasha.com
*Small, well-located hotel with friendly
staff, but rooms are small.*

Kybele Hotel
Mimar Mehmet Ağa Cad. 32/34
Tel: (0)212 5117766/67
Fax: (0)212 5134393
*Very tastefully decorated small hotel near
Yerebatan, with enticing lamp shop below.*

Hotel Nomade
Ticarethane Sok. 15
Tel: (0)212 5111296
Fax: (0)212 5132404
E-mail: nomade@bm.net.tr
*Pleasant cheaper hotel off Divan Yolu,
with rooftop terrace.*

Hotel Hippodrome
Mimar Mehmet Ağa Cad. 17
Tel: (0)212 5176889
Fax: (0)212 5160268
*Cheaper hotel with rooftop terrace behind
the Blue Mosque.*

Arasta Guest House
Mimar Mehmet Ağa Cad. 32/34
Tel: (0)212 5162320
Fax: (0)212 6383104
Cheap accommodation with pleasant café.

Youth Hostel
Caferiye Sok. 6/1
Tel: (0)212 5136150/51
Fax: (0)212 5127628
*Clean, friendly, efficient with all facilities,
and excellent value for money. Book ahead.*

Sultanahmet Sarayı Hotel
Torun Sok. 19, 3400 Sultanahmet
Tel: (0)212 4580460
Fax: (0)212 5186224
E-mail: saray@sultanahmetpalace.com
Website: www.sultanahmetpalace.com
*Elegant 19C mansion converted to a
sophisticated hotel in the heart of
Sultanahmet. The 36 rooms each have a
traditional Turkish bath and views across
the Sea of Marmara or of the Blue Mosque.*

Hotel Armada
Ahırkapı, 3400 Istanbul
Tel: (0)212 6381370
Fax: (0)212 5185060
E-mail: info@armadahotel.com.tr
Website: www.armadahotel.com.tr
Well-appointed larger hotel located near the Sea of Marmara alongside the Byzantine city walls. Wonderful views of the Blue Mosque and St Sophia from the roof terrace.

BEYOĞLU/GALATA

Intercontinental
Asker Ocağı Cad. 1
Tel: (0)212 2312121
Fax: (0)212 2312180
Top of the 5-star range. City Lights, the top-floor cocktail bar, has excellent views over the water in all directions.

Pera Palas
Meşrutiyet Cad. 98/100
Tel: (0)212 2514560
Fax: (0)212 2514089
E-mail: perapalas@perapalas.com
Website: www.perapalas.com
Agatha Christie was among visitors who arrived on the Orient Express to stay here. A must, if only for a drink, to see the décor and the lovely old lift. Wonderful breakfasts.

Richmond
Istiklal Cad. 445
Tel: (0)212 2525460
Fax: (0)212 2529707
Nicely converted building on the main road, with a good coffee bar and patisserie on the ground floor.

Büyük Londra
Meşrutiyet Cad. 117
Tel: (0)212 2450670
Fax: (0)212 2450671
Just up the road from the Pera Palas, this has a great façade complete with caryatids. Shabby splendour inside. Ask for a room on the front, for views over the Golden Horn.

Galata Residence
Hacı Ali Sok., near Voyvoda Cad.
Tel: (0)212 2924841
Fax: (0)212 2442323
E-mail: galataresidence@galataresidencehotel.com
Website: www.galataresidencehotel.com
Aparthotel in Galata, off Karaköy Square, well-appointed but not cheap. On the site of the former residence of a prominent Jewish banking family, and one of the earliest apartment buildings in Istanbul.

BEYOND

Kariye
Kariye Camii Sok. 18
Tel: (0)212 5348414
Fax: (0)212 5216631
E-mail: kariyeotel@superonline.com
A quiet option next to Chora Church and some way from the centre of town, the Kariye is another restored wooden house. From here, the Land Walls and Mihrimah Camii may easily be visited.

Çirağan Palace

Çirağan Cad. 84 Beşiktaş
Tel: (0)212 2583377
Fax: (0)212 2596686
E-mail: ciragan@ciraganpalace.com.tr
Website: www.ciragan-palace.com
*Probably the most luxurious of Istanbul's
hotels. For those who cannot afford to stay
in this beautifully restored waterside
palace, brunch or a drink may suffice.*

Halki Palace

Refah Şehitleri Cad. 88, Heybeliada
Tel: (0)216 3510025
Fax: (0)216 3518483
*Best and most relaxing place to stay on
the Islands – a large mansion with
gardens, sea view and small pool – a
15-minute walk from the ferry.*

Saydam Planet

Iskele Meydam, Büyükada
Tel: (0)216 3822670
Fax: (0)216 3823848
*Newly converted to a family-run hotel,
opposite the landing stage, with bar below.
Rooms are comfortable and spacious. Not
cheap, but a good option.*

Splendid Palace

23 Nisan Cad. 71, Büyükada
Tel: (0)216 3826950
Fax: (0)216 3826775
*Once splendid and still redolent of the
grand old days, now the summer haunt of
elderly widows. Fair price, usually full,
swimming pool.*

Food and restaurants

Eating out in Istanbul is a delight; Turkish food draws on different cultural traditions to produce a delicious variety of dishes. Burger culture may be on the rise, but has yet to make serious inroads into Turkish eating habits, and fresh food bought from the market predominates. Restaurant prices are very reasonable by European standards, even at the top of the range. Istanbul has something for all palates and pockets. Fish, lamb and chicken (as a Muslim country, pork is avoided), vegetable dishes, fruit and puddings are all to be had in abundance. The Turks are very fond of *meze*s (starters) and good restaurants offer a mouth-watering range of hot and cold starters from which you are expected to take your pick. For vegetarians there are a number of meatless dishes. Although many restaurants now add a service charge, tipping is still a custom.

Restaurants are called either *lokanta* or *restoran*. A proper restaurant will serve a selection of cold and hot *meze*s, followed by fish or meat cooked to order, fruit and coffee. Some specialize in meat, others in fish, of which there is a huge variety. 'Counter' restaurants have pre-cooked dishes on display, from which you take your pick. As menus are not a Turkish tradition, they are found only in tourist areas. *Meyhane*s (taverns) are another Turkish institution; traditionally, these are serious men-only drinking haunts. In Istanbul many have gone upmarket and not only admit women, but also provide an excellent meal to be washed down with quantities of *rakı*. Kebab houses are everywhere, less common are the *işkembeci*, which serve offal, in particular tripe soup which is renowned as a cure for hangovers! Turkish pizza is called *pide* and *lamacun* is a kind of *pide* topped with mincemeat, onions and tomatoes. *Mantı* is a ravioli served warm with yoghurt. There are also pudding shops (*muhallebici*) which offer milk and rice puddings and even one made out of chicken! In the streets little boys hawk *simit*, sesame coated bread rings delicious when fresh. Sweets like baklava and other pastries, not forgetting *halva* and Turkish Delight (*lokum*) are popular, and the ice cream man in his colourful costume and great tub of *dondurma* (ice cream) is a familiar figure in the streets of Istanbul.

Alcohol is easily obtained in Turkey, but is not served in all restaurants and certainly not in those linked to mosque complexes. Beer and wine (*şarap*) are produced locally, as is *rakı*, a grape spirit flavoured with aniseed, which is drunk with ice and water. Unusual non-alcoholic drinks include *salep*, a warming winter drink made from ground orchid root, and *boza*, the drink of the Janissaries, a fermented millet concoction not unlike semolina. *Ayran*, a refreshing yoghurt drink can be bought in cartons. Coffee is a great tradition: small cups of black coffee are served sweet (*şekerli*), medium (*orta*) or without sugar (*sade*). Sweet tea is drunk in small glasses, and fruit juices are also available.

Four Seasons
Tevkifhane Sok. 1
Tel: (0)212 6388200
In the courtyard of the hotel behind St Sophia, excellent chef.

Yeşil Ev
Kabasakal Cad. 5
Tel: (0)212 5176785
Hotel bar and restaurant in shady courtyard near Hippodrome.

Ayasofya Büfesi
Yerebatan Cad. 58
Fresh orange juice near the Byzantine cistern.

Sultanahmet Köfteci
Divan Yolu Cad. 12
Excellent service, good lunch break – köfte highly recommended; many locals eat here.

Darüzziyafe
Şifahane Cad. 6
Tel: (0)212 5118414
Former imaret of the Süleymaniye complex, no alcohol. Tables around the courtyard, fair prices.

Zeyrekhane
Opposite Pantocrator Church
Tel: (0)212 5322778
Wonderful views of Süleymaniye, no alcohol.

Pandeli
Spice Market
Tel: (0)212 5273909
Turkish tiles and reasonable food above the Spice Market.

Hamdi Et
Kalcin Sok., near Spice Market
Tel: (0)212 5280390
Great Turkish lunch place for tired shoppers with lots of kebabs.

Merit Antique
Ordu Cad. 226
Tel: (0)212 5139300
Kosher, Chinese, Italian and Turkish restaurants at 5-star prices.

Şehzade Mehmet
Tel: (0)212 5262668
Former medrese of the Şehzade Mosque, tables round the courtyard; excellent lunch venue with good traditional Turkish cuisine, but no alcohol.

Balikci Sabahattin
Cankurtaran and Sehit Hasan Kuyu Sok.
Tel: (0)212 4581824
Very good fish restaurant near the railway and Sea Walls, not cheap.

Armada Bahce
Tel: (0)212 6381370
(specify Armada Bahce Restaurant)
Walled courtyard by the Armada Hotel open only in summer; good food, lovely atmosphere and fair prices.

Kumkapı
Numerous fish restaurants in the old port area, now very touristy.

Magnaura
Akbiyik Cad. 27
Tel: (0)212 5187622
Reasonably priced European-style menu (salads, espresso coffee) but rather smoky.

Café Du Levant
Hasköy Cad. 27
Tel: (0)212 2508938
Next to the Koç Museum, a delicious meal in this French café/restaurant is an excellent end to a morning in the museum.

Med Cizir Café
Tevfikhane Sok.
Tel: (0)212 5172267
Pleasant, small café/bar opposite the Four Seasons hotel.

Konyalı
Tel: (0)212 5139696
*Expensive café/restaurant in the Topkapı
Palace, but with lovely views across the
water to the Asian side.*

BEYOĞLU

Boncuk
Nevizade Sok. 19
Tel: (0)212 2431219
*Less touristy than Çiçek Pasaji, this
restaurant in a street of meyhanes has an
excellent selection of starters and service
with a smile. Many Turks eat here.*

Refik
Sofyalı Sok. 10–12
Tel: (0)212 2432834
*Friendly owner, wide range of Black Sea
mezes. Sit in the little back-street in
summer in this quaint district.*

Yakup 2
Asmalımescit Cad. 35/7
Tel: (0)212 2492925
*Similar to Refiks, good food, but on the
expensive side.*

Rejans
Emir Nevruz Sok. 17
Tel: (0)212 2441610
*Something of an institution after many
years here, a Russian restaurant off
Istiklal Cad. Lemon vodka a speciality.*

Zindan
Olivia Han Gecidi
Tel: (0)212 2527340
*Friendly basement restaurant near
Rejans with reasonably priced set menu.*

Haci Abdullah
Sakizagaci Cad. 17, Istiklal Cad.
Tel: (0)212 2938561
*No alcohol, but traditional Ottoman
cuisine and efficient service.*

Pano
Hamalbaşı Cad. 26
Tel: (0)212 2926664/5
*A long-established winery run by a Greek
family, wonderful atmosphere if crowded.
Opposite British Consulate.*

Haci Baba
Istiklal Cad.
Tel: (0)212 2441886
*Always busy, choose from the counter and
the wide range available.*

Saray
Istiklal Cad. 102
Tel: (0)212 2923434
Good pudding shop.

Gramofon
Tünel Meydanı 3
*Café/bar at the end of Istiklal Cad. where
you can often find late night jazz after a
meal out.*

My Moon
Bekar Sok. 18
Tel: (0)212 2431108
Friendly modern café/bar off Istiklal Cad., sometimes has live music and entertainment.

Çep Sanat Galarisi
Sweet little teahouse amid the art galleries of Sofyalı Sok. near Refiks. Beer and snacks also available.

Kelif
Just off Sofyalı Sok.
Tel: (0)212 2921609
Opposite Çep Sanat, quiet back street, good service, vegetarian option available.

Nature And Peace
Büyük Parmakapı Sok. 21–23
Tel: (0)212 2528609
Old-style vegetarian dishes, friendly and popular, off Istiklal Cad.

EYÜP

Mihmandar
On the central square
Tel: (0)212 6125998
Spacious clean restaurant and garden with good food for very reasonable prices.

BOSPHORUS

Malta Köşk
Tel: (0)216 3410483
In the grounds of Yıldız Park above the Çirağan; a delightfully restored 19C villa, once the property of the sultan. An excellent place for breakfast or lunch, with a shady terrace which looks out over the Bosphorus.

Cadir Köşk
Pretty pink pavilion offering teas, coffees, cakes and ice creams on the terrace.

ÜSKÜDAR

Kız Kulesi
Tel: (0)216 3410403
On the coast road towards Kadiköy, a good place to eat fish and enjoy the views.

Kanaat
Selmanipak Cad. 25
Tel: (0)216 3333791
Family run business near the market, always busy and good Turkish food.

KADIKÖY/MODA

Koco
Moda Cad. 265
Tel: (0)216 3360795
Extremely popular Greek-run restaurant with delicious food and a holy well in the basement. Sit on the terrace overlooking the sea.

Baylan Pastanesi
Muvakkithane Cad. 19, Kadiköy
Tel: (0)216 3466350
Greek coffee house and patisserie with a long history as meeting place of Istanbul artists and intellectuals.

PRINCES' ISLANDS

Başak
Seafront restaurant, Heybeli
Tel: (0)216 3511289
Excellent meal, imaginative food all for very reasonable prices.

Other practical matters

LANGUAGE

Turkish belongs to the Turkic family of languages, which are spoken by well over 100 million people from south-east Europe to China. Since the time of Atatürk it has used the Latin alphabet, while under the Ottomans it was written in Arabic script. Many words are Arabic in origin. Most letters of its alphabet are recognizable; some have umlauts, as in German, others are specific to Turkish. It is an 'agglutinating' language, in which prefixes, infixes and suffixes are attached to a root, and it has a certain melody because of vowel harmony rules. With a small dictionary and phrasebook it is possible to learn a little Turkish during your stay: any attempt at speaking Turkish will be warmly welcomed.

BATHS

Prices should be posted near the entrance, check rather than ask (they may rise spontaneously on sight of a tourist). The women's section may well have a separate entrance. Allow two hours for a relaxing experience. English will probably be spoken only at the bigger baths. Lockers, towels, slippers and soap should be provided, though you may want to take your own shampoo. Evenings are the busiest times. The routine is to sweat in the hot room, then have a scrub to get rid of a layer or two of skin, and then a massage. In between, rest and wash. Finish with a rest in the camekan or entrance room; feeling squeaky clean and relaxed you should sleep well that night. Here are a few addresses:

- Çemberlitaş Baths, Vezirhanı Cad. 8: One of the most popular with tourists, open till midnight, separate sections for men and women.
- Cağaloğlu Baths, Prof Kazim İsmail Gürkan Cad. 34: 18C baths with separate sections for men and women. Very much on the tourist beat.
- Gedikpaşa Baths, Hamam Cad. 65–67 Gedikpaşa: One of the oldest *hammam*s in the city, built in 1475. Off the beaten track on the way down to Kumkapı, and consequently a lot cheaper.
- Turnaçıbaşı Baths, off Istiklal Cad.: On the expensive side, but clean. Try bargaining.

MUSEUMS, CASTLES AND PALACES

Museums and, more particularly, palaces may charge extra if a camera is to be taken in, and there are even higher rates for video cameras. The alternative is to leave them at the entrance and collect them on exit. Museums are mostly closed on Mondays.

Archaeological Museum

9.30 am–4.30 pm, closed Tuesdays
A must on any visit to Istanbul, this stunning collection contains a wealth of artefacts and information from the past. Highlights include the Alexander Sarcophagus and the Çinili Kiosk. Unfortunately, at any one time a number of sections are liable to be closed due to financial constraints and rearrangement. Check before purchasing tickets whether the Çinili Kiosk is open.

Topkapı Palace Museum

9.30 am–5.00 pm, closed Tuesdays, Harem is open 10.00 am–4.00 pm
A treasure house of a museum full of wonders, priceless collections of ceramics, Turkish miniatures, Ottoman arms, jewellery and Iznik tiles in the buildings of the palace, also the harem.

St Sophia

9.00 am–4.30 pm, closed Mondays
Having been both church and mosque, St Sophia is now a museum.

Museum of Turkish and Islamic Art

9.00 am–4.30 pm, closed Mondays
Housed in the palace of Ibrahim Pasha overlooking the Hippodrome, good on textiles and carpets and with a good arts bookshop.

Mosaic Museum

Arasta Sok., behind the Blue Mosque
9.00 am–4.30 pm, closed Mondays
Houses the Byzantine mosaics which once paved the peristyle of the Great Palace.

Calligraphy Museum

Beyazıt Square
9.00 am–4.00 pm, closed Sundays and Mondays
In part of the complex of the Beyazidiye.

Museum of Cartoon and Humour, Kovacilar Sok.

Open 10.00 am–6.00 pm daily
Delightful little museum in the medrese of the White Ağa's mosque which nestles up against the Aqueduct of Valens near the colourful meat-market on Itfaiye Sok.

Fire Brigade Museum

Free. Closed Sundays
Itfaiye Sok. next to fire station. 2 rooms of 18C–20C fire wagons, carts and pumps polished up to the nines.

Church of St Saviour in Chora

9.30 am–4.30 pm, closed Tuesdays
Wonderful mosaics and frescoes in this eleventh-century Byzantine church, not to be missed on any trip to Istanbul.

Military Museum

Vali Konaği Cad.

9.00 am–5.00 pm, closed Tuesdays

Enormous museum, the impressive Janissary band plays there 3-4 pm daily. The singers, horns, drums and cymbals make a terrific spectacle. The huge cannons used in the siege of Constantinople are there, also a range of swords, shields, firearms and tents.

Naval Museum, Beşiktaş

9.00 am–12.30 pm,
1.30 pm–5.00 pm, closed Wednesdays and Thursdays

Most interesting for the collection of sultans' galleys and caiques housed in the first section.

Rahmi M. Koç Museum

Hasköy Cad., Golden Horn

10.00 am–5.00 pm, closed Mondays

An old anchor foundry beautifully converted by one of Turkey's wealthiest entrepreneurs, this collection focuses on science and technology and has the added benefit of an excellent French restaurant next door. Pride of place is given to steam engines.

Sadberk Hanım Museum

Piyasa Cad., Büyükdere

A family collection in two yalis by the Bosphorus at Büyükdere. Combines well with a trip up the straits by boat.

Sabancı Museum

Emirgan

10.00 am–6.00 pm weekdays,
11.00 am–5.00 pm weekends,
closed Mondays

Collection of Ottoman calligraphy and 19C-20C Turkish painting in Bosphorus mansion.

Yıldız Palace Museum

Open 9.00 am–4.00 pm,
closed Mondays

Dull collection of Yıldız porcelain on one side, City museum on the other, neither very interesting. What is worth a visit is the sultan's theatre beyond Kücük Mabeyn. Brave the staff and ask for it to be opened – the little theatre, built in 1889, is beautifully decorated.

Yıldız: Şale Kiosk

Rather ugly, rambling 'Swiss Chalet'. A guide will give you the tour, but may not speak English.

Dolmabahçe Palace

9.00 am–4.00 pm, closed Mondays and Thursdays

Grandiose nineteenth-century pile by the water, guided visits only.

Beylerbey Palace

9.30 am–5.00 pm, guided visits only, closed Mondays and Thursdays

Prime waterside location with pretty gardens although now overshadowed by the bridge. Gilt furniture, Bohemian glass chandeliers and Hereke carpets, all that money could buy.

Ihlamur Kasrı
Ihlamur Tesvikiye Yolu
9.30 am–5.00 pm, closed
Mondays and Thursdays
'Pavilion of the linden tree', highly
baroque in style near the fashionable
Maçka district.

Aynalıkavak, Golden Horn
9.00 am–4.00 pm, closed
Mondays and Thursdays
Once, this charming pavilion was a place
of retreat and relaxation, now it is
hemmed in by industrial buildings and
the views of the Golden Horn are blocked
by shipyards. Houses a collection of
musical instruments.

Küçüksu
9.30 am–5.00 pm, closed
Mondays and Thursdays
Former hunting lodge converted to a
rococo jewel, on the Asian side of the
Bosphorus. Guided visits only.

Rumeli Hisarı
Closed Wednesdays
Mehmet's Bosphorus castle, built with
astonishing speed for the siege of
Constantinople. Prison and fortress in the
Land Walls with a grim history.

COMMUNICATIONS
The code for Turkey is 90. Istanbul
area code is (0)212 for the European side and (0)216 for the Asian
side. Phone cards are now widely
available and are the best deal as
hotel charges are often high. Cards

can be bought at the Post Office and
at some street kiosks. For directory
enquiries phone 118.

The central Post Office (a grandiose, turn-of-the-century block) is
in Sirkecı on Mevlana Sok./Büyük
Postahane. Note the art deco Flora
Han on the other side of the street
towards Sirkecı Station. There is
also a Post Office off DivanYolu in
Imran Okret Cad. (in the basement
of a government building), and
another on Istiklal Cad.

There is no shortage of internet
cafés in Istanbul.

Emergency Numbers:

Police	155
Ambulance	112
Fire	110
Tourist police	
(Yerebatan Cad.)	(0)212 5274503

Tourist Information Offices:

Atatürk Airport	(0)212 6630793
Sirkeci Station	(0)212 5115888
Divanyolu Cad. 3	(0)212 5181802
Hilton Hotel	
Arcade	(0)212 2330592
Karakoy Sea Port	(0)212 2495776

LEAVING TURKEY
Remember to confirm your flight
before departure. Allow plenty of
time at the airport as queues are
long and there are security checks
too. The phone number for British
Airways in Istanbul is **0212 2341100**;
Turkish Airlines is on **0212 6636363**.

APPENDICES

Glossary of Ottoman and architectural terms

Apse – *semicircular end of church or chapel.*

Ayazma – *sacred well or spring.*

Baptistery – *part of church containing the font, often separate.*

Barbican – *fortified gatehouse.*

Bedesten – *market building for safe storage of goods, usually domed.*

Caique – *skiff or rowing boat used on the Bosphorus and Golden Horn.*

Camekan – *disrobing room of a Turkish bath.*

Cami, Camii – *mosque.*

Caravansaray – *roadside inn.*

Çarşı – *market.*

Çeşme – *drinking fountain.*

Chancel – *east end of church, reserved for the clergy, site of the altar.*

Chevron – *decorative element forming a zigzag.*

Cornice – *moulding running along the top of a wall or arch.*

Daruşşifa – *hospital, part of a mosque complex.*

Dershane – *lecture hall in a mosque school.*

Devşirme – *levy of young Christian boys for service in the Ottoman Empire.*

Divan – *Ottoman state council which met in the Topkapı Palace to deliberate on administrative and legal affairs.*

Exonarthex – *outer narthex.*

Firman – *Ottoman imperial decree.*

Hammam, Hamam – *Turkish baths, sometimes part of a mosque foundation.*

Han – *commercial inn with accomodation for merchants and facilities for storage, sale and manufacture of goods.*

Harem – *female part of a house or palace, strictly private.*

Haremlık – *private rooms of a house or palace where the women of a household live.*

Haseki – *sultan's favourite concubine.*

Hippodrome – *large arena for chariot racing, also used for other entertainment, called* Atmeydan *in Turkish.*

Iconostasis – *in Orthodox Christian architecture, a screen across the chancel.*

Imaret – *mosque kitchen.*

Ka'ba – *holy shrine at Mecca into which the black stone is built.*

Kapı – *gate.*

Kathisma – *royal box in the Hippodrome.*

Kiosk – *Ottoman pavilion.*

Kösk – *Turkish for kiosk.*

Külliye – *dependencies of a mosque complex, e.g. library, hospice, kitchens.*

Kütüphane – *library.*

Lunette – *semicircular space between a doorway and the arch above.*

Martyrium – *church or chapel usually containing the bones of a martyr, often circular.*

Medrese – *mosque school or college.*

Mekteb – *primary school.*

Mihrab – *niche in the qibla wall of a mosque which indicates the direction of Mecca.*

Minaret – *spire of a mosque from which the müezzin gives the call to prayer; only imperial mosques were entitled to more than one.*

Minber – *pulpit of a mosque, usually to the right of the mihrab.*

Müezzin – *cleric who calls the people to prayer from the minaret.*

Muqarnas – *decorative honeycomb mouldings typically found over niches and on capitals.*

Narthex – *transverse vestibule at the entrance to a church, west of nave and aisles.*

Nave – *central division of a church, usually flanked by aisles.*

Ocak – *hooded fireplace or hearth; also, division of the Janissary corps.*

Opus Sectile – *decorative stone or marble paving laid in geometric shapes.*

Parecclesion – *funerary chapel attached to church.*

Pendentive – *corner support for a dome over a square room, thus ensuring the transition from the square to the round.*

Pier – *square or rectangular free-standing support.*

Portico – *roofed porch or walkway, often supported by columns.*

Qibla – *wall of the mosque which faces Mecca and therefore has the mihrab placed in it.*

Şadırvan – *courtyard fountain.*

Saray – *palace.*

Sebil – *water tank with grilled windows from which an attendant would offer water to passers-by.*

Selamlık – *male or public rooms of a house or palace.*

Semahane – *dervish dance hall.*

Şerefe – *minaret balcony from which the müezzin calls the faithful to prayer.*

Şeyh ül-Islam – *head of the Islamic clergy in Istanbul, Grand Mufti.*

Soffit – *underside of an architectural element.*

Squinch – *arch placed, like a pendentive, in the corner of a room to bear the dome.*

Tabhane – *hospice, accommodation provided in a mosque for dervishes, free for three days.*

Taksim – *water distribution point.*

Tekke – *dervish lodge.*

Timarhane – *lunatic asylum or hospital.*

Tuğra – *sultan's signature, a highly decorative motif.*

Türbe – *tomb or mausoleum.*

Tympanum – *semicircular space between lintel and arch.*

Valide Sultan – *mother of the reigning sultan.*

Voussoir – *stones of an arch.*

Yalı – *Ottoman mansion, especially along the Bosphorus.*

Useful words and phrases

FOOD
Cold mezes
Bamya – *okra*

Beyaz peynir – *white goat, sheep or cow's cheese*

Biber dolması – *stuffed capsicums*

Cacık – *tzatsiki*

Humus – *chickpea paste*

Imam Bayıldı – *(the imam fainted), aubergine filled with onions and tomatoes*

Midye dolması – *stuffed mussels*

Patates – *potatoes*

Patlıcan salatası – *baked aubergines with yoghurt*

Yaprak dolması – *stuffed vine leaves*

Zeytin – *olives*

Zeytinağlı fasulya – *green beans in olive oil*

Hot mezes
Börek (peynirli, etli, ispanaklı) – *flaky pastry stuffed with cheese, meat or spinach*

Kalamar – *fried squid*

Çorba – *soup*
Domates çorbası – *tomato soup*

Işkembe çorbası – *tripe soup*

Mercimek çorbası – *lentil soup*

Sebze çorbası – *vegetable soup*

Salata – *salad*
Çoban salata – *shepherd's salad*

Domates – *tomatoes*

Mevsim salatası – *seasonal salad*

Meat
Döner kebab – *slices of lamb carved from a spit*

Işkembe – *tripe*

Köfte (izgara) – *meatballs (grilled)*

Kuzu – *lamb*

Şiş kebab – *lamb and tomatoes grilled on a skewer*

Tavuk – *chicken*

Balık – *Fish*
Alabalık – *trout*

Barbunya – *red mullet*

Hamsi – *anchovies*

Kalkan – *turbot*

Kılıç – *swordfish*

Levrek – *sea bass*

Lüfer – *bluefish*

Mercan – *bream*

Palamut – *bonito*

Miscellaneous
Biber – *pepper*

Ekmek – *bread*

Lahmacun – *Turkish pizza (with minced meat, tomatoes and onion)*

Mantı – *ravioli in yoghurt sauce*

Pide – *a kind of pizza*

Pilav – *rice*

Şeker – *sugar*

Tuz – *salt*

Yumurta – *eggs*

Meyve – *Fruit*
Elma – *apple*

Erik – *plum*

Karpuz – *watermelon*

Kiraz – *cherry*

Muz – *banana*

Portakal – *orange*
Şeftali – *peach*
Üzüm – *grape*

Tatlı – *Puddings*
Aşure – *dried fruit and beans*
Kazandibi – *milky pudding sprinkled with cinnamon*
Keşkül – *blancmange*
Krem Şokola – *chocolate blancmange*
Muhallebi – *white, corn-starch pudding with rose water and lots of icing sugar*
Sütlaç – *cold rice pudding*
Tavuk göğsü – *'chicken breast' pudding*

Drinks
Ayran – *cold yoghurt drink*
Bira – *beer*
Boza – *fermented millet drink*
Çay – *tea*
Kahve – *coffee*
Meyve suyu (portakal, elma, vişne) – *fruit juice (orange, apple, sour cherry)*
Rakı – *grape spirit flavoured with aniseed*
Salep – *hot drink made from ground orchid root*
Şarap (kırmızı or beyaz) – *wine (red or white)*
Su – *water*
Süt – *milk*

GENERAL
Numbers
Bir – *one*
Iki – *two*
Üç – *three*
Dört – *four*
Beş – *five*
Altı – *six*
Yedi – *seven*
Sekiz – *eight*
Dokuz – *nine*
On – *ten*
On bir – *eleven*
Yirmi – *twenty*
Yirmi bir – *twenty-one*
Otuz – *thirty*
Kırk – *forty*
Elli – *fifty*
Altmış – *sixty*
Yetmiş – *seventy*
Seksen – *eighty*
Doksan – *ninety*
Yüz – *hundred*
Yüz elli – *one hundred and fifty*
Iki yüz – *two hundred*
Bin – *thousand*
Üç bin üç – *three thousand and three*
Bir milyon – *one million*

Useful phrases
Yes – *evet*
No – *hayır*
Please – *lütfen*
Thank you (very much) – *(çok) tesekkür ederim*
Don't mention it – *bir sey değil*
Do you speak English? – *ingilizce biliyor musunuz?*

I don't speak Turkish – *turkçe bilmiyorum*

I speak a little Turkish – *çok az turkçe biliyorum*

I don't understand – *anlamıyorum*

I'm English – *ben ingilizim*

Good morning – *günaydın*

Good day/afternoon – *iyi günler*

Good evening – *iyi akşamlar*

Goodbye (to someone departing) – *güle güle*

Goodbye (when leaving oneself) – *allahısmarladık*

Very good – *çok güzel*

Welcome – *hoş geldiniz*

'Well found' – *hoş bulduk (the response to welcome)*

How are you? – *nasılsınız?*

I am fine – *iyiyim*

Police – *polis*

Is there a doctor? – *doktor var mı?*

I want a ticket – *bilet istiyorum*

Where is the ticket office? – *gişe nerede?*

After – *sonra*

Now – *şimdi*

What is your name – *adınız ne?*

My name is Jane – *adım Jane*

Okay, fine – *tamam*

Big/little – *büyük/küçük*

What time is it? – *saat kaç?*

It's one o'clock – *saat bir*

Today – *bugün*

Tomorrow – *yarın*

Eating

The bill please – *hesap lütfen*

What is there to eat? – *Ne yemekleriniz var?*

Knife – *bıçak*

Fork – *çatal*

Spoon – *kaşık*

Glass – *bardak*

Waiter – *garson*

Shopping

Shop – *dukkan*

Market – *çarşı*

Half a kilo – *yarım kilo*

More – *daha*

Money – *para*

Post office – *postane*

Pharmacy/chemist – *eczane*

How much? – *ne kadar?*

How many? – *kaç?*

There is – *var*

There isn't – *yok*

Expensive – *pahalı*

Open/closed – *açık/kapalı*

Hotel

Have you got a room? – *odanız varmı?*

How many people? – *kaç kişi?*

Shower – *duş*

Bath – *banyo*

Soap – *sabun*

Towel – *havlu*

Toilet paper – *tuvalet kağıdı*

Key – *anahtar*

Hot/cold water – *sıcak/soğuk su*

Directions

Left – *sol*

Right – *sağ*

Straight on – *doğru*

Entrance – *giriş*

Exit – *çıkış*

Toilet – *tuvalet*

Square – *meydan*

Street – *sokak*

Road – *yol*

Avenue – *caddesi*

Near the hospital – *hastanenin
    yakında*

Where is the church? – *kilise
    nerede?*

Further reading

ART, ARCHITECTURE & ARCHAEOLOGY

Architecture of the Islamic World edited by G. Michell, London, Thames & Hudson, 1978.

The Art and Architecture of Islam 1250–1800 (Pelican History of Art) by S. Blair and J.M. Bloom, USA, Yale, 1994.

Art of the Byzantine Era by D. Talbot Rice, London, Thames & Hudson, 1989.

Byzantine (Style and Civilization) by S. Runciman, London, Penguin, 1975.

Byzantine Architecture by C. Mango, London, Rizzoli International Publications, 1986.

Constantinople: Byzantium–Istanbul by D. Talbot Rice, London, 1965.

Early Christian and Byzantine Art (Pelican History of Art) by R. Krautheimer, USA, Yale, 1989.

Early Christian & Byzantine Art (Pelican History of Art) by J. Beckwith, USA, Penguin USA, 1998.

A History of Ottoman Architecture by G. Goodwin, London, Thames & Hudson, 1997.

Istanbul by C. Beck and C. Forsting, London, Ellipsis London Ltd, 1997.

Splendours of the Bosphorus by C. Hellier and F. Venturi, London, Tauris Parke, 1993.

A Temple for Byzantium by M. Harrison, London, Harvey Miller, 1989.

The World of Ottoman Art by M. Levey, London, Thames & Hudson, 1975.

HISTORY

The Alexiad of Anna Comnena, London, Penguin Books, 1969.

Byzantium by C. Mango, London, Phoenix Press, 1980.

Byzantium by J. J. Norwich, London, Penguin Books, 1993.

Byzantium, City of Gold, City of Faith by P. Hetherington and W. Forman, London, Orbis, 1983.

Byzantium: From Antiquity to the Renaissance by T. F. Mathews, New York, Abrams, 1998.

The Cambridge Illustrated History of the Islamic World edited by F. Robinson, Cambridge, Cambridge University Press, 1996.

Chronicles of the Crusades by J. de Saint Louis Joinville and G. de Villehardouin, London, Penguin Books, 1963.

Constantinople, City of the World's Desire, 1453–1924 by P. Mansel, London, Penguin Books, 1997.

The Decline and Fall of the Roman Empire by E. Gibbon, Everyman's Library.

The Emperor Constantine by M. Grant, London, Phoenix Press, 1993.

Everyday Life in Byzantium by T. Talbot Rice, New York, Dorset, 1967.

Everyday Life in Ottoman Turkey by R. Lewis, New York, Dorset, 1971.

The Fall of Constantinople 1453 by S. Runciman, Cambridge, Cambridge University Press, 1965.

Fourteen Byzantine Rulers by M. Psellus, Penguin Books, 1966.

The Harem by N.M. Penzer, London, George G. Halrap & Co. Ltd., 1936.

Inside the Seraglio by J. Freely, London, Viking, 1999.

Istanbul by J. Freely, London, Penguin Books, 1998.

Justinian and Theodora by R. Browning, London, Thames & Hudson, 1987.

The Middle East by B. Lewis, London, Weidenfield & Nicholson General, 1995.

The Ottoman Empire 1300–1650 by Colin Imber, Basingstoke, Palgrave Macmillan, 2002.

The Ottomans by A. Wheatcroft, London, Penguin Books, 1993.

The Secret History by Procopius, London, Penguin Books, 1981.

Süleyman the Magnificent by J. M. Rogers and R. M. Ward, London, Wellfleet Press, 1988.

Three Christian Capitals by R. Krautheimer, California, University of California Press, 1983.

TRAVEL LITERATURE, GUIDEBOOKS AND BIOGRAPHY

Blue Guide Istanbul by J. Freely, London, A & C Black, 1997.

Everyman Guide Istanbul, London, Everyman's Travel Guides. 1993.

Eyewitness Travel Guide Istanbul, London, Dorling Kindersley Publishers, 1998.

Istanbul, A Travellers' Companion by L. Kelly, London, Constable, 1987.

The Ottoman Centuries: The Rise and Fall of the Turkish Empire by Lord Kinross, New York, William Morrow & Company Inc., 1977.

The Owl's Watchsong by J. A. Cuddon, London, Century Hutchinson, 1960.

Portrait of a Turkish Family by I. Orga, London, Elsand Books, 1988.

Strolling through Istanbul by H. Sumner-Boyd and J. Freely, London, Kegan Paul International, 1987.

The Sultan's Seraglio by O. Bon, London, Saqi Books, 1996.

Index

Note: where there is more than one page number, **bold type** is used for key text on the item; numbers in *italics* refer to illustrations. Mosques, churches and museums are listed under those headings rather than separately under their own names.